HIGH-TECHNOLOGY-CRIME INVESTIGATOR'S HANDBOOK

HIGH-TECHNOLOGY-CRIME INVESTIGATOR'S HANDBOOK

Working in the Global Information Environment

Dr. Gerald L. Kovacich, CFE, CPP, CISSP

William Boni, MBA

UTTERWORTH
HEINEMANN

Boston   Oxford   Auckland   Johannesburg   Melbourne   New Delhi

Butterworth–Heinemann supports the efforts of American Forests and the Global ReLeaf program in its campaign for the betterment of trees, forests, and our environment.

Library of Congress Cataloging-in-Publication Data
Kovacich, Gerald L.
    High-technology-crime investigator's handbook : working in the
  global information environment / Gerald L. Kovacich, William Boni.
        p.   cm.
      Includes bibliographical references and index.
      ISBN 0-7506-7086-X (alk. paper)
        1. Computer crimes—Investigation.   I. Boni, William.   II. Title.
  HV8079.C65K68   2000
  363.25′968—dc21   99-28243
                                                                                        CIP

British Library Cataloguing-in-Publication Data
A catalogue record for this book is available from the British Library.

The publisher offers special discounts on bulk orders of this book.
For information, please contact:
Manager of Special Sales
Butterworth–Heinemann
225 Wildwood Avenue
Woburn, MA 01801–2041
Tel: 781-904-2500
Fax: 781-904-2620

For information on all Butterworth–Heinemann publications available, contact our World Wide Web home page at: http://www.bh.com

10 9 8 7 6 5 4 3 2 1

Printed in the United States of America

To the security, law enforcement, and investigations professionals in every country who dedicate their lives to protecting their companies, their societies, their nations, and the world from the miscreants who use high technology to violate the laws, ethics, and morality of the human race.

Learning is not attained by chance. It must be sought for with ardor and attended to with diligence.

—*Abigail Adams*

What is most obvious may be most worthy of analysis. Fertile vistas may open out when commonplace facts are examined from a fresh point of view.

—*L. L. Whyte*

Knowing is not enough, we must apply. Willing is not enough, we must do.

—*Johann Wolfgang von Goethe*

Contents

Foreword

It really came as a surprise to me.

I recently found myself with Jerry Kovacich drinking fine British beer in a fine London drinking establishment and he asked if I would pen an introduction to the new book he was writing with Bill Boni. I was certainly honored to be offered that task, but that wasn't the surprise. The surprise was the serendipitous timing of his request and the events that were surrounding me at the time. For, you see, a couple of my associates were themselves immersed in cyber-investigations.

Over the years I have had occasion to be on the trail of "bad guys," both within and outside of an organization, and I have found that in most every case, the procedures followed on the part of the victim firm were ad hoc at best.

"What is your policy for dealing with serious external hacking?" I would ask.

"Uh, er . . . we don't have one," the senior security officer would say.

"Okay, how well tuned-in is your in-house counsel for these sorts of events?"

"He's a bean-counting lawyer . . . he doesn't keep up on this sort of thing. What do you think we should do?" they would ask me.

So, it was odd indeed, that drinking fine beer with Jerry four thousand miles from home should coincide with two ongoing cases I was involved with.

In the first case, a large financial institution found itself under a fairly severe attack that had been going on for nearly two weeks. The security manager came from a legal/law enforcement background and had a healthy dose of street-fighting experience. He immediately commenced an internal investigation. Audit trails from all perimeter systems (firewalls, routers, etc.) and native host and applications were "turned up" to a greater degree of sensitivity, thus gathering greater amounts of raw audit data. Analysis was comprehensive in order to learn about the techniques of the intruder. They wanted, hopefully, to learn what his real goals were and what caliber of attacker they were dealing with.

Secondly, they quickly captured an IP address and began the laborious process of tracing and identifying the intruder who was making substantial progress through the company's very sensitive files. By using "street-smarts" pressure, he got the first ISP in the chain to carry on the trace to the next hop. He called the next hop during the night and was able to identify the real IP, real name, and real physical address of who had been breaking in. Throughout this process, police were neither notified nor invited to help.

Using additional investigative tools and by performing an extensive background check on their suspect, the company was confident to five-nines (99.999%) that they had the perpetrator. The security manager contacted some acquaintances and asked if they could make a house-call on the company's behalf. They did so, and in no uncertain terms, convinced the intruders it would be in their best interest to cease and desist their intrusions immediately. Their not-so-subtle tactics worked.

Problem solved. Not one dime or ounce of time was spent with the police. Whether you approve of these actions or not is immaterial. The company was prepared to conduct an internal investigation without the participation of any outsiders, they implemented their plan, and within days it was over. Best of all, only a small number of top corporate officials ever knew there was a problem. No newspapers or Internet rumors. From the perspective of everyone throughout the company in 50 states and many foreign countries, it was business as usual.

The second case was handled a bit differently. Although a very large company with a large number of trade secrets, they had very little security process or technology in place. They became aware of their problem not because of electronic sensors picking up illicit and abnormal behavior as in the first case, but they had discovered that they had a malicious insider because of a disturbing e-mail that inquired why extensive hacking was coming from their IP address. After a scramble, they traced down some logs and manually found activities they couldn't explain; it did indeed seem that someone was hacking from inside their company.

Meetings were hastily called and the internal lawyer was endlessly stuck in a physical paradigm. He just didn't understand the power of their hacker and the technical limitations the company faced. Everyone did agree to no dealings with the police. They wanted to handle it themselves even though they had little clue as to what steps to take.

I helped them draw up a quick-and-dirty game plan, and we soon found that our likely disgruntled employee had once worked for the company that he was hacking into. Because of California law sensitivities, they did not take my advice: go lock up his machine, get a sector copy of the hard disk, and acquire some forensics tools to see what he's been hiding through erasure, deletion, or other disguise mechanisms. Human Resources was appalled at our decision to fire the employee. They told us every reason in the book why we couldn't do what we knew we had to do to build a case against their hacker.

Intense frustration grew on all sides as it became quite clear that none of the senior management had ever considered or discussed the possibility they now faced. Time wore on, and it was at least three weeks before they all agreed on how to handle the case. It was quiet, politically correct, but more than 100 MB of information had been sent via ftp to the other company. They are still trying to figure out what happened.

Two different approaches, both in their own ways unsatisfactory: one in its outcome, the other perhaps in its method. And that is exactly why *High-Technology-Crime Investigator's Handbook* is so valuable a contribution to the field of information security and corporate asset protection management awareness. Very few companies have well thought-out plans on how to deal with contingencies such as I described above. While we have pretty well learned how to handle the Acts of God, such as hurricanes, floods, and fires, we are still in our infancy when it comes to coping with the Acts of Man.

What Jerry and Bill are providing you with is an excellent overview of the entire issue ranging from the new information age environment in which we all now live, who is doing what to whom, a basic outline on how to protect your information assets, and a look into the future.

Most companies I know are loath to enjoin law enforcement in an internal corporate investigation unless it becomes absolutely necessary. A majority of people I know say the police cannot be trusted to keep secrets. Public relations is a critical component of company image and spin control is hard enough without compromising leaks about embarrassing company events. Law enforcement is broadly viewed with technical disdain, often called clueless, mindless, or atavistic in their antedated approaches to cyber-investigations. In addition, you, as a private individual or company, often have a lot more leeway in the sorts of things you can do in an investigation. Due to legal procedural impediments faced by law enforcement, bringing in the police at too early a stage can doom a situation to failure.

Cyber-crimes involve technical staff, security management, senior executives, legal counsel, and often human resources. Because of the nature of the medium, the analyses and investigative processes are often nonlinear and parallel tracks must be taken simultaneously. It is a complex process and must be planned for.

Whether you take every word of *High-Technology-Crime Investigator's Handbook* and use it to gain a better understanding of this new information age environment and build it into your company's procedures or not is inconsequential. The point is that you build and install a process that is right for your company and your company's goals.

This book is also an "Internet crimes awareness handbook" for security professionals, law enforcement personnel, managers, and anyone else interested in this fascinating topic. You could not ask for two better guides than Jerry Kovacich and Bill Boni. I am proud to call them friends and col-leagues who are making great contributions to the field.

Winn Schwartau

President, Infowar.Com, Inc., and author; his most recent book is *Time Based Security*, which provides a quantifiable process and metric for defining an organization's security level

Preface

Crime and illegal activities in the global information environment are growing rampant. Because of the rapid growth of high technology, targets of crime are becoming more plentiful and complex. Today's criminal— whether a company employee, petty thief, con artist, corporate executive, gang member, or professional thug—is far better prepared to meet the challenges of his or her vocation. Criminals use all forms of modern technology— computers, pagers, scanners, cellular phones, faxes, and color printers—to commit simple or complex crimes. They commit complex economic crimes using modern processes, sophisticated devices, and highly technological equipment that frequently delays or prevents detection.

These high-technology miscreants often are better equipped than agencies responsible to enforce the law and investigate their wrongdoing. Unfortunately, many federal, state, county, and local law enforcement agencies and civilian investigative organizations lag far behind in their procurement and use of high-technology equipment and methods for conducting high-technology-crime investigations.

Many investigative units today use outdated procedures, processes, and tools. This leads to prolonged investigations, delays in the preparation and delivery of investigative reports, inability to accurately collect and track data, inadequate case management, poor development of statistical trends, and substandard data analysis.

The managers and supervisors who oversee investigative units, in the law enforcement and other government and civilian business worlds, often lack expertise or are hesitant to use many of the high-technology automated tools and processes now available to the investigative community.

Management, confronted with personnel reductions and frequent funding cuts, is reluctant to realign its priorities and provide the badly needed, up-to-date resources, especially when the people and their politicians want to stop drugs, violent crime, and gangs.

Quite often updating statistical collection methods involves nothing more than the development or implementation of a simple database or spreadsheet application. The most complex case management systems used by many agencies can be simplified and automated to provide a wealth of information with little or no effort. Most software applications produced today have excellent tutorials to help even the most computer-illiterate high-technology-crime investigator learn program basics and develop solutions to meet everyday operational needs.

Colleges and universities offer courses in nearly every aspect of high technology except those related to high-technology-crime investigation. Although many of today's law enforcement and civilian training agencies provide basic and advanced instruction in modern methods and technologies, very few offer in-depth, technical training in high-technology-crime investigations.

Such is the world in which those interested or charged with the responsibility of investigating high-technology crimes and criminals must work—the global information environment.

If read in the order presented, the reader should be able to proceed through

- Understanding the global information environment.
- Developing a high-technology-crime investigation career plan.
- Developing and managing a high-technology-crime investigations unit.
- Establishing a high-technology-crime prevention program.
- Looking into the possible future world of the high-technology-crime investigator.

The book consists of four major sections incorporating 23 chapters.

PART I. INTRODUCTION TO THE HIGH-TECHNOLOGY-CRIME ENVIRONMENT

The objective of this part is to provide the professional high-technology-crime investigators, managers, and supervisors, in either a business or government agency, a basic understanding of the new environment in which we live, work, and play. For investigators to successfully establish and manage a high-technology-crime investigative unit, they must have a basic understanding of the topics discussed in the following chapters:

- Chapter 1. "The Changing World: An Introduction to High Technology." This chapter presents the fundamentals of the high-technology world in which we live and its impact on the criminal justice and law enforcement systems. The chapter gives a basic overview of high technology based on the computer, the microprocessor, and its peripherals. It places "high-tech" crime in a sociological context as well, something inherently fundamental to understanding the role of the high-technology-crime investigator.

- Chapter 2. "The Global Information Infrastructure, the Internet, and a Nation's Information Infrastructure." Having an understanding of the high technology that fueled the fire of global change and the new global environment, the high-technology-crime investigator must be aware of the massive integration of networks occurring on a global scale. This knowledge is needed because it is where he or she will work, now and long into the twenty-first century. This is the new crime scene, because in today's global and networked environment, high-technology miscreants can strike, often with impunity, from anywhere in the world, attacking anywhere in the world. This chapter discusses this new crime scene environment.
- Chapter 3. "The High-Technology Miscreants: Profiles, Motives, and Philosophies." To be successful in conducting high-technology-crime investigations and managing a high-technology-crime investigations unit, the investigator must have a basic understanding of the miscreants, their motives, profiles, and philosophies. This chapter will provide an overview of such individuals.
- Chapter 4. "The Basic Techniques Used by High-Technology Miscreants." This chapter provides the high-technology-crime investigator a nontechnical overview of some of the basic methods high-technology criminals use.
- Chapter 5. "The Basic Information Systems Security Techniques Used Against High-Technology Miscreants." The part culminates in a chapter that provides the high-technology-crime investigators an overview of the basic protection philosophies, methods, and processes used to guard the valuable assets of the global information environment's businesses and government agencies.

PART II. OVERVIEW OF THE HIGH-TECHNOLOGY-CRIME INVESTIGATIONS PROFESSION AND UNIT

This part discusses the profession of the high-technology-crime investigator. The objective of this part is to provide professional high-technology-crime investigators, managers, and supervisors, in business or government, an overview of the profession and how to establish and manage a high-technology-crime investigative unit.

- Chapter 6. "Developing a Career as a High-Technology-Crime Investigator." This chapter provides the investigator a career plan outline to use in developing a career as a high-technology-crime investigator.
- Chapter 7. "Marketing Yourself as a Successful Investigator." The objective of this chapter is to explain some of the more unique methods

to prepare for a high-technology-crime investigation job and the "interview by portfolio" method to get an investigative position.

- Chapter 8. "The Global Enterprise Corporation." This chapter describes a fictional company in which the investigator or investigative manager will work. This approach provides the reader a practical, baseline model on which to build a company high-technology-crime investigative program.
- Chapter 9. "Understanding the Role of the High-Technology-Crime Investigator and Prevention Unit in the Business Environment." This chapter defines the role the high-technology-crime investigator will play in a corporation or government agency; in this case, for GEC. The duties and responsibilities of a high-technology-crime investigator vary depending on the place of employment. However, we assume the high-technology-crime investigator has the perfect position.
- Chapter 10. "The High-Technology-Crime Investigations Unit's Strategic, Tactical, and Annual Plans." The objective of this chapter is to establish plans for a high-technology-crime prevention organization, with subsets of the GEC strategic, tactical, and annual plans. These plans set the direction for GEC's high-technology-crime prevention program while integrating the unit into GEC's plans, thus indicating that the crime-prevention program is an integral part of GEC.
- Chapter 11. "High-Technology-Crime Prevention and Investigative Program and Organization." This chapter discusses the establishment and management of the organization chartered with the responsibility to lead the high-technology-crime prevention effort for GEC, including structuring and describing the organization and the job descriptions of the personnel to be hired to fill the positions within it.
- Chapter 12. "High-Technology-Crime Investigative Functions." This chapter discusses the major investigative functions to be performed by the high-technology-crime investigations unit and describes the flow processes that can be used to establish a baseline in performing the functions.
- Chapter 13. "Sources, Networking, and Liaisons." The objective of this chapter is to identify and discuss various types of sources, networks, and liaisons with outside agencies.
- Chapter 14. "High-Technology-Crime Investigation Unit's Metrics Management System." The chapter discusses the identification, development, and use of metrics to assist in managing a high-technology-crime investigations unit and prevention program.
- Chapter 15. "Final Thoughts, Problems, and Issues." This chapter discusses what may happen in a dynamic, international corporation that drastically changes the high-technology-crime investigations unit, prevention program, and unit manager's position.

PART III. HIGH-TECHNOLOGY CRIMES
AND INVESTIGATIONS

The objective of this part is to provide a sample of actual high-technology crime. This crime is happening daily around the world. The purpose of this book is to provide a basic overview of the profession of high-technology-crime investigator and the global information environment in which the investigator works, so it would not be complete without at least an overview of investigating high-technology crime.

- Chapter 16. "High-Technology Crime: Case Summaries." The chapter uses a range of cases to illustrate the types of incidents that may be encountered under the general grouping of high-technology crime. Although not exhaustive, they provide a sense of the many challenges that face high-technology-crime investigators in both the public and private sectors.
- Chapter 17. "Investigating High-Technology Crime." This chapter provides an overview of the important concepts associated with "computer forensics." It describes the potential sources of evidence available in the typical microcomputer and how to conduct a search for evidence in a systematic and effective manner.

PART IV. HIGH-TECHNOLOGY-CRIME
INVESTIGATION: CHALLENGES FOR
THE TWENTY-FIRST CENTURY

The last section of this book looks into a crystal ball to predict what working in the global information environment will be like for the twenty-first century high-technology-crime investigator.

- Chapter 18. "The Future of High-Technology Crime and Its Impact on Working in a Global Information Environment." The chapter discusses the future impact of technology on individuals, nations, societies, business, and government agencies, based on current trends and some best guesses.

This is not a "how to investigate high-technology crime" book but provides basic information for someone who wants to be a high-technology-crime investigator or is new to this profession. Also, we hope it may provide a few tips or insights for the seasoned veteran—or at least provide some enjoyable reading.

Even though only a small number of investigators officially carry the title of high-technology-crime investigator or a similar title, there is little doubt of the growing need for highly trained, technically competent investigators within the private and public sectors of every information-dependent, information age nation in the world.

No doubt, we have a long way to go. That is obvious when some "computer crime units" are still using Windows 3.11 while others are told to use confiscated software from the evidence locker to run their "new 150 Mhz computers."

We hope this book helps to focus attention and interest on the profession of the high-technology-crime investigator. For, if we are to enter the twenty-first century and rely on the global information networks, the Internet, and other international, national, and intranet networks and global telecommunications systems, professional high-technology-crime investigators, in concert with the information systems security professionals, must have the training, knowledge, and capability to protect this environment from the miscreants who now travel on the information superhighway and attack their victims with impunity.

To those who will take up that gauntlet, good luck and good hunting!

Acknowledgments

As with any large project such as this one, the work requires the support and assistance of many people. Those who deserve a special thanks and appreciation are:

Don Ingraham, Assistant District Attorney, Alameda County, Oakland, California, who for decades has led the fight against high-technology-crime, and who has helped law enforcement professionals and others understand the world of high-technology crime. His advice and assistance over the years have helped make this book possible.

Jerry Swick, Senior Staff Specialist/Senior Investigator, telecom crime fighter, and all-around good guy, of MCI WorldCom, for his valuable input to this project and support over the years. It was based on Jerry's advice that this book has been written.

John Kenney, Ph.D., Professor Emeritus, for his continued counsel and friendship.

Greg Singleton, photographer, security professional, and friend for providing the photographs used in this book.

To the gang at Butterworth–Heinemann, who are the true professionals in their field, and without whose advice and support this book could truly not have been published. A special thanks to Laurel De-Wolf, Rita Lombard, Jodie Allen, and all the other fine professionals who work unselfishly to publish our books.

PART I

Introduction to the High-Technology-Crime Environment

OBJECTIVE

The objective of this part is to provide professional high-technology-crime investigators, managers, and supervisors, in either business or government agencies, a basic understanding of the new environment in which we live, work, and play. For the investigator of high-technology crime to successfully establish and manage an investigative unit, he or she must have a basic understanding of the following topics:

- Chapter 1. "The Changing World: An Introduction to High Technology." The first chapter presents the fundamentals of the high-technology world in which we live and its impact on the criminal justice and law enforcement systems. This chapter gives a basic overview of high technology based on the computer, the microprocessor, and its peripherals. It places "high-tech" crime in a sociological context as well, something inherently fundamental to the understanding of the role of the high-tech-crime investigator.
- Chapter 2. "The Global Information Infrastructure, the Internet, and a Nation's Information Infrastructure." Once you have an understanding of the high technology that has fueled the fire of global change and the new global environment, as a high-technology-crime investigator, you must be aware of the massive integration of networks occurring on a global scale. Such knowledge is needed because this is where the high-technology-crime investigator works, now and long into the twenty-first century. This is the new crime scene because, in today's global and networked environment, high-technology miscreants can strike, often with impunity, from anywhere

in the world, attacking anywhere in the world. This chapter discusses the environment of the new crime scene.

- Chapter 3. "High-Technology Miscreants: Profiles, Motives, and Philosophies." To be successful in conducting investigations of high-technology crime and managing an anti-high-technology-crime investigations unit, you must have a basic understanding of the miscreants—their motives, profiles, and philosophies. This chapter provides an overview of such individuals.
- Chapter 4. "The Basic Techniques Used by High-Technology Miscreants." This chapter provides the investigator of high-technology crime a nontechnical overview of some of the basic methods high-technology criminals use to conduct their misdeeds.
- Chapter 5. "The Basic Information Systems Security Techniques Used Against High-Technology Miscreants." The part culminates in a chapter that provides investigators of high-technology crime an overview of the basic protection philosophies, methods, and processes used to protect the valuable assets of the global information environment's businesses and government agencies.

1

The Changing World
An Introduction to High Technology

**COMPUTERS ARE RAPIDLY CHANGING
THE WORLD**

If you are involved in any activity where technology is used to help accomplish your work, you are aware of the tremendous and very rapid advances being made in that arena. We are in the middle of the most rapid technological advances in human history, but this is just the beginning. We are not even close to reaching the full potential that technology has to offer nor realizing its full impact on all of us—both good and bad.

United States' Vice President Gore during a recent speech stated:

> We are on the verge of a revolution that is just as profound as the change in the economy that came with the industrial revolution. Soon electronic networks will allow people to transcend the barriers of time and distance and take advantage of global markets and business opportunities not even imaginable today, opening up a new world of economic possibility and progress.

It is very important for professional high-technology-crime investigators, supervisors, and managers to understand this new and growing global information age environment, because this is the environment in which they will work.

With this in mind, the nonfiction writing of three renowned authors—Alvin Toffler, Heidi Toffler, and John Naisbitt—comes to mind as acute sociological commentaries applicable to the global information environment.

The Tofflers' writings provide some of the most outstanding looks into the future, not only projecting trends but also explaining why they are occurring. Their books—*Future Shock, The Third Wave, Powershift, War and Anti-War,* and *Creating a New World Civilization,* among others—address the questions of why so many changes are occurring so rapidly and what those trends may mean to our future. Naisbitt's books—*Megatrends*, *Megatrends 2000* (cowritten with Patricia Aburdene), and *Megatrends Asia*—provide a further look at our world environment and the trends transforming our lives.

These books are a "must read" for investigators who want to understand where human societies have come from and where they are headed. This, in turn, will help provide the baseline on which the investigator can develop and manage a *high-technology-crime prevention program* (HTCPP) and *organization* (HTCPPO). Any HTCPP or HTCPPO must be as dynamic and rapidly responsive as the environment of constant change in which it operates. The investigator who does not look ahead will have a stagnant HTCPP that does not meet the needs of the business or government agency. After all, a HTCPPO must be a service and support organization and immediately responsive to its customers.

TOFFLER'S THREE WAVES OF EVOLUTION

The issue of how the dispersal of information—a fundamental element of the high-technology arena—has changed over time can be discussed using the framework of Toffler's Three Waves model of technological evolution.

The First Wave was the agricultural revolution that, according to Toffler, started with the beginning of the human race up to about 1745, at least in the United States. People lived in small and sometimes migratory groups, feeding themselves through fishing, foraging, hunting, and herding. Subsequently, they migrated into clusters, then towns, and then cities. During this period, information was passed by word of mouth or in written correspondence, usually sent by a courier. People were more dispersed and transportation more primitive, which meant less communication among people. During this period, the number of literate people was relatively small in comparison to the total world population.

Therefore, the "threats," such as theft of information in written form, were minimal, although a written message still could be physically destroyed and misinterpreted or changed in some way. By today's standards, high-technology crime per se really didn't exist. The First Wave crime was more personal and physical in nature.

The Second Wave, what the Tofflers call the *rise of industrialized civilization* (Toffler and Toffler, 1994), lasted until just a few years after World War II. This was the age of industrialization: steel mills, oil refineries, textile plants, mass assembly lines, and the like, where people migrated to a centralized location to work in an industry. Its decline, according to the Tofflers, is believed to have started about 1955 in the United States, when, for the first time, white-collar workers outnumbered blue-collar workers.

This was a period of growth in all areas—education, mass transportation, communications, and most important, the sharing of information. For communication protection, cryptography came into its own during this period. This was primarily a government-controlled and -used tool. Although businesses were beginning to look at the use of computers, most found them cost prohibitive. These systems were operated primarily in stand-alone mode as well; in other words, computers did not communicate with other computers.

For much of this period, anti-high-technology-crime measures for businesses and government agencies consisted mainly of some form of physical security; for example, a combination of locks, guards, alarms, and fences. Even as the computer became more sophisticated, the main protection mechanisms changed very little. Reliance was still on *physical security*; and investigations of crime scenes concentrated primarily on the physical aspects such as busted locks or cut wire fences, with theft being the most common reason for the crime. Access control was not an issue, since very few people worked in the computer field and those that did had to know how to "program with punch cards." Initially, therefore, threats to these information systems and their proprietary information were small.

The Third Wave, the age of technology, information, and knowledge, currently is rapidly sweeping worldwide and encompasses more advances than the First and Second Wave periods combined.

The challenge facing the investigator is to assist in deterring and preventing high-technology crimes and violations of business policy and procedures; as well as aggressively investigating and identifying those who violate high-technology-related corporate policy, procedures, and laws. In addition, the investigator is responsible for providing a *cost-effective* high-technology-crime prevention program.

In this Information Age, people everywhere are generally more educated and increasingly more computer literate. This means more access through worldwide networks and more potential criminal acts directed at the investigator's company or government agency. The protection of information systems and the proprietary information they process, store, or transmit is of vital concern in this information world.

In many countries, all three "waves" are simultaneously affecting societies, although with varying degrees of speed and force. With them comes varying degrees of social unrest, conflict, and tension as the "old wave" supporters try to hold on to the past, which also increases the potential for high-technology crimes. In *Creating a New World Civilization* (1994), the Tofflers say that the political tensions of today are primarily caused by the conflict between supporters of the Industrial Age and those of the Information Age. They believe this is the "superstruggle" for the future.

THE CHANGING BUSINESS AND GOVERNMENT ENVIRONMENTS

Businesses can and do adapt to change quite rapidly. However, in government agencies, adaptation comes more slowly and sometimes changes threaten the very existence of the agency. For example, the need for a Department of Education and a Department of Commerce has recently been debated with the advent of each congressional session.

One clear example of these changes is in the U.S. Post Office (USPO). The USPO must now compete with such businesses as Federal Express, DHL, and United Parcel Service (UPS) for the delivery of letters, documents, and packages. However, as more and more people around the world get "on-line" and send electronic mail, legally binding contracts, and other documents through national and international networks, the need for an Industrial Age government agency such as the USPO may become less important as information systems provide immediate, international communication.

To combat this trend, it appears that the USPO is trying to position itself to be the authenticator of e-mail messages. In others words, stay in business by being the intermediary between the e-mail of senders and receivers to verify and validate that the senders in fact are who they claim to be. One does not have to look far to see the vital need for an high-technology-crime prevention program in corporations and government agencies concerned about privacy and liability violations relative to individuals whose information is stored, processed, and transmitted by high-technology systems.

The September 24, 1998, issue of *Washington Technology* (www.wtonline.com) provided a breakdown on the use of intranets and extranets by industry. It indicated the following:

- State and local governments: 35% used extranets and 36% used intranets.
- Health care: 14% used extranets and 21% used intranets.
- Education: 16% used extranets and 51% used intranets.
- Insurance: 25% used extranets and 36% used intranets.
- Law: 18% used extranets and 30% used intranets.
- Finance and banking: 7% used extranets and 54% used intranets.
- National average: 28% used extranets and 38% used intranets.

Look at the information being stored by individuals, including you, on these networked systems and their massive databases. As the systems continue to expand and grow, the violation of privacy rules and laws will increase liability issues. As a high-technology-crime investigator in any of these sectors, you may be called on to conduct an investigation related to such privacy incidents.

Although networking of systems is not yet in place in all the industries' facilities, the majority of U.S. industries are beginning to rely more and more on networks for both their internal and external business communication. Of special interest to the investigator is that the finance and banking industry leads the other industries in the use of *extranets* (networks external to a company but linked to a company's systems networks) and *intranets* (internal company networked systems).

The three primary revolutions taking place as we enter the twenty-first century are the revolution in military affairs (which will not be discussed as it is beyond the scope of this book); the information technology revolution, which is discussed throughout this book; and the economic revolution.

THE ECONOMIC REVOLUTION

Lester Thurow, noted economist and former Dean of MIT's Sloan School of Management, stated in *Winning the 21st Century: New Rules and New Strategies for the New World Economy*, that five fundamental revolutions are changing the nature of the economic game we play:

1. The end of communism as a major world factor.
2. A shift to human-made brain-power industries.
3. Changes in demographics (the population in the United States is moving and aging).
4. The development of a global economy.
5. The dawn of an era with no dominant world power.

Many nations are making foreign trade a national objective to increase their dominant force in the world. One has to look only at Japan and Taiwan to see how economic power can be translated into world power; even if the nations are small in physical size, they can be very large in the economic world.

The majority of the world's largest banks, if not all of them, are in Asia and Europe. Many of the businesses of the world are merging to form global, transnational megacorporations wielding global economic power sometimes larger than the gross national product of many of the world's nations.

A New World Order?

Some say we are in the midst of a new world order. We know that the world is changing rapidly and that change is being fueled by high technology. The end of the Cold War brought in a new era, with new foes, new threats, and more crime. It also heralded such things as information warfare, economic espionage, industrial espionage, new threats to national security, and new challenges to law enforcement, the military, security personnel, and of course, high-technology-crime investigators.

These rapid changes left a void with the demise of the superpowers, also brought on by technology. One may believe that the United States, and possibly China and Russia, are superpowers, at least in a military sense. However, a closer look shows that neither the Chinese nor the Russian military has a global sphere of influence. Even the United States cannot act without support from other nations (e.g., NATO and UN), and new alignments are taking place in Europe, even in NATO. The European Union is beginning to become a world economic force. Islamic fundamentalism is spreading not only in the Middle East but in many parts of the world. New conflicts are taking place in various parts of the former Soviet Union. Change is the cornerstone of the world in which we live. High technology is the cause for much of our changes. So, it is only fitting that high technology should be discussed.

HIGH-TECH FUNDAMENTALS

Today's high-technology environment is primarily based on the microprocessor—the computer. Computers have been around for decades; however, they are now more powerful, cheaper, smaller, and networked nationally and internationally, and these trends are continuing. Computers have become an integral part, a necessity, in our society. We really have entered the Information Age. In the United States and in other developed countries of the world, we have become an *information-dependent* society.

In the past, computerized information (e.g., information stored on disk drives and tapes), was supported by hard copies; however, this no longer is the case. Therefore, information is at greater risk, criminals can cause more damage and destruction, and investigators often lack a paper audit trail from which to develop investigative leads.

Advanced technology is the mainstay of our businesses and the government agencies. Neither business nor government can function without them. Pagers, cellular phones, e-mail, credit cards, teleconferences, smart cards, notebook computers, networks, and private branch exchanges (computerized telephone switches called PBX) all are computer based and all are common tools for individuals, businesses, and public agencies. Criminals also rely more and more on computers. As computers and systems become more sophisticated, so do the criminals. As international networks increase, so does the number of international criminals.

As computers have become more powerful in terms of speed, storage capacity, memory, size, and related software and networks, they have also become more complex. No one can be a technical expert in all of the various operating systems, application software, and communication protocols. However, the investigator of high-technology crime must maintain a current, basic understanding of today's technology, how it functions and its areas of vulnerability, and then rely on *trusted, experienced* specialists to assist in high-technology-crime investigations.

Networking and embedded systems, those integrated into other devices (e.g., automobiles, microwave ovens, and medical equipment), are increasing and dramatically changing how we live, work, and play. According to a study by the National Research Council (1991), financed by the United States Advanced Research Projects Agency (ARPA):

- Computers have become so integrated into the business environments that computer-related risks cannot be separated from normal business risks or those of government and other public agencies.
- Increased trust in computers for safety-critical applications, such as medical monitoring, increases the likelihood that attacks or accidents will cause deaths (Note: This already has happened).
- Use and abuse of computers is widespread, with increased threat of viruses and credit card, PBX, cellular phones, and other frauds, for example.
- An unstable international political environment raises concerns about governments' or terrorists' attacks on information and high-technology-dependent nations' computer and telecommunication systems.
- Individual privacy is at risk due to large, vulnerable databases containing personal information, facilitating increases in identity theft and other types of fraud.

The use of modems now is commonplace; newly purchased microcomputer systems[1] typically come with an internal modem already installed and ready for global access through the Internet or other networks. Therefore, home computers and long distance telephone networks potentially represent some of the most serious and complex crime scenes of the Information Age. This surely will increase as we begin the twenty-first century.

Figure 1–1 depicts a short timeline of significant high-technology events. The Internet is the latest in a series of technological advances being used not only by honest people but also by miscreants, juvenile delinquents, and others for illegal purposes. As with any technological invention, it can be used for good or for illegal purposes. It really is no different than other inventions such as the handgun. The handgun can be used to defend and protect lives or to destroy them. It all depends on the human being using the technology.

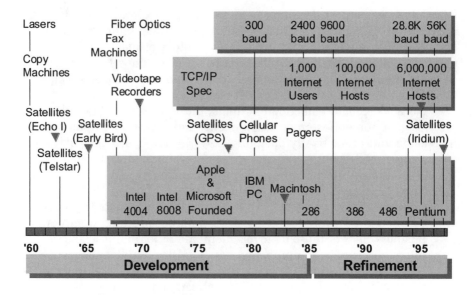

Figure 1–1   Fuel for the fire: the revolution in technology.

It is important for the investigator to remember that one's investigative thinking should not be confused or clouded by the high technology. These are just the "tools of the trade" and will be used by honest people and criminals. The basic investigative questions of who, how, where, when, why, and what still apply. The basic investigative steps, the criminals' motives still apply. The only real change is in the tools, from handgun to computer, as well as the new crime scene environment, a computer (located somewhere in the world).

What Is an Information System?

Today's information system is a computer or computer based. A computer basically is a combination of hardware, software, and firmware that stores, transmits, and processes information or "a device capable of solving problems or manipulating data by accepting data, performing prescribed operations (mathematical and logical) on the data, and supplying the results of these operations."[2]

Basic Computer Components

Computers have three basic components, regardless of size, manufacturer, version, or model: hardware, software, and firmware.[3]

The hardware encompasses the physical components of a computer system. Basically, these are the things you can physically touch and see. They can be subdivided into several main pieces (see Figure 1–2):

- The central processing unit (CPU), which may be synonymous with *computer*, is where the real processing takes place. Can you find the CPU(s) in Figure 1–2? How many are there?[4]
- The keyboard (or mouse or other computer) used as an input device, based on the typewriter keyboard, sends the user's command to the computer. It may have programmable keys. This is important for an investigator to know, as one key may be pressed that would begin deleting all the information stored on a suspect's system. The keyboard may be a separate component of the computer or built in, as in today's notebook computers. Figure 1–2 contains three keyboards and three mouse devices. However, the investigator should never assume that there is one, or only one, keyboard, mouse, or input device for each CPU. In a network, any keyboard may control all the CPUs. Furthermore, one should not overlook the other obvious input device on the desk—the microphone.[5]

Figure 1–2   A portion of a computer layout that a high-technology-crime investigator may encounter during a search. Note that at first glance, one may not be able to determine if the synthesis is stand-alone, networked, has a modem, etc. The first clue is on the lower left, bottom shelf (the hub).

- Storage devices store information for later retrieval. Storage devices range from various types of disks, diskettes, tapes, to compact disks (CDs). This is the major "crime scene" in high-technology-crime investigations, and obtaining evidence from these devices requires computer forensics expertise to be done accurately and legally. Storage devices may be internal to the computer "box" or externally attached. Because of the cheap devices now used by computers to write to CDs, the investigator conducting a crime scene search should not take for granted that CDs labeled as music actually contain music, especially if a CD writer is installed in the suspect's computer (see Figure 1–3).
- The cathode ray tube (CRT) or monitor (see Figure 1–2), as it is usually called today, was developed in 1895.[6] It provides the screen to see information. Although modern monitors rarely suffer the "burned-in screen images"[7] of the past, the investigator should carefully look at the monitor when it is turned off to determine if any images of evidentiary value have been burned into the screen. The monitor may be a separate component or integrated into the computer box as in

Figure 1–3   Examples of various storage devices include hard drives and their disks, tape drives, disk drives, and CD drives. Can you identify each? You must be able to do that and more during a search—and possibly very quickly as the suspect tries to flee with or destroy the evidence (see also Figure 17–4).

today's notebook computers and some of the "old" computers of the 1980s.

- A printer (see Figure 1–2, upper left-hand corner of the rack) prints information on paper. Some printers have memory and may contain valuable information of evidentiary value; therefore, caution should be used during searches so that power is not turned off before the information can be obtained.
- An internal or external modem (see Figure 1–2[8]) is used to transfer information to and from other computers through a telephone line or "Network interface card" to other networks. *Modem* is an acronym for *mo*dulator-*dem*odulator. For the investigator, this is a key element of any search. Such a connection indicates not only that the information of evidentiary value may be transferred to other computers but that the evidence being sought may be have been transmitted via a modem or network and stored on another computer system, somewhere else in the world. Of course, today's systems come complete with modems and software ready for Internet access. Therefore, the problem of "Where in the world is the evidence?" becomes a critical factor, as well as a factor in jurisdictional and search issues.
- Other peripherals and hardware components may include such things as cables, scanners, encryption cards, smart cards, access control devices, biometrics devices.

Software is the written instructions that direct a computer to perform various functions. The two basic types of software are operating system software and applications software.

The operating system software functions as the interface between the computer and the applications software. It controls the operations of the computer and its peripherals, makes directories, organizes files, and so forth. Examples of operating systems are UNIX, MS-DOS, OS/2, Windows, LINUX. When conducting a search, use a specialist in the operating system that is the subject of the search to prevent damage, destruction, or modification of information, as well as to avoid many of the possible defense attorney claims about the accuracy of the evidence found on the computer.

Application software is the set of instructions used to perform a specific task. This type of software makes up most of the software used by computers. Examples of application software are programs used for accounting, word processing, spreadsheets, and databases.

Firmware is a combination of hardware and software. It is a series of instructions or programs that have been written onto a read-only device and thus made part of its "permanent memory." Common examples include the game cartridges used in many video game systems. However, one must remember that these read-only-memory (ROM) devices are *programmable*. Therefore, they also may contain information of evidentiary value.

The Three Basic Steps of Computer Operations

The operation of the computer is based on three basic steps:[9]

- *Input.* Using some device such as a mouse, keyboard, or microphone instructions are given to the computer through the application and operating system software.
- *Process.* The information, or input, is processed according to the instructions entered and the applicable software being used.
- *Output.* Once processed, the information output (the result of the processing) is produced based on the instructions that the computer had been given, say, to a disk, printer, modem, monitor, or speakers.

So, from an investigative viewpoint, the very basic investigative steps also can be broken down easily into the same format. For example, the investigator would want to know *who, when, why, where,* and *how* information (input) was entered into the computer, which instructed it to perform, according to what software instructions, the way it did; and what output was produced and sent where.

Storage and Process Capacity

In the "old days" of the computer (up until the early 1980s), the computer users also were the programmers and systems administrators. To use and maintain these old systems, a degree of hands-on experience in mathematics, engineering, or the like was needed. Since the advent of microcomputers, this no longer is the case. However, to have a basic understanding of computers, which is the basis for all high technology, the investigator should understand the difference between a bit and a byte.

The investigator must remember that the computer does only what its instructions tell it to do. In doing so, it can take in only so much input so fast, process only so much information, and produce only so much output at some maximum speed. Such things as the computer's architecture, memory, storage, and program implementation determine what a computer can do and how fast it can do it. To operate efficiently, today's operating systems and applications are greatly affected by the amount of available memory. So, the investigator should know these measurements of memory:

- A *kilobyte* (KB) is 1,000 characters. A character may be a letter, number, space, or symbol like @, #, or %. (Actually, a kilobyte is 1,024 bytes, so 24 K is 24 × 1024 = 24,576 bytes.)
- A *megabyte* (MB) is about 1 million characters.
- A *gigabyte* (GB) is about 1 billion characters.
- A *terabyte* (TB) is about a trillion characters.

If you are using the storage device to assist in your investigative duties, you obviously want to have enough storage capacity to handle your information and investigative analyses. If you were told the size of a suspect's storage devices, this would give some indication as to the "size" of your crime scene. Therefore, you could be better prepared for the search. Once the suspect's system is seized, its size would provide a good estimate of the time and effort required in searching for evidence.

If 2 MB = 958 pages = one book, then

- A 3430 disk pack would store 200 MB or 100 books (95,833 pages).
- A disk platter would store 20 MB or 10 books (9,583 pages).
- A DASD (direct access storage device) would store between 2.5 GB and 5.2 GB or 1,250–2,600 books (1,197,917–2,491,666 pages).
- A floppy disk (360 KB and 1.2 MB) would store between 0.15 and 0.6 books (145–575 pages).
- A 6157 streaming tape would store 55 MB or 27.5 books (26,354 pages).
- A 3480, 24 K cartridge block would store 200 MB or 100 books (95,833 pages).
- A 3420–6250, 24 K block tape would store 165 MB or 82.5 books (79,062 pages).

This information is based primarily on an old "IBM mainframe" facility and peripherals in common use in the mid 1980s. Compare that to what is now available for storage on microcomputers. Common notebook computers can store over 12 GB of information. Using the preceding formula (or, better yet, use 1 MB = 479 pages = one book, maybe a more realistic measurement of a book's pages), determine how many books and pages of a seized 12 GB notebook hard drive would have to be searched for information of evidentiary value.[10]

One of the biggest disadvantages an investigator faces is the rapid increase in computer power and its storage capacity. It once was fairly easy to copy files from a disk drive onto floppies for search and analyses. A 64 K hard drive could be copied onto how many 1.2 MB floppies? How many floppies would it take to copy a 4.2 GB hard drive on to floppies? If you don't want to do the math the answer is simple: Too many.[11] In one major international corporation, the storage capacity of the mainframe systems (the largest computers available on the market), if printed out and each sheet stacked one top of another, would reach over 110 miles high. Investigations with such networked systems as this crime scene would require a major search team of investigators and specialists, possibly over 100 people.

For this reason, investigators must change the way they collect their evidence and increase the time allotted these searches, based on just the sheer volume of information now being stored on these "monster" hard drives. Furthermore, capacity of the computers and peripherals the investigator now requires also has increased, and that need will continue to increase to keep up with the miscreants' computer power.

Changing Technology

The following are some examples of high technology and its possible impact on crime:

- *Bank check printing made easy.* A vendor has developed a cartridge that allows laser printers to produce bank checks with the magnetic ink required by banks. Along with the toner cartridge, you get a special font to produce the little OCR letters at the bottom of the check. What check fraud possibilities does this provide a criminal?
- *A major vendor to increase storage 30-fold.* The 3.5-inch disk will contain all the text for 10,000, 300-page novels. Current storage is 350 million bits per square inch. By the year 2000, it will increase to 10 billion bits per square inch. Using a blue-laser optical recording system, the vendor was allegedly able to read and write information at a density of 2.5 billion bits per square inch. At that rate, 6,500, 250-page novels could be stored on one double-sided 5.25-inch-diameter optical disk. How long would it take to search for evidence on such devices?
- *Storing information.* An "old" IBM 3380 disk drive contained 2.6–7.25 gigabytes, 36,000–116,000, 250-page books. In the near future, it has been reported that a vendor will have available for storage a device the size of a "sugar cube." Six of these cubes are estimated to be able to store the information now contained in all the libraries of the world. Imagine searching that for evidence!

TELECOMMUNICATION TECHNOLOGY

Telecommunications basically is the transmission of information, including voice, data, or graphics, over telephone lines. Today's telecommunication technology has blurred the distinction between computers and telecommunications because telecommunication equipment today is based on the microprocessor, the computer. The switches, routers, bridges, and the like, now coupled with cellular phones and in the future television, will make these all the same in a process called *convergence*. We already can make telephone calls through the computer on the Internet. We also can surf the Internet through our television. Even pagers are becoming more sophisticated and integrated in watches and cellular phones.

Cellular Phones and Private Branch Exchanges

Cellular phones are rapidly changing from analog to digital.[12] They are beginning to be networked to satellites on a global scale through such consortiums as Iridium and Globalstar. Analog and digital cellular phones both have advantages and disadvantages.

Analog cellular phones have relatively good voice quality and they currently enjoy the widest coverage in the United States. Their disadvantages include a lack of wide coverage in Asia and Europe. They cannot transmit digital images such as graphics or even alphanumeric characters. In addition, they lack the rudimentary encryption and other security capabilities, as well as sophisticated features, available with digital cellular phones.

A digital cellular phone is actually a wireless computer and can transmit better quality voice as well as other digital information such as alphanumeric characters and graphics. Digital phones provide extensive coverage throughout most of the world. They also provide phone features such as caller ID, call forwarding, call waiting, and voice mail. Digital cellular phones have some disadvantages. They currently cost more to buy or lease. Also, they currently have limited coverage in the United States. Obviously, eventually these disadvantages will not be a factor.

Another major piece of telecommunications hardware is the *private branch exchange*. The PBX is a computerized telephone switchboard privately owned by a business or government agency. It allows a more cost-effective means of handling telephone calls within the company or agency. However, outward bound calls still must go through a telecommunications provider such as Sprint, MCI WorldCom, or AT&T.

In developing countries, pagers and cellular phones have been rapidly adopted and are more widely used than in the United States. This is because the need for telecommunications is great in these developing nations; however, their information infrastructure is not as developed as in the United States and European nations. Consequently, very few telephone lines run throughout the nation, specifically in the rural areas.

Indonesia, the fourth largest nation in the world with over 200 million people, is an example of the high-technology "leap forward" of a nation. The people are scattered over 17,000 islands. To establish and maintain a ground-based telephone information infrastructure complete with telephone poles, switch boxes, and other facilities would be cost prohibitive, if possible at all. Therefore, cellular telephones are used extensively, eliminating the restrictions, time, and costs of an Industrial Period[13] telephone system.

We usually think of cellular phones as a high-technology tool for voice communication—not any more. According to "Voice Takes Backseat to Computing Functions in Cellular Phones," a May 14, 1998, article in *TechWeb News* (http://www.techweb.com),

Voice telephony is becoming a less prominent feature of the latest generation of cellular phones, which are bearing a closer resemblance to computing devices . . . Cellular phones are taking on a new role, beyond basic telephony, and becoming mobile "information browsing tools" . . . Motorola's d50 mobile data module, a PC card containing both a modem and a cellular phone. The device slots into a laptop computer PC card docking port, and enables direct dialing to the Internet and other data and voice communications sources without the need to connect an external phone line.

The impact of these new technologies on professional investigators is significant. If you were conducting an investigation into allegations that an employee, who used such a company-provided system, was selling company secrets, would you know the impact such a device would have on your investigative approach? Do you know what investigative steps to take because the suspect had such a device? Is it a factor in how you would approach the investigation? Are you currently prepared and confident that you can successfully conduct such an investigation?

Pagers and Beepers

Pagers once were *the* method of communication, before the cellular telephone. Pager costs have come down dramatically, and even grade school children have pagers, along with such miscreants as drug dealers. To this day, millions of people rely on pagers; however, increasingly in the future watches, cellular phones, and notebook computers will add paging features integrated into their other functions.

If one were to take an example of how we in a global information environment and information-based nation depend on high technology, just look at the "pager failure of 1998." In May 1998, the PanAmSat's Galaxy IV satellite rotated out of position after what was determined to be (allegedly) an "onboard computer control system" failure.[14] This failure knocked out the pager service of approximately *45 million* customers in North America. How bad was it? An article on the *Wired* magazine website dated May 21, 1998 (http://www.wired.com) gave some examples of our dependency on the pager:

It is very scary, said Mark Rizzo, manager of network operations for Ultima Online, an online gaming service . . . his network team extensively uses pagers linked to network monitoring equipment to sound the alarm about any urgent issues in the mammoth Ultima Online system. It's really important to provide 24/7 uptime, and we rely on automated systems that page us if anything goes wrong . . . It is really vital to our support.

A technician from a Web hosting, New York-based company stated that

We monitor our servers, as well as customers of ours for connectivity, and correct operation . . . If one of them fails, it's a loss of money for us or our customers. If we miss a page, a customer could be down and not realize it for hours . . . he used Sky Tel's e-mail-to-pager gateway exclusively for system notification . . .

A simple pager that we all take for granted has taken on added importance and functionality. Like most of our high technology, it has turned into a tool that we rely on and, when taken away, can cause a great deal of chaos and economic damage not thought of until something happens.

Here is something to consider: Suppose you were the high-technology-crime investigator for PanAmSat. You were notified that the satellite had failed and it was believed that someone had hacked into the systems and changed its orbit. Would you know how to investigate the incident? Think about it? Are you up to the challenge of high-technology-crime investigations?

Computers are electrical devices that, when broken down into basic components, are fairly easy to understand. In computers, the microprocessor—the heart of the computer system—drives much of today's processes. These systems are growing in power, connectivity, and speed, while their prices are declining. Our dependency on high technology continues to grow to such an extent that their failure has major personal, business, and national repercussions, something that the high-technology-crime investigator must keep in mind.

ELECTRONIC COMMERCE

Electronic commerce (e-commerce) is the new buzz word of the information age. The term refers to the use of computers, telecommunications, and related high-technology devices to conduct business transactions and communicate between entities to conduct business. This is the beginning of the use of electronic cash and will usher in a "cashless society," where the electronic signals transmitted and received between computers will represent money.

A broad definition of *electronic commerce* is provided by Electronic Commerce Australia (ECA, formerly EDICA) in its 1994 annual report as "The process of electronically conducting all forms of business between entities in order to achieve the organization's objectives."

Electronic commerce embraces electronic trading, electronic messaging, electronic data interchange (EDI, which allows the transfer of documents over networks), electronic funds transfer (EFI, which allows transfer of funds via computer networks), electronic mail (e-mail), facsimile, computer-to-fax (C-fax), electronic catalogues and bulletin board services), shared databases and directories, continuous acquisition and life-cycle support (CALS), electronic news and information services, electronic pay-roll, electronic forms (e-forms), on-line access to services such as the Internet, and any other form of electronic data transmission. The ECA annual report continues:

> For example, medical and clinical data, data related to taxation, insurance, vehicle registration, case information involving legal proceedings, immigration and customs data, data transmitted for remote interactive teaching, videoconferencing, home shopping and banking, EDI purchase orders and remittance advice—are all applications of electronic commerce.
>
> The term "electronic commerce" is sometimes incorrectly used as an alternative to EDI. EDI, a subset of electronic commerce, refers specifically to the inter-company or intra-company transmission of business data in a standard, highly structured format. Electronic commerce, however, includes structured business data and unstructured messages or data, such as electronic memos sent via e-mail.
>
> Another term, "electronic trading," is commonly used to refer to electronic transactions which occur in the procurement of goods and services. Electronic trading uses structured and/or free-form messages. Electronic trading is also a term for stock trades via the Internet and can also be considered a sub-set of electronic commerce.

THE IMPACT OF HIGH-TECHNOLOGY CRIME ON THE CRIMINAL JUSTICE AND LAW ENFORCEMENT SYSTEMS

The criminal justice system is a social system established to maintain social stability and order. If a society is stable and orderly, the criminal justice system will not be challenged or overburdened. It would run rather smoothly. It is a mirror of society.

In *Creating a New World Civilization*, the Tofflers write:

> The conflict between Second and Third Wave groupings is, in fact, the central political tension cutting through society today. . . . On one side are the partisans of the industrial past; on the other, growing millions who recognize that the most urgent problems of the world can no longer be resolved within the frame work of an industrial order. This conflict is the "super struggle" for tomorrow . . .

The current criminal justice system was formed during the First and Second Waves. As society embraces the Third Wave, it does not wait for the two prior waves' processes to catch up. Therefore, one can see the trend of a disintegrating United States criminal justice system, where crime increases faster than the criminal justice system can deal with it.

More discretionary arrests and plea-bargaining prosecutions, over-burdened court systems, and early release of convicted criminals from jails and prisons are indications of this change to a Third Wave society. Yet, we seem to be trying to use Second Wave criminal justice system processes and functions to handle Third Wave problems, and it doesn't seem to be working. In the United States, one may argue that major crimes are decreasing; however true it may be, high-technology crimes seem to be increasing.[15] A disadvantage to being a leading technology-based country such as the United States is that one has no opportunity to learn from the mistakes of others more advanced.

The local, state, and federal lawmakers; law enforcement officers and high-technology-crime investigators; prosecutors; judges; and the corrections officers are faced with learning and adopting technology as a tool to assist them in working in a more effective and efficient manner. This is increasingly important as budget constraints continue to cause criminal justice professionals to rethink and reengineer their processes to do more with less. This includes those in related professions in the business world as well.

No section of the criminal justice system (e.g., law enforcement, prosecution, courts, corrections) appears to have any cohesive plan to address the issues of technology as a support tool for either criminal justice professionals or to address the problem of high-technology criminals. Each is decentralized and addressing technology on a piecemeal basis in our decentralized criminal justice environment.

Five basic problems must be addressed if we are to win the battle against high-technology crimes and the high-technology criminal:

1. Law enforcement agencies often lack the budget, training, expertise, and technology to adequately conduct investigations of high-technology crime.
2. High-technology crimes are being committed faster than law enforcement officers and high-technology-crime investigators can even investigate them, let alone counter them.
3. The laws relative to high-technology crime often are insufficient or nonexistent vis-à-vis new high-technology crimes.
4. Prosecutors generally lack the skills, experience, and understanding necessary to effectively prosecute high-technology criminals.
5. Judges often lack the technical knowledge and skills to fully appreciate high-technology crimes and interpret applicable laws.

We seem to be losing the fight. One may wonder why this seems to be happening. It could be for the same reason we seem not to consider white-collar crimes, like fraud, as seriously as drug trafficking, robbery, assault, or theft. White-collar crimes are considered to be less serious than violent crimes against persons. After all, there are no "people victims" in white-collar crimes. The victims are businesses, insurance companies, government agencies, financial institutions, and the like. Society has come to look at these crimes with less severity and therefore less punishment—

after all, no one was hurt or killed. The high-tech criminals committing these white-collar crimes very often could be our neighbors, sometimes "pillars" of the community (e.g., the banking and financial community), church members, even our own computer "whiz kids."

This perception of the impact of high-technology crime is naïve, since in reality it can devastate its victims. For example, money invested in a fraudulent scheme may represent the loss of someone's life's savings or the money to send a child to college. Victims may be forced to cancel their medical insurance or the company that went bankrupt because of high-technology crime may leave its employees destitute. When these crimes occur, they cause damage on a grander scale, even more so as countries become increasingly competitive in what is turning out to be the twenty-first century form of war, the economic war.

The economic war can be just as damaging to a country as any traditional war. Pierre Marion, the former director of France's Direction Generale de la Securité Exterieure, was quoted as saying, "It would not be normal to spy on the U.S. in political matters or military matters. But in economic competition, in technical competition, we are competitors. We are not allied." What this means to the investigator is that he or she may be investigating at the local, state, and federal levels the "techno-espionage" agents of the world.

As discussed earlier, the future includes electronic commerce. Neither the criminal justice system nor any of its individual parts is currently prepared to deal with the high-technology crimes and issues related to contract disputes based on allegations of changed contracts or forged signatures when these are done through the global information infrastructure. What constitutes an original signature or original contract in such an environment?

History of High-Technology-Crime Laws in the United States

Without the proper tools, law enforcement cannot adequately investigate high-technology crime. One necessary set of tools are clear and concise laws relative to high-technology crimes that can stand close scrutiny in the courts of law. In 1976, the U.S. General Accounting Office (GAO) issued "Computer-Related Crimes in Federal Programs." The report identified 69 computer-related crimes involving federal computer systems. The study concluded:

> It is clear that the potential for computer-related crimes exists especially since reliance on the computer is increasing . . . Consequently, computers have added a new dimension to the potential for crimes. They can make crimes harder to detect because computer-based systems usually provide fewer records of transaction. These systems naturally concentrate processing in fewer hands and make proper separation of duties more difficult to

achieve. The concentration of asset information in easily changed form increases the potential size of each loss . . .

Based on that report and other information, the Federal Computer
Systems Protection Act was proposed in 1977. Congress did not approve
the bill; however, it was used to assist in writing future computer crime
bills. It seems that most high-technology-crime laws are conceived, written,
and enacted only after activities considered criminal by society are found
not to be illegal because they do not violate any existing law.

The first high-technology-crime law passed in the United States was
enacted by Florida in 1978. This was enacted after insiders in a racetrack
in Florida stole several million dollars between 1974 and 1977 by manipulating the computer to show they had won horse races when in fact they
had lost their bets.

One United States senator found that many government agency computers are vulnerable to destruction and theft. Twice in the last decade he
has recommended tighter controls, but the legislature failed to act. Over
time, these high-technology laws have been tested and are gradually being
refined and updated.

This senator found that welfare clerks were accused of conspiring
with more than 90 welfare recipients to defraud one state of $2.2 million.
After surveying several state agencies, he found lax computer security in
motor vehicle records and medical records, therefore, this could assist in
perpetuating high-technology crimes.

In the United States, the definition of *high-technology crime* varies
from state to state. In some states, using a computer to defraud or commit
other crimes may make it a special type of violation. Certain high-technology crimes are specified by federal legislation, such as attacks on or misuse of government-owned systems.

Some of these new laws have been tested in court, while others have
not. Note that many of the noncomputer crime laws are often used to prosecute high-technology criminals. This happens because the old laws have
been tested and validated in court over the years while the new high-
technology-crime laws have not. Additionally, older laws are often easier
for prosecutors, judges, and in the United States, juries to understand.
When it comes to high-technology crimes, the KISS (Keep it simple, Stupid)
principle still applies. In the United States, the elements of proof vary depending on the laws; for example, various federal and 49 different state
statutes relate to high-technology crime.

U.S. Federal Laws

The violation of older, nontechnology federal laws is cited in many cases
as the reason why an investigation is to be conducted or a computer is to
be searched. The use of such laws offers a "simpler" case to present in

courts. Many times, it avoids the complications associated with computer terminology and use. Some of the laws that have been applied are

- 18 U.S.C., Section 1343, Wire Fraud.
- 18 U.S.C., Section 1341, Mail Fraud.
- 18 U.S.C., Section 2314, Interstate Transportation of Stolen Property.
- 18 U.S.C., Section 1961, Racketeer Influenced and Corrupt Organizations (RICO).
- 18 U.S.C., Section 2510, Wiretap.
- 42 U.S.C., Section 2000aa, Privacy Protection Act.

Some technology-related laws are

- 15 U.S.C., Section 1693n, Electronic Funds Transfer Act.
- 18 U.S.C., Section 2701, Stored Communications Access.
- 18 U.S.C., Section 1029, Electronic Communications Privacy Act.
- 18 U.S.C., Section 1030, Fraud in Connection with Federal Interest Computers (Computer Fraud and Abuse Act).

Statutes of the United States

Some individual states also have enacted new legislation specific to high-technology crimes, while others amended their current statutes. At last check, 49 of the 50 states had either amended their current statutes or enacted new legislation. The state of Vermont is the only state that has not.

Some states use separate codes and others use categories such as "crimes against property." The offenses under state statutes include

- Unauthorized access.
- Computer fraud.
- Crimes against computer users.
- Crimes against computer systems.
- Interruption of services.
- Tampering.
- Misuse of information.
- Theft of services.

The punishment for violation is based on the type of crime and the harm caused. The statutes also provide civil remedies and forfeitures in many instances. These new laws include a duty to report the violation in some instances as well as evidentiary provisions. The laws must be clear and concise, provide deterrence, and provide a tool to the criminal justice system professionals.

What Constitutes High-Technology-Crime Laws?

The laws can be divided into four sections: knowledge, purpose, malice, and authorization.

Knowledge means knowingly and willfully committing the offense and knowing it was an offense. The high-technology criminal must be shown to have a *purpose* in mind when committing the violation of law. *Malice*, the intent to do harm, often also must be shown, as well as the lack of *authorization* to access the system or information.

The Criminal Justice Triad: Law Enforcement, Prosecution, and the Judicial System

The police are involved in the broad functions of keeping the peace, preventing crime, and supporting the government and the people in creating and maintaining a secure and stable environment. This includes the protection of the innocent and their civil liberties. As part of that role, police have the authority to apprehend those that commit crimes and enforce a host of both criminal and regulatory laws.

This role will not change. Based on the length of time the process takes, the crimes will exist before laws are enacted. We already see signs of this. Therefore, technology crimes will be committed and we may have difficulty finding an applicable law on which to base an arrest.

In performing their assigned duties, police have discretionary powers that often put them in a difficult position of determining the parameters of the crime and criminality in a community and the country. This does not appear to hold true for high-technology crimes. For example, the FBI sometimes pursues hackers, regardless of their (hackers) apparent intention. That is like using the FBI to go after graffiti writers.

The role of crime prevention by law enforcement personnel is a concept still clouded by a lack of definition and understanding. This concept sometimes is confused with crime suppression, which is the short-term effort to reduce specific crimes or crime in general in a specific location.

John P. Kenney, professor emeritus (University of Southern California, California State University–Long Beach, and August Vollner University) and a world-renowned criminologist, spoke several years ago in Bangkok on the concept of policing. He said that the police have two major tasks: the prevention of crime and the prevention of criminality.

The prevention of crime results from long-term efforts of the police in all activities oriented toward crime control and crime repression. The prevention of criminality requires support of the people of the country and the community. It is a community effort in cooperation with the police, the judiciary, and the correctional agencies. It is an effort to help in the criminal justice process of arrest, incarceration, treatment, and rehabilitation of criminals and to redirect their lives away from criminal activities so they can take their place as viable members of our society.

In this effort, the use of technology may be helpful, such as the use of devices worn by released prisoners under house arrest. The police or corrections center would be notified when the prisoner leaves his or her approved location, for example, when under house arrest. Technology such as this also would save money. Some of these monitoring functions are being contracted out to civilian contractors in an effort to save money.

As high-technology-crime investigations become more complex and the relative expertise of many law enforcement officers and high-technology-crime investigators to investigate such crimes declines, consultants are likely to be hired to assist law enforcement officers and high-technology-crime investigators. In addition, businesses, not wanting to deal with the criminal justice system, will hire more high-technology-crime investigators and handle such crimes in-house, through outside consultation or civil courts.

We have to only look at the United States to see the growing industry of private security to augment or even replace public police in many areas. The police of modern countries also are becoming more involved in security-related matters, which helps to create a secure and stable social environment. So, the tasks of law enforcement and crime prevention are merging and go hand in hand with business security functions. This relationship will continue in the future.

For example, the use of computer technology for sophisticated alarms and the enhanced communication that results from technology will enable security and law enforcement officers and high-technology-crime investigators to better coordinate their efforts in responding to calls and fighting crime.

How police officers conduct their duties will be affected in part by how many and different criminologists' theories are put into practice. Just as we are entering the next century, some argue that, in some modern, technological countries such as the United States, one criminological era may be ending and another beginning. If so, this also may affect how we conduct our duties: how we deal with crime and criminals.

There may be no direct relationship between criminology and computer technology but there is an indirect one. As we carry out our responsibilities in the next century, the computer technology that may support our work will vary depending on the methods we use.

As alluded to previously, we all know that a gun can be used for good or bad. For example, a gun can be used to hunt animals for food. It has a use that benefits people. A person can use a gun to rob or kill another person. Therefore, criminals use it as a tool to violate the law. That, of course, is a bad use of the gun. Going one step further, a gun, in the hands of a law enforcement officer or high-technology-crime investigator, with probable cause and justification, can be used to protect society, by that officer killing someone who is about to kill another person.

The same concepts can be applied to the use of technology. It can be a tool used by a person to help society. If technology can help society, then there would be a better chance of social stability and social peace, thus less necessity for the involvement of the police. It can be used as a tool by a criminal to steal and possibly kill; for example, using the computer to embezzle from a bank or to modify hospital records of patients to cause doctors and nurses to take the wrong action, which may kill a patient. It can be used as a tool by the law enforcement officers and high-technology-crime investigators to function in a more effective and efficient manner.

What law enforcement does—the basic functions of crime prevention, crime control, investigations, and maintaining order and social stability— will not change. However, technology is likely to have an ever-increasing impact on *how* law enforcement personnel do their job, as it will have on every other profession in a technologically advanced society. Therefore, it will require us to make some very serious decisions as to our law enforcement priorities.

If we use other modern countries as examples, we see that with the technology comes an increase in technology-based white-collar crimes and fraud, such as embezzlement, unauthorized money transfer, theft of sensitive information, and illegal computer access. All these are facilitated through the use of the computer and all are very difficult to prove.

Our basic investigative techniques, which have proven successful throughout the years, still can be used; however, law enforcement officers and high-technology-crime investigators must learn how to deal with the new, technology-oriented environment. The crime scene is different. So are the crime methods used, as well as the jobs and even vocabulary of witnesses and suspects.

High-technology crimes, due to their sophistication and complexity, require longer investigations. So, assuming no increase in budget and personnel, other cases will be backlogged and at some point the backlog will become unacceptable. What then? More budget? More personnel? Resetting the priorities of cases? We don't know what the overall impact will be or best course of action at that time; however, we can speculate that such a scenario is probable.

The increased use of networks for international connections provides more opportunity for international criminals, for which law enforcement jurisdiction will be an issue. With the rapid increase in technology to modernize our country, law enforcement officers and high-technology-crime investigators may fall further behind in technological knowledge, making it more difficult to conduct investigations into technology-related crimes.

With modernization comes a larger financial gap between people, until the people on the lower end of the economic scale can progress to at least middle-class status. In the interim, crimes such as burglary, robbery, and theft will probably increase. The "have-nots" will try to take from the "haves." Therefore, demands on law enforcement will increase, and we will have to reset our work priorities.

Law enforcement officers and high-technology-crime investigators, based on budget constraints and lack of technological know-how, will concentrate their expertise on violent crimes. This will continue to be the desire of our society. Technology-related crimes and other white-collar, "victimless" crimes will hold a lower priority, if any priority at all. More and more of them will likely never be investigated. It will fall on the organizations being victimized to conduct their own investigations through their own security officers and take more action through civil lawsuits. With limited capabilities, personnel, and budget, the concentration must focus on prevention and control of crimes that are more people oriented, where people have been physically harmed. This is a monetary consideration when one takes into account how it contributes to the outside perception of the United States as a "safe" or "unsafe" place, which affects tourism among other things.

If we are to prevent criminality, or at least to minimize its occurrence, as it relates to the high-technology-related crimes of the twenty-first century, our law enforcement personnel must receive training, equipment, and funding to be in a position to perform in the next century.

Law Enforcement and High-Technology-Crime Investigators

Law enforcement faces two major challenges in confronting technology: conducting high-technology-crime investigations for subsequent prosecution and applying high-technology to support law enforcement functions.

On more than one occasion, evidence was accidentally destroyed because the investigating officer did not know how to properly handle the computer and retrieve the evidence. As technology and high-technology crimes become more complex, the law enforcement officers and high-technology-crime investigators investigating these crimes must become familiar with the basic technology and the methods used to commit such crimes. In addition, they must become familiar with the elements of proof in the new high-technology-crime laws being implemented.

The training must include courses in computer and telecommunication basics, computer and telecommunication security, and the unique aspects of high-technology-crime investigations, which includes how to properly conduct crime scene searches, including computers and telecommunications equipment.

To emphasize what was stated earlier, an important point to remember is that, no matter how complex the high-technology crime, the basic investigative techniques still apply. Essentially, only the environment is different.

Technology can be as much of a tool to law enforcement officers and high-technology-crime investigators as to criminals. Some of the technology used by law enforcement includes the most obvious: automated report writing and the use of spreadsheets, link analyses, and database applications to help analyze complex fraud investigations and support budgets.

TECHNOLOGY AS A TOOL

Some of applications of technology that can be used as tools for law enforcement include:

- "Teletrac" devices placed in vehicles, which can be monitored when stolen and tracked throughout the area.
- Firearms analysis software to analyze results of firearms and ballistics tests.
- Automated warrant and search documents.
- Law enforcement computer-based training programs.
- Link analysis software to automatically link, through commonality factors, information from one or multiple crimes, suspects, or documents.
- Analysis of evidence such as DNA, blood, hair, dirt, and fingerprints.
- The use of laser guns for training police in how to handle dangerous situations.
- Keeping track of arrest and crime records.
- Maintaining wanted persons records, tracking, and on-line advertising.
- Tracking transport of prisoners.
- Maintaining and tracking parking tickets
- Maintaining an informants database and linking informants.
- Maintaining a gang activities file and linking associates.
- Management of evidence.
- Computer-aided dispatching.
- Computerized sketching.
- Maintaining criminal histories.
- Maintaining a criminal associates database and linking associations.
- Maintaining a missing persons database.
- Maintaining a modus operandi database and analyses.
- National Criminal Information Center (NCIC) entry.
- Maintaining a pawned articles database.
- Maintaining a stolen property database.

The Internet, as previously explained, is a worldwide network. One of its main capabilities is the electronic mail system. The National Institute of Justice (NIJ) established a project to take advantage of that Internet capability by initiating an on-line, moderated discussion group. This group, which was by invitation only on a compartmented segment of the Internet, discussed technology and law enforcement through e-mail. The author, Dr. Kovacich, was a member of that group.

In the NIJ project, Computer Crime, Police Use of Computers, and the Impact of Technology on Law Enforcement in an Information Age: An Electronic Conference to Discuss Current Issues and Assess Future Implications, seven topics were addressed:

1. The prevention, investigation, and prosecution of computer crime.
2. Legislation, research, and policy development.
3. Training and technical assistance.
4. Community policing and collaboration using computers.
5. Organizational response and police operations.
6. Physical and electronic security.
7. Scanning for and sharing innovations on the Internet.

The NIJ hoped to publish two documents relative to the project: (1) the ideas and comments of the members of the project team (approximately 100 people in law enforcement, security, and education) relative to the topics and (2) the lessons learned from conducting this type of electronic group project.

This was the first time this electronic approach to a research project was undertaken by the NIJ. However, it will probably not be the last. The advantages of such an electronic project are that it can be done quickly (all written comments are transmitted electronically and immediately), cheaply (no travel expenses, no time away from the member's primary job), and allows some of the most knowledgeable people in a field to share their thoughts on particular topics.

The use of technology for such endeavors is an excellent example of how law enforcement officers, high-technology-crime investigators, and other members of the criminal justice system can use technology to support their activities.

Another example of the use of technology happened when the Mount Kisko, New York, police officers were given notebook computers and wireless modems. They now can access police databases while moving freely within their assigned areas either on patrol or in vehicles. They can check wants and warrants and even call up a photo of a person. This use of technology provides more flexibility for the officer than the patrol car computer (*U.S. News and World Report*, August 21, 1995).

Even some United States government agencies may not be immune from the temptation of using high-technology crime for personal gain, e.g., to gain more budget. The following scenario is offered as a possible use of the Internet robberies for gaining more budget:

> Discretionary spending, the amount Congress budgets every year for such programs as roads, fighter planes and education programs, has declined steadily to the point it is 12 percent below the 1990 level, according to a congressional study . . . In inflation-adjusted 1998 dollars, discretionary outlays dropped from $630 billion in 1990 to $553 billion this year, the joint Economic Committee study said. Discretionary spending, those programs in the federal budget that Congress must vote on each year, now comprises only one-third of all federal spending. The other two-thirds goes to fixed entitlement and mandatory programs.[16]

So, less discretionary budget means more agencies fighting over their share of the third that is left. Now, looking at the latest Department of Justice and, specifically, the apparent FBI public relations efforts before congressional committees relative to economic espionage, hackers, techno-terrorist threats, and so forth, one could easily imagine using those briefings and hacker cases to obtain more money, especially when major crimes are decreasing and Congress may consider using some of the Department of Justice's allocated funds for other projects. The FBI's new "Internet crime center," with an alleged startup budget of $30–40 million to catch hackers, is one part of that budget battle.

One person wrote to a computing help column in the *San Francisco Chronicle* (computers@sfgate.com), asking for help in getting his or her address off a website. It seems that someone had listed the address as a place to get a massage. Over 50 men showed up at the front door at all hours of the day and night. This may seem funny but not if it is your address.[17] Is this the type of high-technology crime that the FBI will fight or is this type better left to others?

The following statement on U.S. congressional funding for law enforcement was reported by the Associated Press on July 15, 1998:

> The Senate has voted to set aside $250 million over five years for police agencies to upgrade technology and make it easier to exchange information about criminal history records in job and security clearances . . . authorized grants over five years for police to buy systems that would improve the sharing of criminal identification including DNA information and automated fingerprinting . . . Timely and dependable communication is a cornerstone of effective crime-fighting.

PROSECUTORS

Many prosecutors seem reluctant to prosecute individuals under the high-technology-crime laws. This is because these laws have not been used or not used often. The concern is with being the first or one of the first prosecutors to try a case under these "new laws." Another problem is understanding the crime itself. To prepare an adequate prosecution, the prosecutor must have a reasonable understanding of technology. An additional problem is trying to explain the intricacy of the technology and the crime to a judge or jury.

Defense attorneys appear to have a slight advantage in these cases due to the lack of effective security controls on the systems being attacked as well as their inherent vulnerability.

Attorneys, like law enforcement officers and high-technology-crime investigators, have been slow to integrate technology into their work. However, prosecutors and defense attorneys are beginning to adopt the technology into some aspects of their work. A survey of prosecutors showed that 75% of prosecutors' offices use a computer for a variety of purposes:

- 72% for case management.
- 65% for form and letter preparation.
- 51% for prewritten motions.
- 36% for subpoena preparations.
- 30% for witness information.
- 29% for discovery requests.
- 23% for information on individual criminal matters.
- 33% for arrest of individuals.
- 23% for case processing and tracking outcomes.
- 34% for office management.
- 25% for budgeting.
- 23% to track expenditures.

They also are used to model crimes.

Another example is when prosecutor requires the examination of hundreds, if not thousands, of documents. Using technology, the documents could be scanned into the computer, searched by key words, and analyzed more efficiently and effectively.

JUDGES

Judges are usually not technology literate and are relatively slow to adapt to the use of technology in performing their duties. This lack of knowledge can adversely affect high-technology-crime cases that go before the court for prosecution.

In a recent case, a judge dismissed the case against a college student who sent e-mail on the Internet, in which he talked about raping and killing a classmate. The case was dismissed because no "intent" was proven.

Judges can use the technology for writing case notes, opinions, and decisions. They also can use them to look up previous cases for precedence and to communicate with their staffs, do research, and transmit information to other judges.

"High-Tech, Low-Tech Mix Within a State's Bureaucracy"

In Florida, judges access a defendant's arrest record through the Florida unified network of criminal justice information, CJNET.[18] The system also allows them to contact more than 600 law enforcement offices around the state, as well as the court clerks.

The Florida computer system further provides for a digital fingerprint check by rolling a person's fingers across a glass plate connected to a computer. The fingerprint is recorded and checked against a fingerprint database in Tallahassee.

Technology-Created Crime Visuals

In Queensland, Australia, law enforcement officials have developed an "interactive crime scene recording system" that integrates crime scene photographs so that the crime scene can be viewed at any angle, a 360° view. According to a report, "The technology had the potential to cut back the crime scene paperwork swamping courtrooms, and present the same information in a simple and compact computer presentation."[19]

CORRECTIONS

The incarceration and corrections part of the criminal justice system often is overlooked when it comes to technology. However, technology tools are being developed that can help the prison, parole, and probation processes.

Corrections agencies must deal with prisoners once the rest of the criminal justice system has finished with them. The agencies have less of a problem in dealing with high-technology crimes than high-technology criminals. Most high-technology criminals are classified as white-collar criminals and, therefore, usually are not considered as dangerous to society as rapists, murderers, and others who commit violent crimes.

According to a study done by the National Institute of Corrections and the California Department of Corrections Technology Transfer Committee, some of the following technologies should be considered to support the corrections processes:

- Use of magnetic resonance imaging for use in nonintrusive body searches to detect hidden contraband.

- High-speed neural networks employing artificial intelligence and fuzzy logic in conjunction with biometrics to identify individuals, process prisoners, and perform similar jobs.
- Use of artificial intelligence and image recognition to assist in tutoring prisoners and enhancing their education.
- Drug detection through retinal scans, breath analyzers, and air samplers.
- Computer-based automation of prison records, training, work schedules, inventory, population projections, and the like.
- Computer simulation and modeling of riots and other disturbances to help in contingency planning and guard training.
- Zero fault–tolerant perimeter security and alarm systems.
- Robotics for perimeter patrols and surveillance.
- Composites to manufacture safer and stronger items that cannot be turned into weapons.
- Infrared devices to detect chemical plumes of drug manufacturing.
- Use of satellite technology to analyze areas where a potential prison may be constructed.

Technology can play an important role in the criminal justice system. One technology in use is electronic monitoring; for example, placing a criminal not in prison but under house arrest. The advantage of such a process is that it saves prison space to house the more violent offender. Also, with fewer prisoners in prison, the number of guards can be reduced, and money would be saved by not having to provide for that prisoner.

Under the electronic monitoring system, the prisoner would have to take care of himself or herself and still be confined away from society as punishment. Prisoners confined under the use of this type of technology of course would be those accused of a nonviolent crime. The limitations, or the lack of them, is under the jurisdiction of the individual judicial system. However, like all technologies, electronic monitoring is not well liked by all members of the criminal justice system. In some areas, guards' unions are very strong and may argue against the use of the technology if jobs are lost.

WHAT OTHERS ARE DOING

The United States Federal Bureau of Investigation

The FBI appears to be positioning itself to be the dominant law enforcement authority in the United States and the world. Therefore, it stands to reason that the FBI wants to be the leading investigative agency when it comes to high-technology crimes. Because many of the high-technology criminal acts use the global or national information infrastructure or the

Internet, they are interstate crimes, so there seems to be clear evidence that the FBI, by its charter, would have investigative responsibility.

However, the federal government follows certain guidelines to determine jurisdiction; for example, the Department of Defense normally investigates those high-technology crimes within its jurisdiction and authority, as it does other crimes. In addition, the United States Secret Service, Customs, and other federal agencies usually also control some "piece of the high-technology-crime action."

So what has the FBI been up to vis-à-vis high-technology crime?

- It has placed many of its investigative files on individuals, as well as other information, on its website (http://www.fbi.gov).[20]
- Since the FBI's National Computer Crime Squad (NCCS), part of the National Information Infrastructure Protection Agency, began in 1992, it has been involved in investigations of high-technology crime related to child porn, fraud, and gambling. Computer and computer-related crimes average approximately 5% of its investigations.[21]
- It continues to ask for more power related to faster and easier remote wiretaps, requiring Internet Service Providers (ISPs) to rapidly trace hackers through the Internet, access to encrypted communication and files through key escrow, and development of a technology that would track hackers automatically through the identification of their telephone numbers.
- As part of the Department of Justice, the FBI was involved in an agreement to improve cooperation with seven other nations in fighting high-technology crime and harmonizing their high-tech-crime laws.[22] The countries are the United States, the United Kingdom, Germany, Japan, Italy, Canada, France, and Russia. The agreement calls for

  Training experts to battle high-technology crime.

  Establishing around the clock cooperation.

  Developing faster methods to track Internet hackers.

  Prosecuting the alleged offenders if they cannot be extradited.

  Developing methods to preserve computer evidence.

  Reviewing national laws to "boost" enforcement of high-technology-crime laws.

  Working with businesses to detect and punish criminals.

- The Internet Fraud Council, an anti–on-line crime collaboration between the FBI, the national White Collar Crime Center, and the National Fraud Center was unveiled on May 10, 1999. A complaint center that allows consumers to lodge complaints about on-line fraud is also part of the initiative. The West Virginia–based center will house 10 analysts initially, but up to 130 more may eventually be funded, says Richard Johnston, director of the White Collar Crime

Center. William Boni of PricewaterhouseCoopers likens the initiative's operational approach to that of the Centers for Disease Control. "A central response center will collect data, track the problem, and do intervention," Boni says. Corporations, higher-education institutions, government agencies, and the media will be offered the chance to become members of the council, for a fee of $5,000 to $25,000. Membership entails the use of the council's "best practices" website seal, access to Internet-related legal and legislative information, and education and training.[23]

- The FBI's Computer Investigations and Infrastructure Threat Assessment Center (CITAC) joins its new National Infrastructure Protection Center (NIPC) with subdepartments for analysis and warnings, a watch and warnings unit, and a training, administration, and outreach unit.
- The NIPC is deploying a program called InfraGuard, which was originally developed in Cleveland for use in more than 50 cities. The program is used by companies to report high-technology crime through an electronic report.[24]

Independence County, Missouri

Other law enforcement agencies have also considered or implemented new technologies to combat crime. Criminal justice departments are using 64 Kbps ISDN lines for videoconferencing to arraign prisoners, interview them, and communicate among the various officers.[25]

United Kingdom Customs Officials Check Computers for Porn

Allegedly, the customs officials in the United Kingdom had begun to use a "special scanning" software to inspect travelers computers for pornography.[26] Based on recent conversations with British authorities in London, the idea has been dropped.

Canadian Police Struggle in Their High-Technology-Crime Fight

Due to a limited staff, the Canadian police are having a difficult time keeping up with the growth of crime on the Internet and other high-technology crimes.[27] "We're not actively investigating Internet fraud. There is no Internet unit in Toronto," says Toronto police detective constable Wolfgang Lott. The Internet, he adds, "is just a new tool for criminals committing the same old scams."

European Union Will Not Establish a "Cyberpolice" Force

European Union officials decided that they would not establish an "cyberpolice" force; however, they were looking at methods to provide "efficient public protection, in particular against the use of telecommunications for the benefit of criminal organizations."[28]

Pittsburgh Police Using Wireless Data System

Police in Pittsburgh use a wireless system installed in laptop computers and handheld units.[29] It is used to access wants and warrants, local and state databases, license plate information, vehicle information, and the like.

Department of Justice to Assist State and Local Law Enforcement in Purchasing High-Technology Equipment

Under its More Cops program, the United States Department of Justice will supply grants for high-technology equipment to local and state law enforcement officials as long as their agencies provide a minimum of 25% in matching funds.[30]

Technologies and Agencies Converge

In a cooperative effort, the Sacramento, California, Police Department and the Sacramento County Sheriff's Office are working together in a multimillion dollar effort to upgrade and improve their high-technology systems to reduce the paperwork and paperwork time of its officers.[31] The upgrades and new technology will include a digital mug-shot imaging system.

Convicted Murderers Sue over DNA Database

In Massachusetts, four convicted murderers are suing the state due to a law that mandates collection of DNA from prisoners.[32] They claim it violates their constitutional rights and is the same as an illegal search and seizure. The information is stored in a database for future comparisons with crime scene evidence.

Law Enforcement Officials Add Information Technology

Due to lower costs of high technology, state and local law enforcement agencies are buying computerized dispatch systems, mobile data terminals, and other such equipment.[33] The spending has gone from $1.29 billion in 1997 to an estimated $2.59 billion in 2002.

Suspect or Prisoner Identification Key Evaluations Systems

"Small police forces have a new weapon. It's called SPIKE [suspect or prisoner identification key evaluations] . . . SPIKE combines the face, voice and fingerprint recognition into a single ID system that can be shared over the Net, via a service called SPIKENET'"[34] (see True Touch Technologies, Inc. at http://www.truetouch.com).

SUMMARY

All members of the criminal justice system, private security, or investigative personnel, when confronted with a problem that can be solved or mitigated by high technology, should conduct an Internet search. Chances are that others have a product or proven solution. It is only logical that high technology be used to assist in the fight against all crime and specifically high-technology crime, since it is being used against you and your business or government agency.

Someone once said that the future is what we make it. Those involved in the criminal justice system face a myriad of challenges ahead as technology evolves. It is the responsibility of all those in society to minimize the use of high technology to commit crimes by safeguarding that technology and information and to minimize the opportunity for high-technology criminals to commit their illegal acts.

NOTES

1. The term *microcomputers* has been used to differentiate the computers on our desks from minicomputers and mainframe computers. The computers' power and what the manufacturer decided to call them differentiate these systems. However, with the power of today's microcomputer equaling that of larger systems, the issue is unclear and no longer very relevant. The terms for these systems, coupled with

notebooks, PDAs, workstations, and desktops, are not that important since basically they all operate the same way.

2. Donald D. Spencer, *The Illustrated Computer Dictionary* (Columbus, OH: Charles E. Merrill Company, 1980).

3. As part of their "crime scene toolkit," investigators should have a good computer dictionary and as much documentation as possible for the various devices available on the market today. Information should be stored in a database and readily accessible by investigators that describes the memory capacity and unique aspects of various components, such as keyboards and printers that may contain information in memory.

4. There are three. One is below the desktop CRT on the right; one is the "box" in the lower right-hand corner of the rack; and the third is the horizontal box on the lower left-hand corner of the rack.

5. The microphone is programmed so that we can say one word and begin the deletion of the hard drive and destruction of all evidence as we walk away from the computer. The investigator may think that, because no one is touching the systems, no evidence "tampering" is taking place.

6. October 1998 issue of http://www.govtech.net.

7. When the computer was left on for an extended period of time with the same image on the screen, it tended to "burn-in" that image. It was then visible when the CRT was turned off. Screensavers were developed to eliminate this problem. For today's modern monitors, this no longer is a problem.

8. A high-speed modem is located on top of the CPU, directly under the desktop monitor. Another modem, internal, is located inside the CPU and not visible from the outside.

9. This also applies to cellular phones and pagers. Can you identify the input, process, and output of these devices?

10. Don't look here for the answer. If you cannot figure this one out based on the information provided, it is very, very strongly recommended that you take an introductory course on computers or at least read a textbook used in one of those classes.

11. Remember that, although we are discussing general computers, the same holds true for cellular phones and other high-technology devices.

12. This information is based on "Smart Phones," *Computerworld* (April 13, 1998).

13. Read the Tofflers' books identified in the References and Recommended Reading chapter at the back of this book for additional information.

14. *Orange County Register* (May 23, 1998), p. 24.

15. The process of gathering statistics may be faulty, as well as how the statistics are interpreted and reported. Remember that these statistics

are reported by the FBI and they can also be used as a political tool by those in office. Therefore, all statistics, including those reported in this book, should always be taken as "best guesses" during the time and place they were developed.

16. *The Orange County Register* (April 7, 1998).
17. *The Orange County Register, Connect* (August 16, 1998).
18. Information received from the High Technology Crime Investigator Association listserv, credited to April 20, 1998, 2:02 A.M. EDT at http://www.nando.net.
19. "New Technology Developed to Recreate Crime Scenes," *Xinhua* (August 3, 1998).
20. *The Orange County Register* (June 14, 1998), p. 46.
21. *Computerworld* (April 27, 1998).
22. *Washington Technology* (December 18, 1997).
23. *USA Today* (May 10, 1999).
24. See Winn Schwartau's site at http://www.infowar.com (May 11, 1998).
25. *LANTIMES* (May 12 1997).
26. See Winn Schwartau's site at http://www.infowar.com (August 19, 1998).
27. See Winn Schwartau's site at http://www.infowar.com (August 19, 1998).
28. See *San Jose Mercury* newspaper site at http://www.sjmercury.com/business/tech (July 28, 1998).
29. *Communications News* (December 1997).
30. *Washington Technology* (June 4, 1998).
31. *Government Technology* (April 1998).
32. *Information Security* (March 1998).
33. *Washington Technology* (July 2, 1998).
34. *The Orange County Register* (November 24, 1998).

2

The Global Information Infrastructure, the Internet, and a Nation's Information Infrastructure

THE GLOBAL INFORMATION INFRASTRUCTURE

The global information infrastructure (GII) is a massive international connection of the world's computers that carries business and personal communication as well as that of the social and government sectors of nations. Some say it could connect entire cultures, erase international borders, support "cybereconomies," establish new markets, and change our entire concept of international relations.

The Internet is the basis for the GII. It allows the sharing of information and interaction on a real-time basis. What is interesting to note is that the estimated largest percentage of growth is in what we call *Third-World* countries, such as Argentina, Iran, Peru, Egypt, Philippines, Russia, Slovenia, and Indonesia. The Asian Internet, the GII baseline, is expected to rise 63% for the period 1995 to 2001.[1]

Why Is It Important to Us?

The GII is important to the high-technology-crime investigator because

When fully realized, the GII will be a vast network consisting of hundreds of thousands of networks. These networks will run our factories, process our financial transactions, organize our work, increase our productivity, instruct us and our children, help physicians and hospitals to care for us, connect us more closely with friends and family wherever they may be, entertain us, and perform a myriad of other services not yet conceived.[2]

In other words, it is increasingly the heart of our nonphysical world and also supports much of our processes in the physical world. Therefore, it also will be where the world's miscreants ply their trade.

What Are Its Advantages?

The GII has many significant advantages:

- Instant global communication.
- Instant global transfer of information.
- Increase global responsiveness.
- Lower cost of communications.
- Reduced cycle time to develop and deliver new products.
- Global electronic commerce.

What Are Its Military Uses?

Because the GII is based on the Internet, which was developed primarily for the military by the United States government's Department of Defense (DoD), and because it connects nations of the world for personal, business, and government agency use, it has many military uses and implications:[3]

- The United States military uses it for the DoD's continuous acquisition and life-cycle support (CALS), a 1980s effort to reduce costs and time for weapons systems procurement; "creating an infrastructure to enable improvement in core processes."
- It also is used for CALS contractor-integrated technical information service (CITIS), a 1990s vision of "a global information infrastructure linking customers and suppliers into virtual enterprises that can rapidly design, build, and support complex products."
- With United States government support, the GII also is being used for "collaborative design, engineering, manufacturing, and product support services accessible over global network."
- The CommerceNet CALS special interest group pilot project is designed to "develop and test the architecture for a network of Intelligent Hubs that is open, extensible, and 'scaleable' to support a distributed global enterprise integration business model."

What Are Its Implications?

From a high-technology-crime investigator's viewpoint, the GII has four primary implications of concern:

1. *Industrial and economic espionage.* Criminals can gain competitive advantage through penetration of the GII and theft of information. Because it is a global repository of "public" information, it offers access to information, some of which is not intended for general access.
2. *Terrorism.* Dependency on the GII means physical or logical attacks on it will have an impact on the "enemy."
3. *Military.* A target of opportunity, poorly protected since it was never intended for conflict, the GII could be vulnerable to even limited military systems.
4. *Fraud and other criminal acts.* The GII provides a vehicle for the world's miscreants to use in perpetrating fraud, on-line global stalking, identity theft, stock scams, and other crimes now being perpetrated in the "real," physical world.

THE INTERNET

The pace of evolution in communication and other technologies accelerated during the early years of the Information Age with the advent of satellites, fiber optics connections, and other high-speed, high-bandwidth telecommunication technologies.

In the context of this phenomenal growth of technology and human knowledge, the Internet arose as a mechanism to facilitate sharing information and as a medium that encourages global communication. According to a U.S. General Accounting Office report to Congress,[4] the rapid developments in the telecommunication infrastructure in the United States resulted in the creation of three separate and frequently incompatible communications networks: wire-based voice and data telephone networks; cable-based video networks; and wireless voice, data, and video network.

In the future, this problem will diminish as integration and commonality, forced by business and government needs for total information compatibility, takes place. As discussed earlier, this already is happening in many areas; for example, cellular phones and notebook computers, television and Internet access.

Birth of the Internet

The collection of networks that evolved in the late twentieth century to become the Internet represent what could be described as a "global nervous system," transmitting facts, opinions, and opportunity from anywhere to anywhere. However, when most security, law enforcement, and high-technology-crime investigative professionals think of the Internet, it seems to be something either vaguely sinister or of such complexity that it is difficult to understand. Popular culture, as manifested by Hollywood and network television programs, does little to dispel this impression of danger and out-of-control complexity.

The Internet arose out of projects sponsored by the Advanced Research Project Agency in the United States in the 1960s. Originally an effort to facilitate sharing of expensive computer resources and enhance military communication, over the ten years from about 1988 until 1998, it evolved rapidly from its scientific and military roots into one of the premier *commercial* communication media. The Internet, which is described as a global metanetwork, or network of networks,[5] provides the foundation on which the global information superhighway is being built.

However, not until the early 1990s did Internet communication technologies become easily accessible to the average person. Prior to that time, Internet access required mastery of many arcane and difficult to remember programming language codes. However, the combination of declining microcomputer prices, enhanced microcomputer performance, and the advent of easy-to-use browser software[6] were key enabling technologies to mass Internet activity.

In the United States alone, tens of millions of people access the Internet on a regular basis. Millions of others around the world are logging on, creating a vast environment often referred to as *cyberspace* and the *global information infrastructure*, which has been described as the virtual, on-line, computer-enabled environment—distinct from the physical reality of "real life." The growth of the Internet continues to surpass expectations, and therefore, any projections here would be of little use. Suffice it to say that the current estimates put its growth at a rate of approximately 7% per month. That is phenomenal and the growth may slow down in the near future; however, it is too unpredictable to guess.

The most commonly accessed application on the Internet is the World Wide Web. Originally developed in Switzerland, the Web was envisioned by its inventor as a way to share information. The ability to find information concerning virtually any topic via search engines, such as Alta Vista, HotBot, Lycos, InfoSeek, Yahoo or others from the rapidly growing array of web servers, is an amazing example of how the Internet increases the information available to nearly everyone. One gains some sense of how fast and pervasive the Internet has become as more TV, radio, print, and even billboard advertisements direct prospective customers to visit their business or government agency website. Such sites typically are named http://www.companyname.com for private businesses or http://governmentagency.gov for government agencies.

By the year 2000, worldwide revenues from Internet commerce are expected to reach perhaps hundreds of billions of dollars, an unparalleled growth rate for a technology that was effective only since the early 1990s. The "electronic commerce" of the early twenty-first century is expected to include everything from on-line information concerning products, purchases, services, to the development of entirely new business activities like Internet-enabled banking

The Web truly is global in scope. Physical borders and geographical distance are almost meaningless in cyberspace; the distant target is as easily attacked as a local one.

The annihilation of time and space makes the Internet an almost perfect environment for Internet thieves. When finding a desired server located on the other side of the planet is as easy and convenient as calling directory assistance for a local telephone number, Internet thieves have the potential to act in ways that we can only begin to imagine. Undeterred by distance, borders, time, or season, the potential bonanza awaiting the Internet thief is a chilling prospect, not only for those responsible for safeguarding the assets of a business or government agency but also those who must investigate violations of company policy or criminal acts.

What Are Its Uses?

The Internet has as many uses as one's imagination has vision. It currently is used for such things as

- Worldwide electronic mail.
- Business.
- Research.
- Crime.
- Travel reservations.
- Weather reports.
- News.
- Clubs and associations.

Internet Access

Internet access usually is from one of two sources: a business or government agency network interface to the Internet or an Internet service provider (ISP), of which there are hundreds if not thousands in the United States alone.

Internet Tools

The investigator should be familiar with the "tools" available for Internet users. Although not all inclusive, some of the more common ones are

- The World Wide Web is a screen leading to other screens using hypertext.
- File transfer protocol (FTP) transfer files between computers.
- Browser software is a client that enables access to websites.
- Telnet is used to log on to other computers to get information and programs.

Domain Names

The Internet is segregated into logical divisions known as *domains*. Because the Internet is the baseline for the GII, additional domain name extensions were required that would identify the countries' addresses. Such extensions include *uk* for United Kingdom, *ca* for Canada, and *us* for the United States, for example. A complete list of these designations can be found on the Internet. The investigator is challenged to find this list, which is located at more than one site.[7] The primary high-level domains are designated by describing their primary focus:

com for commercial businesses.

edu for educational institutions.

gov for government agencies.

int for organizations established by international treaty.

mil for military services.

net for network backbone systems, information centers.

org for nonprofit organizations.

Future Shock

With appreciation for Toffler's, *Future Shock* (1971), the reaction of people and organizations to the dizzying pace of Internet "progress" has been mixed. Although some technologically sophisticated individuals and organizations were very quick to exploit the potential of this new technology, many others have been slower, adopting more of a wait-and-see posture.

Sometimes lost in the technological hype concerning the physical speed of Internet-enabled communication is that it provides unprecedented *access* to information. The access is unprecedented in the breadth of the total volume of information that is moving on-line and may be tapped for decision making. In addition, it allows for communication among people.

Also unprecedented is the increasing percentage of the world's population that enjoys the access. As more and more information moves on-line and becomes available to more and more people, it is causing some fundamental changes in how we communicate, do business, and think of the world we live in. Consequently, it also is causing fundamental changes in how criminals and miscreants commit crimes.

Throughout much of human history, the educated elite of every culture has jealously guarded its knowledge. Access to knowledge, whether in written or spoken form, often was the source of the elite's privileged position and allowed it to dominate or control of the great uninformed masses of humanity—information was and still is a means to power. "Outsiders" were never granted access to the store of wisdom unless they were inducted into the privileged elite. Now, however, the average Internet traveler, wherever resident, with little more than a fast modem and a mediocre microcomputer, can access, analyze, and distribute information around the world on almost any topic.

Some pundits have concluded that we now live in an era where there are "no more secrets." By some estimates, early in the next century more information will be published and available on-line than ever available in all the libraries on earth. The primary objective of every security, law enforcement, and high-technology-crime investigator whose business or government agency travels the Internet is how this torrent of information will be managed to ensure that the Internet thieves do not wreak havoc and dominate the Internet or have power over others, in violation of local, state, national, and/or international laws.

Roadmap for the Internet

To better explain the Internet, it can be compared to a roadmap for a superhighway. Some basic examples will help explain the Internet in common terms.

When multiple computers (whether microcomputers or larger) are linked together to allow digital information to be transmitted and shared among the connected systems, they become a network. The combination of tens of thousand of organizational networks interconnected with high-capacity "backbone" data communication and the public telephone networks now constitutes the global Internet. However, there is a major difference in this environment that is important for security, law enforcement, and high-technology-crime investigators to consider.

When the isolated "byways" of individual business or government agency networks become connected to the global Internet, they become off-ramps, accessible to other Internet travelers. The number and diversity of locations that provide Internet "on-ramps" is vast and growing. Today, one can access the Internet from public libraries, "cyber" cafés in many cities around the world, even kiosks in some airports. These and other locations provide Internet on-ramps to anyone who has a legitimate account or an Internet thief who can "hijack" one from an authorized user.

Typically, a business or government agency will use centrally controlled computers, called *servers*, to store the information and the sophisticated software applications used to manage and control its information flow. These systems could be equated to a superhighway interchange.

Business and government agency networks commonly are considered private property and the information they contain proprietary, for the exclusive use of the organization. These business and government agency "networks" are connected to large networks operated by Internet service providers (such as UUNET, GTE, AOL, AT&T, and others) that provide the equivalent of toll roads and turnpikes for the flow of information.

The Internet: No Traffic Controls

The Internet challenges security, law enforcement, and high-technology-crime investigators with an array of new and old responsibilities in a new environment. From the perspective of managing risks, this new access to information creates new kinds of danger to businesses and government agencies. It also allows well-understood security issues to recur in new or unique ways. No longer can organizations assume they will obtain any security through obscurity, no matter where they are located physically. In other words, because there is an Internet off-ramp they will be visible to Internet thieves. Everything from a nation's most critical defense secrets to business information is vulnerable to easy destruction, modification, and compromise by unauthorized Internet travelers.

Too often careless managers fail to take adequate measures to safeguard sensitive information, which results in premature disclosure, with the attendant adverse impact. The major part of the controllable risk arises from inadvertent disclosure to the ever-vigilant eyes of the Internet thieves and others such as competitive intelligence analysts with Internet access.

No Central Management or Internet Police

One of the most fascinating aspects in the Internet growth saga is that it developed largely through the collaborative and unregulated efforts of the interested parties. Self-appointed leaders and task forces worked together to address the tricky technical details of the design and operation of this environment.

When the Internet was limited to scientists, academic researchers, and government employees, such a collaborative framework probably was a very cost-effective means of controlling the virtual world. However, in the early 1990s, for the first time, more commercial sites than educational and government sites were using the Internet. Since that time, matters have become increasingly complex. The informal array of social sanctions and technical forums for cooperation no longer can ensure a modicum of civilized behavior.

THE U.S. NATIONAL INFORMATION INFRASTRUCTURE

The U.S. information infrastructure,[8] also called the *national information infrastructure* (NII), generally is described as the total network of computers and telecommunication systems used to maintain, support, and service the needs of a nation.

The U.S. Critical Information Infrastructure

As the United States began to develop its information infrastructure, protection of the NII became a concern to many businesses and government agencies. The President's Commission on Critical Infrastructure Protection (PCCIP) was the first national effort to address the vulnerability created in the new Information Age. The commission, established in July 1996 by Presidential Executive Order 13010, had the task of formulating a comprehensive national strategy to protect the infrastructures we all depend on from physical and "cyber" threats. The final report was completed in October 1997. (See http://www.PCCIP.gov for additional information. A copy of the report may be available on-line—the unclassified version.)

Of course, no government study or commission would be worth its weight in bureaucracy without recommending and subsequently assisting to form government organizations, commissions, task forces, and the like to expand government influence into more and more of the private sector, based on some government study. The PCCIP was no exception. The Information Infrastructure Task Force (IITF) was formed to articulate and implement the administration's vision for the national information infrastructure.

The IITF consists of representatives of the federal agencies that play a major role in the development and application of information and telecommunications technologies. Several IITF committees have been established: Telecommunications Policy, Information Policy, and Applications and Technology.

The Infrastructure Protection Task Force (IPTF), a multiagency task force, was created on July 15, 1996, by Executive Order 13010 to identify and coordinate existing expertise and capabilities in the government and private sectors from both physical and cyber threats.

Critical infrastructures are systems whose incapacity or destruction would have a debilitating impact on the defense or economic security of the nation. They include telecommunications, electrical power systems, gas and oil, banking and finance, transportation, water supply systems, government services, and emergency services.

PCCIP Working Definitions

The following definitions were taken directly from the PCCIP website:

- *Telecommunications.* The networks and systems that support the transmission and exchange of electronic communications among and between end users (such as networked computers).
- *Electrical power systems.* The generation stations and transmission and distribution networks that create and supply electricity to end users so that users achieve and maintain nominal functionality, including the transportation and storage of fuel essential to that system.
- *Banking and finance.* The retail and commercial organizations, investment institutions, exchange boards, trading houses, and reserve systems, and associated operational organizations, government operations, and support entities, involved in all manner of monetary transactions.
- *Transportation.* The aviation, rail, highway, and aquatic vehicles, conduits, and support systems by which people and goods are moved from a point of origin to a destination point in order to support and complete matters of commerce, government operations, and personal affairs.
- *Gas and oil production, storage, and transportation.* The holding facilities for natural gas, crude and refined petroleum, and petroleum-derived fuels; the refining and processing facilities for these fuels and the pipelines; ships, trucks, and rail systems that transport these commodities from their source to systems that are dependent on gas and oil in one of their useful forms.
- *Water supply systems.* The sources of water, reservoirs and holding facilities, aqueducts and other transport systems, the filtration and cleaning systems, the pipelines, the cooling systems and other delivery mechanisms that provide for domestic and industrial applications, including systems for dealing with wastewater and fire fighting.
- *Emergency services.* The medical, police, fire, and rescue systems and personnel called on when an individual or community is responding to a public health or safety incident where speed and efficiency are necessary.
- *Continuity of government services.* Those operations and services of governments at federal, state, and local levels critical to the functioning of the nation's systems; that is, public health, safety, and welfare.

Organization of PCCIP Sector Teams

The commission is divided into five teams, representing the eight critical infrastructures. Each team evaluates the growing risk, threats, and vulnerabilities within its sector. The sector teams and their industries include

- *Information and communications* monitors telecommunications, computers and software, the Internet, satellites, and fiber optics.
- *Physical distribution* monitors railroads, air traffic, maritime trade, intermodal traffic, and pipelines.
- *Energy* monitors electrical power, natural gas, and petroleum production, distribution, and storage.
- *Banking and finance* monitors financial transactions, stocks and bonds markets, and the Federal Reserve Bank.
- *Vital human services* monitors water, emergency services, and government services.

The PCCIP study and final report found the following:

- *Interdependence of critical infrastructures.* Electrical energy, communications, and computers now are an interrelated trio.
- *New threats.* Physical threats have expanded to include cyber threats, and these new threats are wide-ranging.
- *Lack of awareness.* The general public is unaware of the nature and extent of the dependency of modern society on the critical intrastructures.
- *No national focus.* No single element of government has primary responsibility for security to critical instrastructures.

The study concluded that new thinking is required. With escalating dependence on information and telecommunications, U.S. infrastructures no longer enjoy the protection of oceans and military forces. The public and private sectors share responsibility for this protection.

The country must act now to protect the future. Waiting for disaster will prove to be expensive and irresponsible. Information assurance is a shared responsibility—it's not just the military's job. Protection cannot be based on who the attacker is or from where the attack originates.

The study recommended a broad program of awareness and education and information protection through industry cooperation and information sharing. Such structures would provide for the partnership needed to assure our future security.

The following immediate actions were suggested:

- Isolate critical control systems from insecure networks.
- Adopt the best practices for password control and protection.

- Provide for individual accountability through protected action logs.
- Reconsider laws related to infrastructure protection. Present laws have failed to keep pace with technology.
- Revise the program of research and development to provide resilient system and response capabilities.
- Establish a national organization structure composed of sector coordinators and lead agencies, such as the National Infrastructure Assurance Council (which includes CEOs, cabinet secretaries, representatives of state and local governments), the Information Sharing and Analysis Center, the Infrastructure Assurance Support Office, the bulk of the national staff responsible for continuous management, and the Office of National Infrastructure Assurance (as the top policy making office).

One Last Word of Gloom to Put This in Perspective

The United States still is not prepared for cybercrime, according to participants of the Thirteenth Annual International Symposium on Criminal Justice Issues. According to some, who of course have vested interests, "It's going to take a major high-tech disaster to shake up corporate and government officials enough to work together in fighting high-tech crime." Corporate management is willing to accept the risks because the costs of such crime is prohibitive—and comes out of shareholders' values: profits and dividends.

A major complaint of government officials, such as those in the FBI, is that the corporations are unwilling to report high-technology crimes. Probably, they are right in not doing so based on the costs, bad publicity for the company, length of time to conduct the investigation, and the potential lawsuits from the alleged miscreants.

The article also pointed out some other interesting "news":

- Jurisdiction in cyberspace appears to be an issue as both state and local police seem unwilling to concede to the FBI.
- Despite the fact that only about 1 in 20 cases of computer break-ins is reported, the FBI is quickly becoming swamped. The new FBI organization has more than 500 cases of computer crime pending, up 130 percent from 1996.
- Because the United States economy depends on the Internet and computers more than any other country, it has the most at risk. Other nations—including Israel, Canada, France and Germany—seem ready to learn from the United States' problems. Concerns over cybercrime have even reached the hinterlands of the Internet. Five officers from the Botswana police department attended the conference.

"We have had many problems with banks and computer crime," said Officer Tabathu Mulale.

To summarize thus far, it is imperative that anti-high-technology-crime professionals understand this global environment of networks, users, technology, threats, areas of vulnerability, risks, global miscreants, and how to successfully work in this environment.

NOTES

1. CNN at http://www.customnews.cnn.com/cnews (February 4, 1998).
2. *Understanding the Global Information Infrastructure*, IBM Living in the Canadian Information Society. (See http://www.CAN.IBM.com.)
3. The quotes are from *Formtek Journal* 28 (Fall 1996), p. 3.
4. Information Superhighway: An Overview of Technology Challenges, GAO-AIMD 95-23 (Washington, DC: GAO, 1995), p. 12.
5. Ibid., p.11.
6. Software that simplifies the search and display of World Wide Web-supplied information.
7. A helpful hint when looking for something on the Internet, start by accessing a "search engine" and search using key words such as . . . well, you're an investigator, investigate.
8. The information relative to the NII and PCCIP was taken directly from various websites. We suggest using a search engine and searching for PCCIP. Numerous sites are available on this topic.
9. "US Still Not Prepared for Cybercrime," *ZDNet* (August 10, 1998), at http://www.infowar.com/law.

3

High-Technology Miscreants
Profiles, Motives, and Philosophies

HISTORY OF HIGH-TECHNOLOGY CRIME
AND ITS MISCREANTS

As stated earlier, the environment really is the only major difference between high-technology criminals and the other miscreants found in society today. The change in environment does not change the type of people nor their motives. They still are the same scoundrels who want something someone else owns or, out of jealousy or just plain meanness, want to deprive the owner of that thing of value. Others soon will want, and will try, to kill someone through telemedicine.

The juvenile delinquents, economic and espionage spies, hackers, PBX and cellular phone fraudsters, sexual deviants, and other miscreants that commit high-technology crimes generally represent a cross-section of those that have always been around. Known generally as *threat agents*, all of these miscreants pose threats to the businesses, government agencies, and honest citizens in today's high-technology environment.

In the 1970s, high-technology crimes such as computer fraud were rare, and those that did occur rarely were reported because the company or government agency did not want the public to lose confidence in it and in its newly installed computers. After all, these groups were touting the dawn of the computer age, at a cost of millions of dollars.

Perpetrators generally were computer specialists: programmers, computer operators, data entry personnel, systems analysts, and computer managers—insiders. After all, they were the only ones who knew how to operate and use the technology and the only ones able to gain physical access to them. The threats were internal, because there were no physical connections of these systems to the outside world. In addition, these systems cost millions of dollars and were extremely heavy and difficult to move. So, even theft generally was not an issue. As the technology and systems evolved, limited networking took place; however, most were the Arpanet connections, which was the "father" of the Internet.

In the 1980s, the type and frequency of high-technology crime changed, brought about by the personal computer, telecommunication advancements, and networking. The internal types of perpetrators were expanded to include workers suffering financial or personal problems, disgruntled, bored, tempted by curiosity, or challenged. This also was the time of the external hacker. During this period, external threats began to grow. Most information systems security professionals during that period and into the early 1990s placed the threats at approximately 80% internal and 20% external.

In the 1990s and into the twenty-first century, international crime and fraud developed, and will continue to develop, due to increased international networking—the global information infrastructure based on the Internet.

Also, the new technologies of the private branch exchange (PBX; a telephone switching device) and cellular phones, both based on computers (microprocessors), brought with them the telecommunications criminals, who increased in number as the technology became cheaper, more powerful, and more widely used.

The perpetrators generally are the same as in the past but now include more international criminals, hackers, and phreakers because of this ease of international access. With the integration of telecommunications and personal computers into the Internet, the threats appear to be approaching an equal split between internal and external agents: 50% internal and 50% external.

WHAT CONSTITUTES A HIGH-TECHNOLOGY CRIME

To commit a high-technology crime, three requirements must be met. According to the Association of Certified Fraud Examiners and members of the criminology profession, these three requirements are the same regardless of the crime to be perpetrated:

- *Motive.* One who is not motivated to commit a crime will not commit a crime.
- *Rationalization.* One must be able to rationalize the crime to be committed. The rationalization need not be logical or make any sense to anyone else, but the "criminals" must believe it.
- *Opportunity.* Even if one is motivated and able to rationalize a high-technology crime, one needs the opportunity to commit that crime with at least the thought of not getting caught.

When discussing this "triad," it is important to remember that we all probably could commit a crime under the "right" circumstances. For example, consider the following hypothetical scenario. Steve has a family with kids getting ready for college, a mortgage, car payments, and the normal other bills. He worked for a company for about 25 years and is about 54 years old. He is called into the boss' office one Friday and told that the company is downsizing and terminating his employment. He is being given 60 days notice since federal law requires it (the company is firing over 500 people). He knows that he will have difficulty finding another job, especially at his age, and his skills are somewhat outdated and not in great demand. He doesn't know how he will make it. Money put aside for college would have to be dipped into. He will have to sell one car, as he can't afford two. Also, he is concerned about other finances. In other words, in about 60 days, Steve's entire world will be turned upside down and he doesn't know how he will survive.

For most people that would be enough to start thinking somewhat negatively about his or her place of employment and its managers, company president, and so on. However, to really push Steve over the edge, let's say, the next morning, he reads in the business section of the paper that company he worked for was having greater sales than ever and record profits. In fact, the company president is getting a $2.5 million bonus and the executive managers are getting $1 million dollars each for saving the company so much money over the years and increasing profits.

Steve now is motivated to get what he can from that company in the next 60 days. "You deserve it" becomes the rationale. So now, he has the motive and the rationalization. Some people use violence as a means of retribution, such as the office worker who kills the manager that yelled at him or her; others use fraud, theft, or whatever opportunity gives them.

As a high-technology-crime investigator, keep the triad in mind when investigating a high-technology crime, and try to identify it when searching for a suspect.

INSIDER THREATS

Still the most serious threats and the highest risks are from the business's or government agency's employees. These individuals have access to the physical and intellectual property of their employers. Furthermore, they are *trusted.*

Who Is an Insider?

An insider is a company or government agency's employee or a person on contract to the company, such as a contract programmer. To make a clearer distinction, it is defined, at least for our purposes, as one who receives payment directly from the business or government agency that employs him or her. An insider is anyone who has access to the high technology, intellectual property, and other sensitive information residing on high-technology equipment (e.g. information system networks) as well as to input or output documents. These include, but are not limited to, the following:

- *Auditors.* Auditors have the authority to gain access to many sensitive areas and sensitive information. Furthermore, they conduct audits of computers, PBX systems, and other high-technology processes, depending on the business, that identify areas of inadequate controls. They are some of the most trusted employees within a business.
- *Security personnel.* Security personnel are the people on the defensive frontline against high-technology crime. They, like the auditors, know what areas are vulnerable, where security may be weak, and the security controls in place in all areas of the business. They, like the auditors, are some of the most trusted personnel within a business.
- *Marketing.* The marketing people have access to computer systems, dial-out access through the PBX, use cellular phones, pagers, and the like, both in the office and when they travel on company business. They have access to customers' listings, long-range plans, and marketing concepts now and into the future.
- *Accountants and financial personnel.* Accountants and financial specialists have access to automated financial accounts, check writing, financial analyses of the business, accounts payable, accounts receivable, and the like. In many companies, they also are responsible for distributing to employees, and controlling, company credit cards.
- *Management.* Managers, by the very title, have access to sensitive information and finances, via their budgets; and they generally have more access authority on information systems. Also, they have the authority, depending on the management level, to waive controls—physical, administrative, and logical.
- *Inventory and warehouse personnel.* These individuals have access to physical property and the inventory records maintained on the business's computer network. High-technology devices often are a tempting item for theft.
- *Human resources.* HR people have access to much of the company's information; at a minimum, information concerning salaries, home addresses, social security numbers, and other information of a private nature, which is worth money to businesses building marketing databases of potential customers. In companies going through downsizing, HR personnel have been known to sell computerized listings of these individuals.

Now, place yourself in one of the preceding or another position, and think of how you could use these high-technology tools to perpetrate a high-tech crime. Then, think of how you would investigate such a crime. You will probably find that you can at least develop a logical set of questions to ask as you interview employees. If so, that is a good start. If not, then at least you'll realize you have much to learn and can go about acquiring that knowledge.

Insider Motivations, Rationalizations, and Opportunities

Some possible motives for insider crime could be financial gain, revenge, the challenge of getting away with it, or curiosity.

Some rationalizations for committing the crime could be that the insider felt underpaid, denied a deserved promotion, or that his or her work goes unrecognized.

The company or agency provides the opportunity, which could include a lack of audit trails, no access controls to systems or files, a lack of separation of duties, or no method of accountability.

Threat Recognition

Some characteristics or indicators that an insider may pose a threat include

- Bankruptcy.
- Pending divorce.
- Unexplained wealth.
- "Big spending."
- Constant complaining.
- Hostility.
- Emotional instability.
- Signs of extreme stress.
- Profound personality changes.
- Expressed feelings of being victimized by peers, employers, or the organization.

OUTSIDER THREATS

Class of Outsiders

Outsiders have always been a threat, especially now that companies have the Internet, global networks, cellular phones, and PBX systems, but in reality, far more documented high-technology crimes have been perpetrated by insiders than outsiders. Some groups of outsiders are as follows:

- Hackers.
- Phreakers.
- Vendors.
- Former employees.
- Employees of associated businesses.
- Competitors.
- Foreign government agents.
- Customers.
- Subcontractors.
- Terrorists.
- Contractors, such as maintenance personnel.
- Outside auditors.
- Consultants.
- Political activists.

A number of business and technological developments will increase the outsider threats:

- The number of computers internationally continues to increase past 100 million.
- The number of U.S. computers continues to increase past 25 million.
- Computer literacy worldwide in on the rise.
- Telecommunications and networked computers continue to increase worldwide.
- More and more people are telecommuting.
- Outsourcing increases.
- Increased use of technologies such as EDI, EFTS, and POS (point-of-sale; as used by grocery stores and others often coupled with bar-coding systems) systems.
- Strategic, advanced systems become increasingly the target of others as economic competition grows.
- Terrorism is growing, and it is only a matter of time before terrorists begin targeting computers.
- Former Soviet Union countries' intelligence agents are selling their expertise to the highest bidders.

Outsider Motivations

Many outsiders share the same motivations as the insiders, but some others include

- Revenge of a former employee.
- Competitors wanting inside information.

- New employees who provide information relative to their previous employer.
- Former employees' curiosity about their previous access ID and passwords.
- Political agenda.
- Nationalistic economic pressures.

HACKERS, CRACKERS, AND PHREAKERS

The Hackers

One of the biggest challenges facing security, high-technology-crime investigators, and law enforcement professionals today is the hacker. This is not only because of some of the hackers' increasingly sophisticated methods but also because of their sheer numbers.

Initially, hackers were considered just intelligent kids who experimented with the computers (Levy, 1984). Then the term *hacker* began to be used incorrectly as a label for those who illegally accessed the computers for their personal pleasure, vandalism, and later criminal purposes. This usage has now become part of the Internet culture.

Hacker Profile

It is generally agreed among those dealing with hackers that the average United States hacker profile[1] ever since the 1980s is as follows:

- White.
- Male.
- Young (14 to middle 20s).
- Intelligent.
- Avid computer enthusiast.
- Introverted.
- Insecure.
- From a middle- to upper-middle-income family.

The opinion of security professionals and the hackers themselves tend to agree that computer hackers are mostly motivated by their desire to

- Learn about computers as a hobby.
- Defy authority.
- Respond to a challenge.
- "Beat the system."
- Cause disruption.

- Show contempt for others.
- Show how smart they are.

The U.S. Department of Justice[2] describes hackers as

- Between 15 and 45 years old.
- Predominantly men with the number of women increasing.
- Have no prior criminal record.
- Target businesses' and government agencies' systems.
- Bright, motivated, and willing to accept challenges.
- Fear ridicule, exposure, and loss of status.
- Usually work alone but are socially "normal."
- Hold a position of trust, usually are the first to arrive at work and last to leave.
- View criminal acts as a game.

When comparing these two descriptions, one can see that not much has changed over the last 15 to 20 years.

Jerrold M. Post, director of the Political Psychology Programs at George Washington University, described hackers as follows:

- They are creative, individualistic, problem solvers, but from a psychological perspective they are arrogant, loners, and from a broken or troubled home.
- They seem to suffer low self-esteem, have a need to draw attention to themselves, and seek the recognition of their peers.
- The hackers perceive themselves to be intelligent but poor achievers in school; often perceived as misfits, nerds, weirdos, misunderstood; look for challenges; usually are between 12 and 28 years old; from dysfunctional families; inept from a social perspective.
- They are motivated by challenge, excitement, and want to learn for intellectual satisfaction.
- They do not consider themselves thieves but "borrowers" and may be addicted or obsessed by computers.
- They consider themselves civil libertarians, Robin Hoods, and electronic freedom fighters.

There are three basic types of hackers (Levy, 1984; Kovacich, 1994): the curious, the meddlers (or juvenile delinquents), and the criminals.

The curious break into computers to learn more about them. It is generally agreed that the first true hackers came from the Massachusetts Institute of Technology in the 1950s and 1960s. Many of that initial group belonged to MIT's Technical Model Railroad Club. The original "hacker ethic" was "Access to computers—and anything which might teach you something about the way the world works—should be unlimited and total.

Always yield to the Hand-On-Imperative!" (Steele, 1983). With the proliferation of different types of computers and increased security controls to do with licensing and software agreements, the types of hackers changed. They no longer are regarded as simply having an insatiable curiosity.

The meddlers (Steele, 1983) or juvenile delinquents break into computers because they are interested in the challenge of breaking in and looking for weaknesses in the system. In the days of "dial-ups" and before the Internet expanded into what it is today, this inquisitive person might have used a "hacking software" program that continuously dialed telephone numbers looking for a computer modem tone (a "wardialer"). Then the hacker used various types of software or just guesses to identify a user's identification and passwords to gain access. Today, these miscreants use search tools such as Yahoo, Lycos, or Excite; search the Internet for hacking tools; download hacker software programs (or security programs that have been turned into hacking tools); identify a target; and execute the programs. The primary difference between today's hackers and the earlier ones of the 1960s through 1980s is that today's hackers not only access computers without approval or authority, but if they are challenged, they tend to become more vicious and more prone to destruction of information and shutting down systems.

The criminals break into computers to commit a crime: to act for personal gain, destroy information, steal information, or damage system files. As they began to penetrate computers, they bragged about their exploits to fellow hackers, through hacker computer bulletin boards. These hacker computers, linked through telephone lines, "talk" to one another. It is interesting to note that many of the hacker bulletin boards had better security than the billion dollar corporations' systems they had penetrated. Now, these hackers, along with the true hackers and meddlers, often operate their own websites on the Internet.

These penetrations and subsequent unauthorized entry and manipulation of computer files, such as those of credit records, caused harm and increased publicity. Because of public outrage and legislation, hackers found their equipment confiscated by federal and local law enforcement officials, many times to the surprise of their parents.

Although some computer and telephone hackers fit the profile of the hackers of the 1950s, 1960s, and 1970s, the late 1980s saw two new types of hackers. The first were the international hackers that began penetrating computers in the United States from as far away as Europe. In one notorious case, a hacker was traced from Lawrence Berkeley Lab to Hannover, Germany (Stoll, 1989). It was subsequently determined that hackers were being paid by the KGB to break into U.S. computers. Hacking had become an international "profession." The other type of hacker was penetrating telephone switching systems for the sole purpose of selling toll free international telephone calls to anyone with $15 or $20. These became known as *phreakers*.

The challenge is to stop these hackers and phreakers, who are causing annual losses in the billions of dollars. Jerry Swick, a senior investigator at MCI WorldCom, explains,

> According to law enforcement and private sector experts, business losses from telecommunications fraud are estimated at more than $4 billion per year. The average loss per incident to users is in the thousands of dollars. Telecrooks, hackers, and "phone phreaks" are invading corporate telephone and voice messaging systems at an unprecedented rate. This type of activity disrupts an organization's valuable communications network and causes losses of revenue. Telecommunications fraud creates an expensive problem that affects consumers and businesses.

International hackers are a growing concern, and many have targeted systems in the United States, especially those of the Department of Defense. These juvenile delinquents and foreign governments' information warriors have become more sophisticated, better equipped, and more vicious than their predecessors. It was rumored that a group of Dutch hackers offered their support to Iraq during the Persian Gulf War. They denied making any such offer. The financial systems of the United States have come under increased attacks, and some of the most serious are from Russia's criminal elements.

The Phreakers

While the hackers were busy breaking into computer systems, another form of hacker was busy breaking into telephone switching systems and making telephone calls around the world without paying for them. One of the first to gain notoriety was "Captain Crunch." He allegedly found that a free whistle enclosed in cereal boxes, when held to the telephone handset, made the same sound as the telephone switching equipment. It provided him the ability to make free long distance telephone calls. Another, known as "The Cracker," began to explore the telephone switching systems at the age of 14 (Landreth, 1985).

The phreaker is a hacker who specializes in telecommunications hacking. Phreakers prefer private branch exchanges and telephone switches. In writing to one another and others, they exchange the letter *f* with *ph*, which is why they are known as *phreakers*. Today, these juvenile delinquents and criminals pose some of the most serious challenges to security and law enforcement professionals. Some have skills that rival those of engineers at the telecommunications corporations.

Sometimes hackers and phreakers form "hacker gangs" and declare "war" on each other. Some shared information and others were rivals. The rival gangs often attacked each other like the street gangs of today. Gangs, such as Masters of Deception, Legion of Doom, and numerous others, generally were loosely formed groups of young hackers who enjoyed the camaraderie of sharing information and attacking systems together.

PROFILE OF THE HIGH-TECHNOLOGY AND INTERNET FRAUDSTERS

Technology fraudsters, like other technocriminals, can be anyone— organized crime members, white-collar workers, drug dealers, people in debt, people wanting revenge, greedy people—under the right circumstances.

Don't forget that high-technology fraud offenders differ little from the "average" person. According to studies (Association of Certified Fraud Examiners, 1995), most offenders commit fraud for the same reasons most criminals commit crimes: motive, rationalization, and opportunity. These studies also indicate that most computer crimes have been committed for personal financial gain, followed by intellectual challenge, to help the organization, and from peer pressure.

HIGH-TECHNOLOGY TERRORISTS

Terrorism is the use of terror and violence for political purposes, as by a government to intimidate the population or by an insurgent group to oppose the government in power. The FBI defines *terrorism* as "the unlawful use of force or violence against persons or property to intimidate or coerce a government, the civilian population, or any segment thereof, in furtherance of political or social objectives." The U.S. CIA defines *international terrorism* as "terrorism conducted with the support of foreign governments or organizations and/or directed against foreign nations, institutions, or governments." The U.S. Departments of State and Defense define *terrorism* as "premeditated, politically motivated violence perpetrated against a noncombatant target by sub-national groups or clandestine state agents, usually intended to influence an audience. International terrorism is terrorism involving the citizens or territory of more than one country."

A terrorist, then, is one who causes intense fear; one who controls, dominates, or coerces through the use of terror. With businesses, government agencies, and users becoming more and more dependent on the Internet, it is just a matter of time before the Internet terrorists begin committing their acts. However, instead of car bombs, they will use logic bombs and viruses.

Results of Terrorist Actions

Terrorist acts tend to cause an increase in security. It may cause the government to decrease the freedom of its citizens to protect them. This, in turn, may cause more citizens to turn against the government, thus supporting the terrorists. It also causes the citizens to become aware of the terrorists and their demands.

We can see some aspects of this trend in the United States. We are willing to give up some of our freedom and privacy to have more security and personal protection; for example, increased airport security searches and questioning of passengers to avert aircraft hijackings.

Current terrorist targets have included transportation systems, citizens, buildings, and government officials, military barracks, and embassies.

The Environment of Terrorist Technology Threats

Today's terrorists not only are using technology to communicate (e.g., Internet e-mail) and technology crimes to fund their activities (e.g., credit card fraud or illegal bank money transfers), they are beginning to look at the potential for using technology in the form of information warfare against their enemies. It is believed by many security professionals that this will increase in the future.

Internet terrorists can conduct such activities with little risk to themselves, since target systems can be attacked and "destroyed" from the base of a country friendly to them. In addition, they can do so with no loss of life, thus reducing the potential backlash against them that could occur if they had destroyed buildings and people.

HIGH-TECHNOLOGY ECONOMIC AND INDUSTRIAL ESPIONAGE ON THE INTERNET

When we look at rapid, technology-oriented growth, we find nations of haves and have-nots. We also see corporations that conduct business internationally and those that want to do so. International economic competition and trade wars are increasing. Corporations are constantly looking for a competitive edge.

One way to gain competitive advantage is through industrial and economic espionage. Both forms of espionage have been around since there has been competition. However, in the Information Age, competitiveness is more time dependent, more crucial to success, and dramatically more pervasive, largely due to technology. We now have more sensitive information consolidated in large databases on Internet-networked systems whose security often is questionable.

Industrial espionage is the individual or private business entity sponsorship or coordination of intelligence activity conducted to enhance a competitor's advantage in the marketplace. According to the FBI and the Economic Espionage Act of 1996, Section 1831, economic espionage "refers to foreign power-sponsored or -coordinated intelligence activity, directed at the U.S. government or corporations, entities, or other individuals operating in the United States for the purpose of unlawfully obtaining trade secrets" (see http://www.fbi.gov).

Try Catching These Miscreants

Former (as well as active) KGB, CSR, and GRU agents[3] are dangerous, but the most dangerous high-technology spies are Ph.D. computer scientists trained by the KGB, GRU, Chinese Intelligence Service, and others. They have many decades of experience, reverse-engineered IBM mainframes during the Cold War, and are the ones to most fear. These are the agents that, without sheer luck or a lot of money spent on security, will not be detected. If they are detected, it will be a challenge to investigate the matter and be able to build a case that would stand up in court.

Proprietary Economic Information

The new global competitive environment makes a corporation's proprietary information more valuable than ever. According to an unnamed FBI agent this information can encompass

> all forms and types of financial, scientific, technical, economic, or engineering information including but not limited to data, plans, tools, mechanisms, compounds, formulas, designs, prototypes, processes, procedures, programs, codes, or commercial strategies, whether tangible, or intangible . . . and whether stored, compiled, or memorialized physically, electronically, graphically, photographically, or in writing.

This assumes that the owner takes reasonable measures to protect the information and it is not available to the general public. These types of information are key targets for the industrial and economic espionage agents and much of this information is accessible via the Internet or on Internet-connected computer and network systems.

Vulnerability to Economic Espionage

The increase in economic espionage also is due largely to corporate vulnerability to such threats. Many corporations do not adequately identify and protect their information nor do they adequately protect their computer and telecommunications systems. Too many have inadequate security policies and procedures, and employees are unaware of their responsibility to protect the corporation's proprietary information. Many of the employees and managers of these corporations do not believe they have any information worth stealing or believe "it can't happen here."

Therefore, the combination of

- A nation's or corporation's information that is valuable to other nations and businesses,
- The amount of money some are willing to pay for that information,
- The increase in miscreants willing to try to steal that information,
- The increase in Internet connections to businesses and government agencies,
- The vulnerability of systems on Internet connections such as websites,
- The lack of security as a high priority for businesses and government agencies, and
- The ability to steal that information on a global scale

all combine to create conditions that are ripe for criminal exploitation.

All these add up to some very dangerous times for those with information worth protecting and major challenges to the security, high-technology-crime investigators, and law enforcement professionals with the responsibility to protect and investigate incidents.

When corporations fail to adequately protect their information, they take risks that, in all probability, will cause them to lose market share, profits, business, and help weaken the economic strength of their countries.

Infowarriors and Cyberwarriors

Information warfare (IW) is the term used to define the concept of twenty-first century warfare, which will be electronic and information systems driven. Since it is still evolving, its definition and budgets are "muddy" and dynamic.

Federal government agencies and departments within the U.S. Department of Defense (e.g., Air Force, Navy, Office of Secretary of Defense, National Security Agency, US Army) all seem to have somewhat different definitions of IW. As you would expect, these agencies define IW in terms of strictly military action; however, that does not mean that the targets are strictly military ones.

As defined by the U.S. Defense Information Systems Agency (DISA), *information warfare* is actions taken to achieve information superiority in support of national military strategy by affecting adversary information and information systems while leveraging and protecting our information and information systems.

This definition seems to be a good summary definition of all the federal government agencies' definitions.

The federal government divides IW into three general categories: offensive, defensive, and exploitation. For example,

- Deny, corrupt, destroy, or exploit an adversary's information, or influence the adversary's perception (offensive).
- Safeguard ourselves and allies from similar actions (defensive), also known as *IW hardening*.
- Exploit available information in a timely fashion to enhance one's decision or action cycle and disrupt the adversary's cycle (exploitative).

In addition, the military views IW as including electronic warfare (e.g., jamming communications links), surveillance systems, precision strikes (e.g., bombing a telecommunications switching system), and advanced battlefield management (e.g., using information and information systems to provide information on which to base military decisions when fighting a war). The People's Republic of China has the view, as do most other countries, that information warfare will include the civilian community (afterall, it did in WWII, Vietnam, and Serbia):

> The rapid development of networks has turned each automated system into a potential target of invasion. The fact that information technology is increasingly relevant to people's lives determines that those who take part in information war are not all soldiers and that anybody who understands computers may become a "fighter" on the network. Think tanks composed of non-governmental experts may take part in decision making; rapid mobilization will not just be directed to young people; information-related industries and domains will be the first to be mobilized and enter the war . . . (The British Broadcasting Corporation Summary of World Broadcasts [August 20, 1996], translated from the *Jiefangjun Bao*, a Beijing newspaper [June 25, 1996], p. 6).

Remember that these armies of infowarriors are looking at the targets presented along the Internet, and the vast majority of these are commercial, nonmilitary. The weapons they will use can be designed for attack, protection, exploitation, and support. They have the funding and identified targets and are developing plans and sophisticated application programs to attack a nation's information infrastructure, which includes those on the Internet.

SOPHISTICATED DRUG DEALERS' USE OF HIGH TECHNOLOGY

"Drug traffickers no longer use telephones or radios. They have become sophisticated using equipment that codifies their messages," Also Demoz, head of the Latin American and Caribbean division of the United Nations Drug Control Program (UNDCP), told Reuters.[4]

Julio Cesar Araoz, head of Argentina's drug enforcement agency, said, "Drug-trafficking organizations have globalized their task and use high technology," and suggested similar tactics be used by governments to fight the drug war. "Latin America and the Caribbean should likewise have a globalized reaction based on international cooperation. And we have to use the same technology as the traffickers, because otherwise it looks like a lost battle," he said.

SUMMARY

One should not be surprised to see those who are interested in adult or child pornography, racism, bigotry, perpetrating frauds, scams, and others whose behavior has been termed unacceptable by most societies now are involved in high-technology crime. They also are cruising the GII, Internet, NII, and companies' high-technology systems. The people haven't changed, only the modus operandi. The high-technology-crime investigator, to be successful, must know "what makes people tick." Again, people are people. Only the environment has changed.

NOTES

1. Generally accepted profile of hackers by high-technology-crime investigators based on their experiences and others in the early 1980s.
2. Found at http://www.ed.harrison.net. (Ed Harrison is a law enforcement officer and high-technology-crime investigator.)
3. The KGB is the Komitet Gosudarstvennoy Bezopasnosti, the Soviet intelligence agency; the CSR is the Centralnaya Sluzhbza Razvedkyin, the remaining elements of the Committee for State Security; and the GRU is the Glavnoye Razvedyvatelnoye Upravleniye, the Chief Intelligence Directorate.
4. These quotes are taken from Winn Schwartau's website at http://www.infowar.com (October 6, 1997).

4

The Basic Techniques Used by High-Technology Miscreants

INCREASING HIGH-TECHNOLOGY CRIMES

High-technology security problems have increased and high-technology criminals are successful for several reasons:

- A more distributed computing network environment, no longer controlled in one room with dumb terminals in office areas.
- More networking, both nationally and internationally.
- Blurring of computers and telecommunications systems; for example, a PBX is a computer.
- Capability for more remote systems maintenance; anyone who knows the access codes could take over the system.
- Cheaper hardware and software are available to more people.
- Poor high-technology security because it holds a low priority.
- More individuals growing up with high technology have turned into high-technology criminals and vandals; for example, instead of breaking a business's store windows and spray painting walls, they break Microsoft Windows and spray paint websites.
- Opportunity for criminal gain with little international recourse by law enforcement agencies.
- General standardization on specific hardware and software, such as TCP/IP, UNIX, browsers, and Windows 9X, and NT environments, that have known areas of vulnerability that are exploited before vendor patches are implemented.
- Systems generally are easier to use.
- More hackers, although most are much less technically competent than in the past.
- A few, but smart, very sophisticated hackers with a great deal of technical competence.
- More integration of the PBX, computer, cellular phones, and pagers.
- Law enforcement and high-technology-crime investigators lacking the training, knowledge, budget, and other resources to adequately deal with high-technology crime.

It is important to reiterate that these are the same people who, in most cases, would have conducted these criminal acts whether in a high-technology environment or not. They would have found some way to perpetrate their deeds. The high-technology environment, in many cases, provides these miscreants a *better* opportunity to commit their crimes. The environment no longer is just physical. It is a cyberspace environment that has few extensive security measures in place. The United States government passed the Computer Security Act of 1987 with the goal of protecting the sensitive information processed, stored, and transmitted by government systems, but the majority of these systems have yet to meet the spirit and intent of this law.

HIGH-TECHNOLOGY MISCREANTS' BASIC APPROACH TO ATTACKING NETWORKS

Criminals who attack through high-technology systems, especially those that are networked (e.g., to the GII, Internet,[1] and other systems), generally use a common attack philosophy and methodology. Their sequence of attacks usually follows this scenario:

1. *Research target organization.* Identify the target (this also could be a company, government agency, or network) then study it. If it is connected to the Internet, study it as much as possible using one or more of the search engines that can be found on the Internet to collect information; gather documentation and system identification.
2. *Identify the target's areas of vulnerability.* For various types of computer hardware and software, an excellent source of information are the CERT's (computer emergency response team) announcements notifying all those on their Internet subscriber's list as to new-found areas of system vulnerability and how to eliminate or at least mitigate them. Normally, attackers keep up with these announcements from the CERTs and use them to attack systems faster than the Internet-targeted businesses or government agencies can correct the problem.
3. *Attack.* Use the basic software tools, such as the ones identified later, and begin the attack. Once inside, the attackers steal, modify, or destroy information. Depending on the attacker objectives, the attacker may install a covert backdoor that circumvents protection systems for easy access later, search for other systems networked to the system just penetrated and attack them in a similar manner, or log off the system. The attacker may or may not erase the audit trail records identifying what the attacker had done and then log off the network.

BASIC USE OF PHYSICAL AND HUMAN
INTELLIGENCE COLLECTION METHODS:
THEFT AND SOCIAL ENGINEERING

Let us use the example of a high-technology criminal whose goal is to obtain information about a company. Again, we go back to the GII, Internet, and NII, because these massive networks are excellent examples of the new high-technology environment where these miscreants will ply their trade, now and into the future, and where high-technology-crime investigators are expected to spend a great deal of their time.

The Internet itself provides an excellent vehicle for the attackers to collect and share information with others around the world. The information they share may not be about Internet-connected networks or breaking into computer systems but about how to make fraudulent long distance calls or clone cellular phones, provide PBXs' voice mailbox access codes or listings of credit card numbers and owners, even where to buy and sell specific types of drugs. Remember that these massive networks are global *communication* systems. Therefore, the high-technology criminal uses them as he or she would a telephone, telegraph, or letter a few years back.

Sometimes, it may be necessary to gather information directly from the target, whether it is a business or government agency. The basic methods for doing so are by personally collecting the information on the target's site through theft, social engineering, or a combination of both.

You may recall watching a typical television drama where the police, trying to catch a criminal, covertly take the person's garbage and sift through it for information that can be used to help the investigation. High-technology criminals often use the same technique. They frequently rummage through the trash bins of their target looking for clues to assist them in a successful attack.

What are these "dumpster divers" looking for? They are seeking information that will tell them more details about the computing environment of the target. For example, boxes in the trash may have been used to transport new computer hardware and software. One of the boxes may have been used to ship the target's new Internet firewall product, its new network server, routers, switches, as well as the new version of its operating system

In addition, they look for memos, telephone books—anything with names, positions, and telephone numbers that may give a hint as to the user IDs and passwords, possibly the passwords themselves. Even expired passwords provide good information because they may indicate a pattern that would allow easy guessing of the new password. For example, if I am required to change my password every month, I may choose a word with a sequential set of numbers. So when I have to change my password I use "password2" in February. Then in March, I use "password3." This meets the security requirements to change passwords on a monthly basis as well as the security requirement to use alphanumeric characters for passwords, but it also means anyone who finds my old password easily could predict my current and future passwords.

Information also may be gathered by posing as an employee, vendor, prospective employee, or even as a janitor on a night shift (when fewer people probably are around). Typically, all it takes to obtain almost unrestricted access to a target site is either getting hired by the janitorial service or finding out what work clothes the janitors use and stealing or buying a similar set. Photo ID badges used by the organization pose little deterrent to a determined Internet robber. With just a little bluffing, they may tell the security guard that they are a new employee and they have an appointment to get an ID badge in the morning. In the interim, the janitorial company has told them to sign in as a visitor. More likely than not, the guard will allow the access for the single evening, which may be all that is required.

This is only one way of social engineering your way into the targeted facility. The objective is to convince someone to allow you access to the target facility. Once inside, you have many hours to find information that will assist you in breaking in. If you are lucky, maybe someone even left a computer operating and connected to the organization network at the end of the workday. Such a lucky break will allow the fortunate intruder to act as an "authorized" user with access to the system.

Social engineering quite often is used for gathering the information necessary to successfully attack a system on the Internet. Social engineering is nothing more than the ability to "con" information out of someone or make the person do what you want. For example, taking an organization's phone book out of a dumpster may give the Internet robber the names of people who may have the information required to break into a major network or application containing the most critical information of the organization.

Another approach is to call during nonbusiness hours, the later at night the better because all the higher level managers, if not all managers, most likely will have gone home. You call the systems operations group, who typically work 24 hours a day, and tell the person on duty you need access to the maintenance port to do some on-line maintenance. You give as the name of "your" company, the firm's primary computer vendor, such as Sun, IBM, or whatever works.

You know what systems the company has from documentation you obtained in previous searches or by calling up someone in the target company and asking what computers are used there. Again, social engineering techniques apply. You can say you are a high school student or teacher looking for a company for your high school science class to tour that has a certain type of computer. Normally, you will be referred to the public relations or marketing people. In either case, these individuals have been known to give out a great deal of information.

You also can pose as a computer sales representative or anyone else who can get such information. The most essential skill for social engineering is the ability to make other people believe what you are telling them.

If the operations person is hesitant in providing that information, some nice talking may work: "Look, I understand your concern and I appreciate your position, but we both have our jobs to do. Mine is to do some system maintenance for you. Your company called in the first place so it's not like I want to be here this late at night either. Look is Bob Johnson there? [You found Bob Johnson's name in some targeted documentation and found that he was the director of operations.] His name is listed on the work order with telephone number 234-2345."

Normally, the specific and detailed nature of the information provided the contact causes that person to believe the request is legitimate. After all, how could anyone know that much information unless he or she was legitimate?

If that approach does not work, then intimidation may: "Look. If you don't give me the information I need to perform the maintenance, I really don't care. I can go home early, no problemo. Let me have your name and position please so that when my boss—or this Johnson guy—asks why the work was not done, I can tell them to talk to you. I don't care!" That technique works quite often, and once you are in, you are in!

If none of those techniques work, maybe it is time to try an easier target. Unless the high-technology criminal has specifically targeted a business or government agency, the Internet robber generally will move on to an easier target. After all, these people want to spend time on-line "playing" with systems and cruising down the Internet for other systems to attack. Most high-technology criminals don't want to be delayed by talking to people unless it helps get the information they need to mount a successful attack.

Social engineering works because people basically think other people are honest; unless they had some guidance and awareness briefing on what to say and *what not to say*, they normally are very helpful and provide the requested information.

OTHER COMPUTER-RELATED TECHNIQUES
USED BY BOTH INSIDERS AND OUTSIDERS

The following are some methods[2] that may be used by attackers:

- *Data diddling*. Changing data before or during entry into the computer system; for example, forging or counterfeiting documents used for data entry or exchanging valid disks and tapes with modified replacements.

- *Scavenging.* Obtaining information left around a computer system, in the computer room trashcans, and the like.
- *Computer manipulation with data leakage.* Removing information by smuggling it out as part of a printed document or encoding the information to look like something different and removing it from the facility.
- *Computer manipulation with piggybacking or impersonation.* Physical access, for example, following someone in through a door with a badge reader; electronically using another's user ID and password to gain computer access; tapping into the terminal link of a user to cause the computer to believe that both terminals are the same person.
- *Computer manipulation with simulation and modeling.* Using the computer as a tool or instrument to plan or control a criminal act.
- *Wiretapping.* Tapping into a computer's communication links to read the information being transmitted between systems and networks.

SYSTEM MANIPULATION

Many software applications have been written and techniques used by high-technology criminals. The term for these types of application programs have become standardized over the years. Most high-technology criminals use a variation of hacker tools but they generally can be classified as follows:

- *Trojan horses.* Instructions are covertly placed in a program that causes the computer to perform unauthorized functions but usually still allows the intended performance. This is the most common method used in computer-based frauds and sabotage.
- *Trapdoors.* When developing large programs, programmers tend to insert debugging aids that provide breaks in the instructions for insertion of additional code and intermediate output capabilities. The design of computer operating systems attempts to prevent this from happening. Therefore, programmers insert instructions that allow them to circumvent these controls. High-technology criminals take advantage of these trapdoors or create their own.
- *Salami techniques.* This involves the theft of small amounts of assets from a large number of sources without noticeably reducing the whole. In a banking system, the amount of interest to be credited to an account is rounded off. Instead of rounding off the number, that fraction of it is credited to a special account owned by the perpetrator.
- *Logic bombs.* A computer program executed at a specific time period or when a specific event occurs detonates these "bombs"; for example, a programmer would write a program to instruct the computer to

delete all personnel and payroll files if his or her name were ever removed from the file.

- *Computer viruses.* These are malicious codes that cause damage to system information or denies access to the information through self-replication.

USING THE GII, INTERNET, AND NII
TO SEARCH FOR TOOLS

When high-technology criminals need tools to attack their targets, especially those on the massive, global networks, they usually come from three sources: friends, developed by themselves, and the Internet. The first two speak for themselves, so only the Internet will be addressed here. Very little equipment or skill is needed these days to attack systems connected to the Internet. The high-technology-crime investigator must remember that these are just some examples and are not all-inconclusive. Some "network patches" have been developed by manufacturers and others that defend against such attacks. Furthermore, new areas of vulnerability, patches, and attacks are identified on what seems to be a daily basis.

The attacker obviously must have access to the Internet, which usually is through some Internet service provider (ISP), and that is assumed for our purposes. Once on the Internet, the attacker points the mouse to the Search icon and then types in "hacker," "hacker software," or a specific tool that the Internet robber had heard about, such as SATAN. Then, the Internet thief must be able to download the tool. This, too, generally is an easy task, as often the attacker has to just click on the Download icon. The Internet robber then identifies the target or randomly attacks various targets by executing the attack tools programs.

ATTACK TOOLS FOUND ON THE INTERNET
AND USED PRIMARILY TO ATTACK INTERNET-
CONNECTED TARGETS

Most high-technology criminals use programs readily available on the Internet. Many of these programs were intended to help systems administrators identify the areas of vulnerability in their systems so they could "patch the holes." Some of the most common programs used by attackers are SATAN, COPS, ISS, Crack, FBrute, RootKit. Tripwire, and Finger.

SATAN (security administrator tool for analyzing networks) is a testing and reporting tool that collects a variety of information about networked hosts. SATAN was developed to assist security administrators in identifying areas of vulnerability in their systems that would require patching, hence, the name. This tool also is commonly used by hackers to identify and attack areas of vulnerability in networked systems. This public domain tool can be found and downloaded from numerous sites on the Internet.

To show how easy it is to find these software tools, using Search on the Internet for SATAN AND Software, the authors found numerous websites where SATAN was available (after sifting out the ones with religious connotations). The website with the URL http://www.ensta.fr/internet/unix/sys_admin/satan.html was one of several found. This website identified numerous addresses where SATAN could be found. In North America,

ftp://ftp.mcs.anl.gov/pub/security/
ftp://coast.cs.purdue.edu/pub/tools/unix/satan/
ftp://vixen.cso.uiuc.edu/security/
ftp://ftp.acsu.buffalo.edu/pub/security/
ftp://ftp.net.ohio-state.edu/pub/security/satan/
ftp://ftp.cerf.net/pub/software/unix/security/
ftp://ftp.tisl.ukans.edu/pub/security/
ftp://ftp.tcst.com/pub/security/
ftp://ftp.orst.edu/pub/packages/satan/
ftp://ciac.llnl.gov/pub/ciac/sectools/unix/satan/

In Australia,

ftp://ftp.dstc.edu.au:/pub/security/satan/
ftp://coombs.anu.edu.au/pub/security/satan/
ftp://ftp.auscert.org.au/pub/mirrors/ftp.win.tue.nl/

In Europe,

ftp://ftp.denet.dk/pub/security/tools/satan/
http://ftp.luth.se/pub/unix/security/
ftp://ftp.luth.se/pub/unix/security/
ftp://ftp.wi.leidenuniv.nl/pub/security/
ftp://ftp.cs.ruu.nl/pub/SECURITY/
ftp://ftp.cert.dfn.de/pub/tools/net/satan/
ftp://ftp.csi.forth.gr/pub/security/
ftp://ftp.informatik.uni-kiel.de/pub/sources/security/
   MIRROR.ftp.win.tue.nl/
ftp://ftp.kulnet.kuleuven.ac.be/pub/mirror/ftp.win.tue.nl/security/
ftp://ftp.ox.ac.uk/pub/comp/security/software/satan/

ftp://ftp.nvg.unit.no/pub/security/

ftp://cnit.nsk.su/pub/unix/security/satan/

ftp://ftp.win.tue.nl/pub/security/

COPS (computer oracle and password system) is a publicly available collection of programs that attempt to identify security problems in a UNIX system. COPS does not attempt to correct any discrepancies found; it simply produces a report of its findings.

ISS (Internet security scanner) is a software program that checks a range, from beginning to end, of a set of IP logical addresses on a network to determine what systems, by address, are on the network, and whether the systems are vulnerable to specific attacks. It is a commercial and much-improved software similar to SATAN in some respects.

Crack is a software program that attempts to guess passwords based on dictionary entries, user ID, and user name. It requires a password file (/etc/passwd). The new version can be used across an entire network.

FBrute is a software program that can decrypt encrypted password software. It uses a dictionary and is similar to Crack.

RootKit, according to BellCore, was first noticed about 1993. It is targeted to specific systems (originally SunOS 4.1.X, but a new version targets LINUX) and is used as a "patched" login that allows any ID to access the systems through a backdoor password and a combination of attack programs.

Tripwire is a software program that checks file and directory integrity. It is a utility that compares a designated set of files and directories to information stored in a previously generated database. Any differences are flagged and logged, including added or deleted entries. When run against files on a regular basis, Tripwire enables administrators to spot changes in critical system files and to immediately take appropriate damage control measures. Tripwire also is available on the Internet.

Finger is a UNIX protocol that can be used to obtain information about users logged onto a system. It provides information that can be used by attackers, such as when the account was last used and from what location the user last connected.

SOME COMMON METHODS OF ATTACK
FROM THE INTERNET

Some of the more common Internet attack methods cause millions of dollars in lost revenue through denying use of websites or modifying websites to cause embarrassment to their owners. Spoofing, session stealing, and other attack methods plague the Internet. Patches and remedies are available to avoid being the victim of most of these common attacks; however, many businesses and government agencies have not installed them, including many U.S. Department of Defense systems. There is no excuse for such lack of security. Ironically, the Defense Department is supposed to defend this nation but often can't seem to defend its own systems.[3]

Denial of Service

Denial of service means to block the use of the Internet or a related system. Various methods are used to deny service or access to a system on the Internet. One example is to send a big ping packet. The attacker sends a packet (ICMP echo request) larger than 65,507 bytes (ping -1 65510 target system). The reassembled fragments overflow the TCP/IP stack. This attack works on various hardware; however, the vendors and others have been developing patches to prevent such a denial of service.

Web Server Modifications

Attacking web servers has been the latest fad among many of the miscreants on the Internet, generally the juvenile delinquents. However, in the hands of someone more devious, it can be used to make political statements or to divert others through links to a competitor's site. The devious schemes used are limited only by the high-technology criminal's imagination.

The problem is that common gateway interface (CGI) scripts allow for the creation of web pages but are vulnerable to attacks (CGI scripts such as FormMail, convert.bas, .bat files, custom scripts).

IP Fragmentation

IP fragmentation is accomplished by splitting the TCP header into two fragments (fragment 1 is part of the TCP header, and fragment 2 is the rest of TCP header with the port number). For example, in fragment 1, a "phony" port, such as port 80, is added; in fragment 2, the TCP header is used with port 23. When the fragments are reconnected, the port number is overwritten.

Password Sniffing

One technique to successfully attack a system on a busy subnet is to change the system configuration to make it a network sniffer. Thus, the attacker can collect user IDs and passwords flowing through the network (see Figure 4–1).

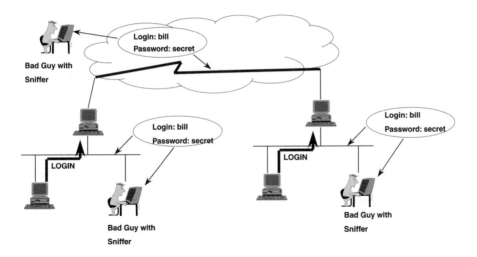

Figure 4–1   A simplified example of sniffing.

ISP Attack

In an ISP attack, the attacker sends a false message, usually to numerous servers that offer newsgroups, and "convinces" them to send back information, such as server passwords.

Spoofing

Spoofing requires the prediction of future sequencing numbers. The attacker spoofs the trusted system into believing that the attacker's system is another, authorized system, while simultaneously blocking that other trusted system (see Figure 4–2).

War Dialers

Prior to the Internet, dial-up systems[4] were the predominant method for high-technology criminals, and authorized users, to gain remote access to the business or government agency computer system. Today, that is still possible; however, it is not as prevalent now that the Internet exists. Hackers wrote programs in BASIC to find those computers and record their telephone numbers for later attack. This method was made famous by the movie *War Games*.

After identifying a computer system through its dial tone, the hacker used other programs or manual guessing to identify a user ID and password

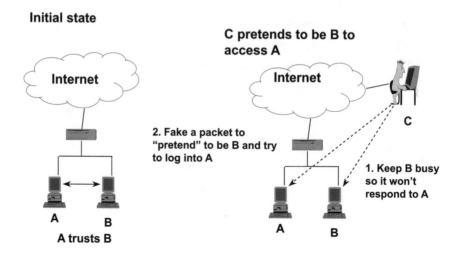

Figure 4–2   A simplified example of spoofing.

that would allow system access. Some systems still can lead the hacker onto an Internet ramp.

Other Methods, Tools, and Techniques

Numerous techniques, methods, tactics, and tools are available to anyone on the Internet. In addition, other sources such as hacker and computer magazines discuss areas of Internet hardware and software vulnerability.

The high-technology-crime investigator should become familiar with the basic information provided on hacker sites. The techniques, methods, and so forth constantly are changing and improving as Internet security improves. Security continues to be an ongoing challenge for everyone on the Internet.

EXAMPLE OF HACKER NAÏVETÉ

One hacker advised others via e-mail: to rent a cheap room at a hotel, such as a "run down motel that you take hookers to." He stated that the motel owners probably won't remember you; they hardly ask for identification, don't take credit cards, and want cash payment. Then go to the room and dial into an ISP using a hacked trial (free use of an ISP's access to the Internet for a specific period of time by using the ISP's CD account (normally given away through the mail, for example), but never your own. If traced back, the investigators would "hit a dead end." This miscreant also recommended using different hotels and different accounts and not bragging about it. This individual also recommended using a laptop in universities and libraries that have phone jacks. "Bring a bunch of textbooks and you'll fit in with everyone else with a laptop there." Suppose you traced this hacker to a motel, library, or a public room of a university. What steps would you take to investigate such a case?

ELECTRONIC MAIL

Electronic mail involves sending and storing written communications through computer networks. Aside from the normal fraudulent uses of electronic mail, e-mail, as it is commonly called, can include a virus. However, in the past, it was a program that the receiver overtly implemented by opening the mail, such as the mail attachments.

There are indications that covert instructions and viruses may be sent through the "cookies" constantly requested of users by various Web site vendors, news agencies, marketing companies, and the like.

Using e-mail through such systems as the Internet creates a risk, in that the true sender of the message can be disguised. This method would work well to assist in the economic sabotage of a business. In addition, because a sender's identity can be disguised, he or she can safely forward sensitive business information to an unauthorized address.

Again, old fraud schemes have surfaced in new ways.

CELLULAR TELEPHONES: CLONING
AND OTHER FRAUDS

Cellular telephones, like any high-technology devices, are both a target and a tool of high-technology miscreants. Cloned and stolen phones are excellent communication devices being used by criminals not only for making illegal, long distance telephone calls but also to communicate such things as drug deals and other criminal activities with impunity.

When we think of cellular phones, we usually don't think of computers and information protection in the "systems" sense. However, the divisions of hardware begin to blur as they are integrated into communication networks. So, we must begin focusing on all aspects of information storing, processing, and transmitting. To do otherwise would be a disservice to our companies and our profession. After all, cellular phones are information systems as well. All one has to do is look at the increase in the forms of wireless communication, such as cellular phones attached to notebook computers, to appreciate the new challenges ahead.

The following information is provided to give you a basic understanding of cellular phone fraud and how you can help protect these systems. The numbers and use of cellular phones continues to increase in our society. All businesses using cellular phones incur a security risk. Any-one, any business, right now could be the victim of cellular phone fraud. This can occur from inside or outside the company. In fact, as you read this book, someone may be illegally charging his or her calls to your cellular phone. Cellular phone fraud costs business and carriers over $1 million a day (Motorola, "Management Report: Cellular Fraud," date un-known).

Threats, Vulnerability, and Risk

What are the threats to this new communications tool? Why and how are cellular phones vulnerable to criminals? How much risk are businesses taking by using them? The following may help answer some of these questions.

The two key elements of a cellular phone are its electronic serial number (ESN) and its mobile identification number (MIN). The ESN is programmed into the microchip installed in each cellular phone by the manufacturer. The microchip is called a *programmable read only memory* (PROM) microchip or *erasable PROM* (EPROM) microchip. The MIN is the "phone number" assigned to the cellular phone by the cellular phone car-rier, such as 310-123-4567.

The ESN is like the vehicle identification number of a car or truck and the MIN is like a vehicle's license plate number. If you are a computer user, think of the MIN as your computer identification (user ID) and the ESN as your password.

When you make a cellular phone call, your phone transmits your ESN and MIN to your cellular phone carrier. The carrier's computer switching system validates that the ESN and MIN, in combination, represent a cus-tomer authorized to make a call through that switch. After verifying the user's cellular phone identity, it puts through the call and tracks usage for billing purposes.

By using electronic equipment, a person near you while you are mak-ing a cellular phone call can identify your MIN and ESN. Then, using other electronic equipment that can program PROMs and EPROMs, a criminal can program your ESN and MIN into another microchip and use it. By "cloning" your microchip information, the criminal can use one or several cloned phones to make calls that are billed back to you (Figure 4–3).

The equipment to clone a chip is readily available and modifying the chip is as easy as changing batteries in a flashlight. The authorized caller may not know his or her chip has been cloned and misused until after re-ceiving the monthly telephone bill.

The FCC rulings on listening in on the airwaves state that you can lis-ten, but you cannot use the information received for personal, profes-

Figure 4–3 A scanner that can pick up cellular phone information.

sional, or monetary gain. How hard is it to scan the cellular airwaves and listen to the conversations? According to John Beecher, a Los Angeles-based telecommunications expert, you can easily purchase the necessary equipment for about $200 at your local electronics store. In addition, your cellular phone easily can be modified to also pick up cellular phone conversations. If you know how to reconfigure your telephone in maintenance mode, you can reconfigure it to act as a listening device on cellular phone frequencies. The maintenance mode passwords are readily available in published documents relating to cellular phones. However, this approach is more difficult than using scanners. According to Beecher, some new cellular phones will make it more difficult to listen in on conversations. Although the new phones are not a quantum leap in protection, they do provide better security.

Cellular phone carriers have established monitoring processes that look for individual cellular phone usage patterns. When a phone exceeds the normal pattern, such as many calls in one day to overseas numbers by someone who never called overseas before, the carrier normally will suspend that phone service and notify the customer. This abnormal increase in phone usage is known as *spiking.* The criminals who clone cellular phones are aware of the monitoring process. They may just take their chances and use the phone as long as they can, or they may keep the number of calls low so as not to attract attention. Because of the difficulty in identifying these criminals, most of them appear to continue to use the phones as long as they can. Some criminals clone the phones and sell them to others, such as drug dealers or operators of prostitution or gambling rings. These people use the phones, which are difficult to trace, to transact their illegal business.

Some of the more sophisticated criminals modify the cellular phone by using a microchip that permits the reprogramming of ESNs and MINs with the phone's keypad. This process of changing the phone's identification is commonly called *tumbling.* If a cellular phone is being used outside the service area of their carrier, the outside carrier normally will allow one call to go through while it checks to validate it is by an authorized user. This use of an outside carrier is generally called *roaming.* A criminal armed with a keypad to modify the ESN and MIN "on the fly" and a list of valid ESNs and MINs can continue to make one call per cellular phone identification. This usage, of course, is charged back to the authorized cellular phone user. The carriers are working to eliminate this vulnerability.

In one instance, a company purchased several new cellular phones that were held in reserve for issuing later. Before the phones were assigned, the company received a bill from its carrier that included over $6,000 in charges to the phones still in their original boxes. The carrier was informed and the company was not charged for the calls, many of which were to overseas locations. The carrier absorbed the costs as a "normal" part of doing business. However, those charges eventually are passed on to all the customers through rate increases—or at least don't allow the carriers to lower the rates as much as they could.

A cellular phone can "leak" information without the knowledge of the sender or receiver. For example, several years ago at a security conference in San Francisco, a friend and Dr. Kovacich were in the hallway outside a conference room. The friend turned on his phone, and as he was about to dial a number, he heard a conversation between a U.S. military captain and general in Washington (names withheld), discussing sensitive contract information and contract bids of potential contractors. This happened purely by accident but proves one very important point: high technology can be vulnerable in ways that we may least expect.

Another major threat to cellular phones is theft. Cellular phones are stolen and used by the thief until the user or the carrier terminates the usage. A criminal may sell time on the phone so people can call nationally or internationally. This type of operation is known as a *call-sell operation* and works with pay phones and telephone calling cards. The cellular phone owner or the carrier picks up the costs. These costs can amount to thousands of dollars in a matter of one or two days. The phones still can be sold and used again after they have been cloned, as previously described.

With basic scanning equipment, an outsider can "listen in" on cellular phone calls and obtain sensitive company information. Remember, as business competition increases, especially in the global economy, the incentive to learn more about what the competition is doing increases as well. This threat may be one of industrial espionage (one company seeking information from another company) or economic espionage (a foreign government seeking information from a company).

Cellular phone calls can be made by authorized employees that are not related to company business. The employee may even let friends and family members make calls on the phone. Employees who are issued a cellular phone can sell it to criminals and subsequently report it stolen.

Information of Investigative Interests

Certain test equipment is used to poll cellular phone cells. If you identify such equipment in the hands of someone not employed by the carrier or a related, legitimate cellular phone business, you can assume the equipment is stolen and being used for illegal purposes.

If you seize a phone and it is necessary to determine its original destination, the manufacturer should be able to tell you the identity of the phone and its destination. For example, Motorola maintains centralized records in Arlington Heights, Illinois.

Check also for the serial numbers on the phone. Obviously, if they are absent, written over, or scratched out, the phone probably was stolen. In addition, an FCC sticker is required. In one case, the lack of the FCC sticker enabled investigators to obtain a felony conviction in Illinois.

If the phone has a locked code or codes, the manufacturer may be able to unlock it. In addition and under certain circumstances, it may even be able to determine the last number called. At a minimum, do nothing to the phone, as this may erase the number. Contact the manufacturer or your carrier to determine if they can help you.

If, during your investigation, you seize a cellular phone that, when turned on, indicates that it is roaming mode, the phone probably is stolen.

If it is important to identify and trace phone numbers called by the cellular phone you have seized, remember that the phones store telephone numbers to make calling more convenient for their owners. Contact the manufacturer for assistance if you don't know how to obtain those numbers from the phone without destroying relevant evidence.

COLORED BOXES AND TELECOMMUNICATION FRAUD

Over the years, phreakers and others have devised various electronic boxes that emulate the sounds used by the telecommunication networks. These "colored boxes" allow the user to circumvent the normal controls and billing for such things as long distance calls. The following descriptions are provided in nontechnical terms.

The blue box in Figure 4–4 allowed the user to make long distance, toll calls, for free. A red box simulates the signals made by coins at pay phones. The black box in Figure 4–5 simulates a toll call being terminated, so the toll no longer is recorded, even though the parties could continue talking. A yellow box indicates "supervision status" to the telephone system.

Other colored boxes have been identified over the years, and these boxes sometimes were called different colors by different phreakers. For example, some call the silver box the predecessor to the blue box; however, others call a silver box the box that can change specific traffic signaling devices. Other colored boxes are white, beige, rainbow, and green

Figure 4–4   A blue box.

Figure 4–5 A black box.

according to at least one individual. For additional information on these devices, use your search engine and search the Internet and hacker or phreaker sites.

PRIVATE BRANCH EXCHANGE ATTACKS

A PBX can be attacked like any other computer and used for various reasons, such as to gain outside calling access to make toll free calls, take over a PBX, or read other people's voice mail. Figure 4–6 A–C depicts three basic methods and reasons a PBX might be attacked.

SUMMARY

High-technology devices are becoming necessary and convenient business communication tools, not only for legal businesses but illegal ones as well. The basic techniques and methods are well known. Whether a miscreant is attacking such devices as a PBX, Internet site, cellular telephone, or other computers, high-technology-crime investigators must learn these techniques and work with the individuals responsible for the protection of these business and government agency assets. In addition, high-technology-crime investigators must understand the techniques or modus operandi to conduct successful investigations.

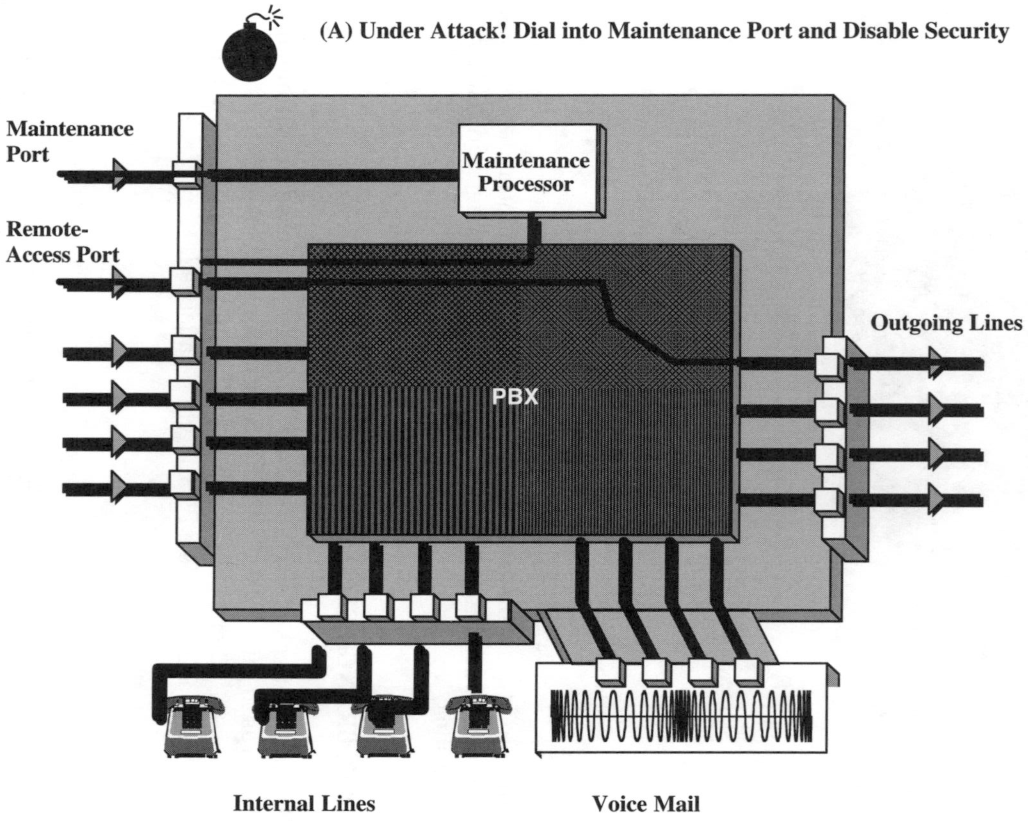

(A) Under Attack! Dial into Maintenance Port and Disable Security

Maintenance
Port

Remote-
Access Port

Maintenance
Processor

PBX

Outgoing Lines

Voice Mail

Internal Lines

Figure 4-6 Attacks on a PBX system.

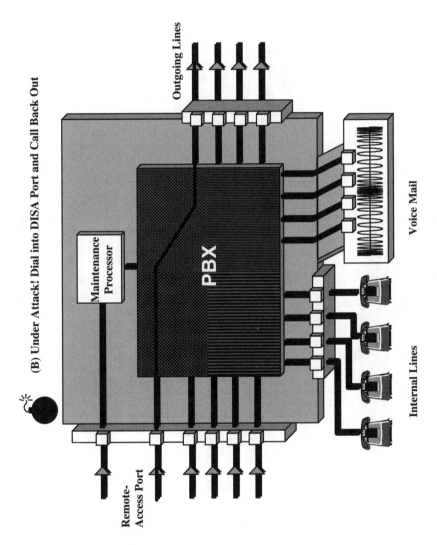

(B) Under Attack! Dial into DISA Port and Call Back Out

Remote-
Access Port

Maintenance
Processor

PBX

Outgoing Lines

Voice Mail

Internal Lines

Figure 4–6   Continued

91

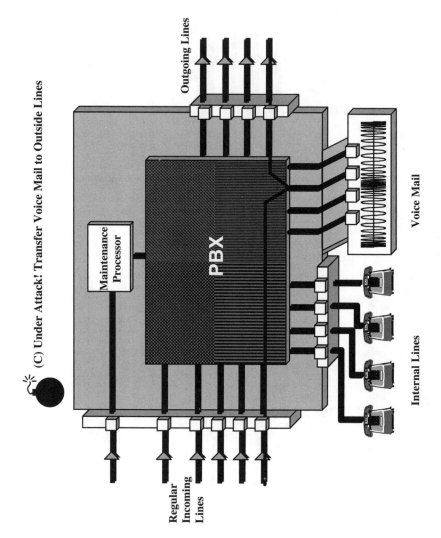

(C) Under Attack! Transfer Voice Mail to Outside Lines

Outgoing Lines

Maintenance
Processor

PBX

Voice Mail

Internal Lines

Regular
Incoming
Lines

Figure 4–6   Continued

NOTES

1. Emphasis is placed on networks related to the Internet, since, for today's high-technology-crime investigators and others, this is the "hot" crime environment and where law enforcement at all levels of government is concentrating much of its efforts, such as against child pornographers and hackers.
2. The terms and definitions are those generally used by the FBI and others. The FBI provided these definitions in 1979 to Dr. Kovacich in their Computer Crime Investigation Course; obviously, not much has changed.
3. Numerous very good technical papers and books have been written on the subjects noted. The authors do not intend to provide a technical discussion of the subject but only an awareness of its existence. The reader should become more familiar with these attack methods by reading some of the excellent material available on the topics. It is recommended that the reader search the Internet for such material. For books on the topic, it is suggested that readers refer to http://www.bh.com and http://www.amazon.com.
4. Dial-up systems accessed a computer via a modem by dialing the computer's telephone number and having it answered through another modem to the system.

5

The Basic Information Systems Security Techniques Used Against High-Technology Miscreants

BASIC INFORMATION SYSTEMS SECURITY CONCEPTS

If high-technology-crime investigators are to support the protection of high technology and related systems used to process, store, and transmit that information, they must be able to identify the weaknesses in the information systems security (InfoSec)[1] processes that allow crimes to occur.

The basic computer protection concepts require a balance between ease of use, cost, capability, flexibility, performance, and protection. Three basic InfoSec principles form the foundation of an InfoSec program: (1) access control, (2) individual accountability, and (3) audit trails.

Access Control

Access control is the first line of defense of high technology and information, for without access (either physical, logical, or a combination of the two), the opportunities to conduct high-technology crimes are drastically reduced—not eliminated but reduced. Physical access is controlled through gates, guards, badge readers, smart cards, biometric devices, and the like. Once the physical access has been obtained, the individual has access to the high-technology devices; for example, telephones, cellular phones, or computer workstations.

The next hurdle for the miscreant to overcome is obtaining the personal identification number (PIN), user identification (user ID), and password or whatever the InfoSec hardware or software requires to gain access to the "tool." So once a crime has been committed, "who" has "what" access becomes an important question.

Individual Accountability

Individual accountability is a major pillar of an InfoSec program and means that all actions related to the high-technology device, system, or whatever can be traced back to a specific individual. However, individual accountability requires such policies, procedures, and processes as separation of functions, unique user IDs and passwords for each individual, unique biometric scans for each individual, unique PINs, unique badges and card readers for each individual, and the like.

As businesses and government agencies downsize and look for more ways to gain efficiency in their processes, it is not uncommon for the employees' responsibilities to cloud or even eliminate the separation of function concept. This is why such things as passwords, smart cards, and PINs, by policy, are never to be used by anyone other than the person to which they were assigned. Nonadherence to this policy makes criminal identification and appropriate disciplinary action extremely difficult.

Therefore, when conducting a high-technology-crime investigation, the investigator should ask a series of questions about policy and procedures related to separation of functions, sharing of passwords, PINs, and so forth. If the "administrative security documentation" (policies, procedures, employee acknowledgment statements) related to the investigation is old, inadequate, or nonexistent, the opportunity to take disciplinary action or prosecute an employee, generally, is drastically reduced if not eliminated all together. Thus, an investigation may be a waste of time.

If passwords were shared by two or three employees and there was corroborating evidence, you may have some hope. However, that is very unlikely, because company lawyers or prosecutors often shy away from high-technology cases in the first place, and when you add the other complications, they may not want to support disciplinary action or prosecution.

Audit Trails

When we speak of audit trails, we are talking about the historical records in any form including, for example, closed-circuit television videotapes, hard-copy sign-in records, computer historical records of what user ID accessed what files or networks or made what telephone calls through the PBX or cellular phone, and any other records that can help prove or disprove allegations against individuals. Computerized records usually do not provide the details that show exactly what specific information in a database was accessed, modified, deleted, or manipulated—who did what with or to the information.

Most of today's modern InfoSec systems have the *capability* to provide a great deal of details; however, most of the information technology people who operate, maintain, and otherwise support the business or government agency will "turn on" only the minimum audit trail features that they can get away with. They continually argue that detailed monitoring adversely affects the performance of the systems and the record keeping takes up too much storage space. They are correct to a point, and generally management will side with them and take the risk that detailed audit trail records will not be needed.

As a high-technology-crime investigator, audit trail records are like fingerprints and footprints at the crime scene. If properly installed in sufficient level of detail, they can be the piece of evidence that leads to suspects. So, when conducting a high-technology-crime investigation, the investigator should ask a series of questions related to audit trail records. All applicable audit trail records should be considered and protected as evidence.

INFOSEC PROCESSES OR FUNCTIONS

The InfoSec program is separated into several basic functions:

- *Physical security.* Those barriers, devices that help protect assets. They include such things as guards, fences, alarms, closed-circuit television cameras, and sensors. In most companies, physical security is the responsibility of the business security management.
- *Personnel security.* This may include background investigations on potential employees and other screening processes. Personnel security, too, generally is the responsibility of business security management.
- *Administrative security.* As the name implies, it consists of the administrative processes, policies, and procedures related to InfoSec. The department responsible for InfoSec generally establishes these policies and procedures. Depending on the business culture, agreements, and company policies, it may or may not be coordinated with the business security management.
- *Communication security.* Generally, the encryption of the information transmitted via telecommunication links; it can be the responsibility of the InfoSec organization or business security management.
- *Risk management.* The management of risks associated with high technology is everyone's responsibility when using or making decisions relative to any high technology. Formal risk assessments and analyses vis-à-vis high-technology protection generally falls within the purview of the InfoSec organization.
- *Disaster recovery and contingency planning.* Planning and preparing for actions to take in the event of disaster (e.g., hurricane, earthquake, or a hacker destroys the business's database) and recovery from such

disaster affecting networks and systems generally falls within the InfoSec organization's purview.

THE INFORMATION SYSTEMS SECURITY OFFICER

The information systems security officer (ISSO) leads the InfoSec effort for a business or government agency. The ISSO position can be summarized as directing, supervising, managing, and administrating an InfoSec program that minimizes threats, vulnerabilities, and risks to the company's sensitive information and high-technology assets.

InfoSec and ISSO Goals and Objectives

The ISSO, through the InfoSec program, generally has some stated goals and objectives. The following are examples of goals and objectives that may be used by an ISSO:

- Administer an innovative information systems security program that minimizes risk with the least impact on costs and schedules, while meeting all requirements.
- Enhance the quality, efficiency, and effectiveness of the organization.
- Identify potential problem areas and mitigate against them before customers identify them.
- Enhance the company's ability to attract customers because of the ability to efficiently and effectively protect their information.
- Establish the organization as the information systems security leader in the industry.

Risk Management

The risk management process is crucial to establishing and maintaining an InfoSec program with the lowest cost while protecting the high technology and information. Risk decisions are based on threats (human caused or natural occurrences with potentially adverse effects on systems and information when combined with specific areas of vulnerability), vulnerability (weaknesses that allow specific threats to have adverse effects on systems and information), and risk (the chance that a specific threat can take advantage of a specific area of vulnerability to have adverse effects on systems and information). The assessments could be qualitative, quantitative, or a combination of both. They often result in a formal report and include identifying costs and benefits.

Other Aspects of an InfoSec Program

There are many aspects to InfoSec, depending on the business, sophistication of the InfoSec program, and most important, how management perceives its importance and allocates resources for it.

Security verifications and validations must be part of a good InfoSec program and include ensuring that InfoSec is in place where needed, its systems are active (configured and operating per security parameters), it is cost effective, and new technology products evaluated for risks and cost-effectiveness.

INFOSEC ORGANIZATION

Continuous debate centers on where the InfoSec responsibility and organization should be located. Regardless of the reporting structure, it should include developing, implementing, maintaining, and administering a companywide information systems security program that includes all plans, policies, procedures, assessments, and authorizations necessary to ensure the protection of the company's and customers' systems and information. Its operations should include

- All functions and work routinely accomplished during the course of conducting the organization's security business.
- System access administration and controls, including the direct use and control of the system's access software, monitoring its use and identifying access violations.
- Access violation analyses to identify patterns and trends that may indicate an increased risk to the systems or information.
- Coordinating computer crime and abuse inquiries with the high-technology-crime investigator when there are indications of intent to damage, destroy, modify, or release information of value to unauthorized people.
- Disaster recovery and contingency planning, including directing the development and coordination of a companywide program to mitigate against the possible loss of systems and information and ensure their rapid recovery in the event of an emergency or disaster.
- An awareness program established and administered to all system users to make them aware of the information systems security policies and procedures that must be followed to adequately protect systems and information.
- Evaluation of the system's hardware, firmware, and software for their impact on the security systems and information. Where applicable, risk assessments are conducted and the results reported to management for risk decisions.

- The system's compliance inspections, tests, and evaluations conducted to ensure that all users and systems are in compliance with security policies and procedures.
- Projects initiated where improvements or other changes will be accomplished.

PREVENTIVE CELLULAR PHONE FRAUD MEASURES

Cellular phone fraud cannot be eliminated but it can be reduced if some simple steps are taken:

- Ensure cellular phones are adequately justified.
- Establish and enforce good security policies and procedures.
- Brief phone users on security requirements.
- Approve phone numbers to be called in advance.
- Limit call areas to only those required for business.
- Establish billing thresholds with the cellular phone provider.
- Secure the phone out of sight when not in use.
- Don't call if suspicious people are near you.
- Use encryption when possible to protect sensitive information.
- Actively monitor the billings and verify the legitimacy of the calls.

SECURITY REQUIREMENTS FOR VOICE MESSAGING OPERATIONS

The uses of telecommunication systems continue to grow rapidly. One aspect of the phenomena is the company-owned telecommunications switchboard. These private branch exchanges (PBX) give the company control over its voice and data communication networks not possible just a few years ago. These modern telephone switchboards are nothing more than another computer. However, like any computer, they come with the potential for exploitation by hackers or, in this case, phreakers.

Although most companies are beginning to secure the computer networks that are "attached" to the outside world, many have failed to realize that the PBX also is a computer that must be secured. In many companies, the organizations responsible for the "normal" computer systems are not those responsible for the PBX. This historically has been the case because computer systems were maintained and operated by data center people while telephone systems were maintained and supported by the telecommunication people. Companies have been slow to recognize the need to integrate these two segregated groups. The lines between telephone switchboards and other types of computers are rapidly blurring. While telecommunication people didn't concern themselves much with threats other than natural disasters, computer technicians for some time have been concerned with both the internal and external threats to their systems.

Until the advent of the PBX, telephone technicians were concerned primarily with ensuring the phone systems were operational. They did not seem to, and some still do not, take the hard-learned lessons of securing their computers and use those techniques to secure the PBX.

The penetration of a PBX still appears to be primarily for using its direct inward system access feature to dial through the switch to a long distance number, with the charges being picked up by the owner of the PBX. The penetration of the PBX to use and store messages in vacant voice mailboxes and listening to and destroying messages in a voice mailbox that has been penetrated are becoming an ever-increasing threat.

To assist in protecting the business's PBX, the following four measures, at a minimum, should be in place:

1. Adopt a corporate remote access policy.
2. Audit the existing system software for configuration and compliance with the InfoSec policy.
3. Establish and maintain a process to maintain a secure PBX.
4. Implement remote maintenance port protection, install call accounting software, and continuously monitor the PBX's parameters.

The following security requirements are provided to assist the high-technology-crime investigator in understanding the protection that should be in place, thus helping minimize the opportunity to take advantage of the system.

Telephone Voice Messaging Operation

Policy

The policy document outlines the minimum security requirements for the telephone voice messaging (TVM) system that supports the services of voice mail, call answering, mailboxes, and call processing. The security controls for TVM, with reasonable dependability, must prevent unauthorized access to company information during or resulting from the processing of such information and unauthorized manipulation of the system that could compromise company information.

The company's PBX security controls and operating procedures must be documented in writing and approved by security personnel. The documentation is to ensure that all security aspects of the systems were addressed, to serve as a baseline for investigation in the event of a penetration or attempted penetration, to assist in conducting a risk analysis, and to assist in conducting damage assessments in the event that information or equipment is stolen or damaged.

Requirements

The following 13 requirements are provided as the baseline for a procedures document:

1. *Identification.* This section provides basic telephone voice messaging system, user, and management identification. First, provide a unique name for the system. Then, identify personnel responsible for maintaining controls and safeguards: the system security manager, security custodian and alternate(s), and owners of hardware and software resources. Specify the physical location(s) of resources and users.

2. *System usage.* This section describes TVM system purpose, sensitivity levels of the information processed, type and usage of electronic media, and the specific mode of operation. Describe the specific services of voice mail, call answering, mailboxes, call processing, and so forth provided to each user or group of users. Indicate the days and hours of operation. List the highest sensitivity level of company information transmitted or stored in mailboxes.

3. *Hardware.* This section identifies TVM system equipment and provides for hardware layouts, configurations, and disconnection methods. Provide a current list of equipment that includes manufacturer model and serial number (and, optionally, any company property tag numbers). Describe company and noncompany premises where all hardware components for the system reside. Provide an inventory of the type and size of internal memory and the type and usage of storage media. Describe all removable and nonremovable media used as well as the configuration management techniques in place to ensure that all hardware components function in a cohesive, identifiable, predictable, and reliable manner.

4. *Software.* This section describes TVM operating system and application software. List all installed software, including vendor and release number. Describe the operating system and messaging security and protective features. Specify the telephone time-out interval and method of warning established for interactive voice messaging.

5. *Teleprocessing.* This section describes TVM communication capabilities and circuits. Provide current network diagrams, schematics, and floor plans of the systems and telephones, as well as capabilities and restrictions on the use of cellular phones, company-owned pagers, and the like, as applicable. Describe the methods of restricting voice messaging to company use only; the techniques for safe storage of all incoming and outgoing message traffic against power or

equipment failure, power surges, or spikes; and the configuration management techniques in place to ensure that all elements and components function in a cohesive, identifiable, predictable, and reliable manner.

6. *Personnel.* This section describes the TVM system personnel access controls. Describe the security responsibilities of the following personnel: the system security manager, security custodian and alternate(s), owners of hardware and software resources, and users of mailbox information. Describe supplemental custodian and user security awareness and training.

7. *Physical security.* This section describes the physical security measures to protect the TVM system. Describe the system hardware and media access controls in place during working and nonworking hours and how all teleprocessing circuits are physically secured against tampering. Provide evidence that equipment carrying sensitive information is not connected to systems not approved to transmit sensitive company information. Also, provide evidence that connectivity to nonsensitive systems or telephone equipment outside approved company areas is accomplished with controls that would preclude the intentional or accidental introduction of sensitive company information.

8. *General access controls.* This section describes TVM controls that restrict access to the system such as passwords, detection of unauthorized use, and sign-on and sign-off procedures. Describe methods for user identification and authentication of employees using the system from outside and inside the company, including all of the following: authorized user identification; restrictions on use of guest mailboxes; automatic password and PIN expiration interval, minimum length, and change interval; restricted mailbox access during nonworking hours; user failed-logon suspend criteria. Describe procedures for periodic review of user mailbox access and call processing authorization as well as mailbox group list update procedure on notification to or by an employee of an organization reassignment or intent to terminate employment. Describe method to prevent audible disclosure of passwords and PIN codes (e.g., conference speaker phones).

9. *Operating procedures.* This section describes TVM system startup, in-process, and shutdown procedures for processing sensitive information. Discuss how security-approved procedures will be used to enforce continuity, accuracy, and protection of mailbox information.

10. *General storage, protection, and control.* This section describes TVM methods of marking, handling, storing, and controlling system media and information. Describe provisions during call answering and call processing for system identification as company business use only, the companywide method to enforce labeling of voice mail as company sensitive, how the owner of each message contained in a mailbox is

captured, and the method for safeguarding operation system software, messaging software, message distribution lists, and mailbox contents.

11. *Audit trails.* This section lists, describes, and provides exhibits of all automated and manual audit trail records to provide a documented history of TVM system use, violations, and maintenance. Describe the audit trail reports and logs used to capture access to the system, attempts to break in, attempts to bypass established system parameters, access to another user's mailbox without proper authorization, and so forth. Also describe the review process for reports and logs. Show how all anomalies or violations of security policies and procedures are evaluated, how the reason for them is determined, and what corrective action will be determined and taken. Provide examples of the following minimum set of audit trail logs and reports: custodian acknowledgment statement, user acknowledgment statement, system access list, mailbox group list request, mailbox access change request, and vital software index.

12. *Subcontracting.* This section describes TVM arrangements for subcontracting time or services, as applicable. Identify all authorized subcontractor(s), vendors, or other noncompany personnel that have any interface with this TVM and the voice messaging services and features authorized for them. Also describe security restrictions unique to noncompany personnel, how they are enforced and so on.

13. *Emergency plans.* This section describes TVM procedures to identify, recover, and protect information during system crashes, security violations, or other emergencies and the backup recovery process for information processed on the system. Specify and set priorities for vital system software, messaging software distribution lists, and mailbox information. Provide a list of personnel to notify in case of emergency, including telephone numbers, fax numbers, home addresses, and the like. Specify emergency procedures for protection of hardware, system software, messaging software, distribution lists, mailbox information, and audit trials. Provide evidence of periodic testing of backup procedures. Specify procedures for rapid resumption of vital voice messaging functions. Document procedures for long-term restoration of normal messaging service levels.

Voice Mail Summary

The establishment of a security policy and procedures documentation for each PBX will help mitigate against, but not prevent, attacks by phreakers and internal threats. This can form the baseline on which to develop a more secure system.

Voice Mail Protection

As with cellular phones, protection methods can be used to minimize losses and damage to voice mail systems:

- Use large passwords.
- Lock all unused mailboxes.
- Search unused boxes for messages.
- Eliminate their use by former employees.
- Don't store personal information.
- Don't store sensitive information.
- Ensure audit trails are in place and active.
- Review audit trails often.

Electronic Mail Protection

To minimize electronic mail problems,

- Don't execute programs received in the mail.
- Verify the sender's identity.
- Establish and maintain current security policies and a user awareness program.
- Establish and maintain system defaults that limit the duration for retaining messages on servers and individual microcomputers.

PROTECTION FOR LAW ENFORCEMENT COMPUTER SYSTEMS: A POLICY PROPOSAL

The objective of this section is to present a policy proposal for the protection of law enforcement computer systems and the information processed, stored, and transmitted by those systems.

The information developed, used, processed, transmitted, and stored on computers by police agencies is extremely sensitive. Much of the information has value to others such as the criminals; for example, identity of police informants, reports of investigation, and addresses of witnesses. Also, information protection is a very real concern, due to the privacy issues involved in such matters as juvenile cases.

For example, unauthorized access by unknown person(s) into the Anaheim, California, Police Department computers gave a pro-life group the address of a pro-choice doctor. The group then picketed the doctor's home. Such events not only cause an embarrassment to the police and the city officials but also could put the doctor's life in jeopardy (*Orange County Register*, May 1993).

Police departments continue to use and rely on computer and information systems to process, store, and transmit sensitive police information. At the same time, they generally lack a basic understanding of these systems and how to adequately protect them. They must begin with a policy directive setting forth the minimum requirements that must be met to protect their systems and computerized information. Based on that policy, a three-pronged program can be established to educate the police administrators and system users, protect the system and information, and prepare the investigating officers to investigate computer-related crimes.

The first purpose of the proposed policy is to provide the justification for the establishment of a computer awareness, protection, and crime investigation training program. The program would consist of three parts:

1. *Computer basics—what is a computer and how does it work?* Explain the hardware (the cathode ray tube, central processing unit, keyboard, random access memory, and read only memory) and output devices (printers, plotters, and modems). Explain the software (the operating system, programming languages, and application programs used for word processing, databases, spreadsheets, graphics, desktop publishing, and communications). Explain how the entire system works (directories, subdirectories, files, and records).
2. *Computer protection basics—what is sensitive information and how can it be protected?* Included here would be access control functions, separation of functions, audit trail records and analyses, identifying sensitive information, and backup and storage of information.
3. *Computer crime investigations—what is a basic approach?* This would include

   Issues affecting investigations and prosecutions.

   Types of criminals and their computer tools.

   Types of computers and computer-related crimes.

   How the investigations are conducted.

   Collection of computer evidence.

   Preparing affidavits and search warrants.

   Obtaining assistance of computer experts.

   Preparing the investigative reports.

   The challenges ahead for law enforcement.

The second purpose would be to establish requirements for the protection of police computer systems and the information processed, stored, and transmitted by those systems.

**Police Department Information Systems
Protection Policy**

Policy Number
    Date

  I. Introduction
     1. *Objective.* The objective is to provide an information systems protection policy setting forth the minimum requirements necessary for the protection of information and information systems used to process, store, and transmit sensitive police department information.
     2. *Scope.* This policy document applies to all employees of the police department as well as any other users of the police department's information systems.
 II. Responsibilities
     1. *Supervisors.* Supervisors are responsible for ensuring that the information systems used by their staffs are protected from theft, misuse, and abuse; and a properly trained system protection custodian is assigned to each system to ensure that they and their information are protected in accordance with this policy document and all related policy directives. On receipt of information that the protection policies and procedures have been violated, supervisors must initiate an inquiry to resolve the issue in accordance with internal investigative procedures.
     2. *System protection custodians.* The systems protection custodians are responsible for ensuring that the systems operate in accordance with all department directives; that they are only used by authorized users; that the users only have access to that information necessary for them to perform their assigned work; and that the system's protection controls are in place and working. At a minimum, on a weekly basis, the systems protection custodian must review the audit trail records for indications of unauthorized access to the systems and files and report to the supervisor any violations of the information protection policies and procedures.
     3. *System users.* Prior to gaining access to any of the department's information systems, the system users must (1) obtain approval to access the specific information systems from their supervisor and the system protection custodian; (2) they must be briefed and acknowledge, in writing, their understanding of the information systems' protection policies and procedures, which must be followed while using the department's information systems; (3) and report any violations of those policies and procedures to the supervisor or system protection custodian.

III. Requirements
1. *Individual accountability.* Each information system must be able to identify each user through a unique user identifier.
2. *Access controls.* Each information system must control system access by preventing unauthorized access and allowing users access only to that information which they need to do their jobs. At a minimum, a logon user identification must be used in conjunction with a one-way encrypted password for access to information systems and sensitive files. The passwords used for access to the systems must be separate from those used to protect sensitive files access. The passwords must be at least six alphanumeric characters in length and unique to each user and sensitive file. In addition, the passwords must not be words easily associated with the user, such as date of birth, middle name, or nickname. Passwords must be changed quarterly and the same password must not be used more than once per year.
3. *Audit trails.* Each information system must maintain automated, manual, or combination audit trails that record the activities of the users on the system, including but not limited to (1) user identification, (2) time and date of access, and (3) the information accessed.
4. *Awareness briefings.* Prior to having access to any of the department's information systems, each user must
   A. Have a working knowledge of the hardware and software he or she will use.
   B. Be briefed on the policies and procedures to be followed for the use and protection of the system and the information processed, stored, and transmitted by it.
   C. Sign an acknowledgment statement relative to the preceding.
5. *Media.* All media (e.g., diskettes, tapes, printer ribbons) will be protected in the same manner as department documents containing similar information. All original software will be secured in a locked container. All software will be used in accordance with the licensing agreements accompanying the software product. All media will be labeled with, at a minimum, the following information:
   A. The sensitivity designation of the information contained on the media. The designation will be the same as used for documents.
   B. The name of the organization and the identity of the information system used to generate the information or media.
   C. The name of the system user responsible for the media.
6. *Information System Protection Procedures.*
6.1. An information system protection procedures (ISPP) document must be developed by the information systems protection custodian and approved by the supervisor prior to the operation of any information system within the department.

6.2. The ISPP must use the following format and include, at a minimum, the following:

A. *Identification.* The name of the department's organization that will use the system, the system's physical location, the name and telephone number of the supervisor and custodian of the system, and the type of information the system is authorized to process, store, and transmit.

B. *Hardware.* List and describe all the equipment that makes up the information system, including the printers, plotters, keyboard, cathode ray tube (CRT), and the like. The listing must include the make, model, and serial number of the equipment.

C. *Software.* List and describe all the software that will be used by the system, including company name, name of the software, and version number.

D. *Telecommunications and networking.* Describe how the system is connected to other systems, its purpose, and any telephone numbers called by the system, their location, and purpose of the connection.

E. *Personnel access.* Explain who has access to the system, what controls are in place to ensure only authorized users can access the system, and what procedures are in place to identify and delete users who no longer require access to the system.

F. *Physical protection.* Describe the physical controls in place to ensure that the hardware and software is protected from theft, modification, and abuse.

G. *Operating procedures.* Describe the procedures used during system operation to include how the system is accessed and how sensitive information is accessed and protected from input through hard-copy output. Explain the steps to be taken when protection procedures have been violated.

H. *General storage protection.* Describe where and how removable media (e.g. diskettes and tapes) are stored and protected.

I. *Audit trails.* Identify and describe the system's audit trails, the process for reviewing them, and include a sample copy of each as an attachment to the ISPP.

J. *Emergency plans and disaster recovery.* Describe what procedures are in place in the event of an emergency or disaster, the procedures to be used to recover from an emergency or disaster, and the procedures used to backup and store additional copies of important software and information files.

If a policy like the one just presented is not written on the police department's own initiative, it may well be forced on it by lawsuits from people whose privacy has been violated or, worse, who have been harmed due to the release of sensitive information. It also could be brought about because of the destruction of such information or the system.

Is this really needed? Let's look at another example. The county provides the computers and information technology support for the police systems, which are networked to its various locations. As part of an inmate's rehabilitation, he learns computer operations. He gets out of prison on parole, and his parole officer gets him a job on the midnight shift, working computer operations in the county's computer operations facility.

On midnight shifts only a minimal crew is around. After all, who wants to work that shift? So the parolee now has access to the county's computer systems and, therefore, all the information residing on those systems.

Is this possible? Is this likely? Yes. Of course, it is dependent on the type of InfoSec in place, authorized access given the parolee, and other factors. However, by the very nature of the parolee's computer operations' position, he has a certain level of access, which is required to properly perform his duties. That access is much broader in scope than any user's.

A convicted felon who has served his time is entitled to work and be considered as having paid for his crimes. Therefore, no future guilt should be imposed on the individual. However, we all know that recidivism and other factors could make a felon return to crime. So the question is twofold: (1) Does the police department know who has access to the system it uses? (2) Is it worth the risk to have such a person working in a facility that would give him access to a police computer system and, through it, other systems (e.g., DMV records, court records, and other criminal justice records)?

PROTECTING SEMICONDUCTORS: MICROCARVING

For those high-technology-crime investigators who may investigate the theft of semiconductors, the following information was gleaned from the Internet (source unknown):

> Selling stolen semiconductors is about to get a lot harder. An electronic industries association has adopted a new technology, data matrix, that engraves an indelible microscopic code on the outside of chips. It works like a tiny bar code but contains 100 times as much information. This lets manufacturers mark each chip with individual serial numbers. Thieves can't remove the code without ripping off the chip's casings, which in most cases would destroy the device.

SUMMARY

InfoSec's key principles are access control, individual accountability, and audit trails. This would apply to all high-technology equipment, including computer networks, PBX, cellular telephones, electronic mail, voice mail, electronic mailboxes, and other devices.

Police computers also should be secured and protected, especially if they are operated and maintained by those outside the police department.

InfoSec's functions, duties, and responsibilities will vary, depending on the culture and management support given to it.

NOTE

1. Several terms are used interchangeably to describe the protection of the information systems and the information that they store, process, and transmit. Among the more common are *computer security, information systems security (InfoSec), information systems protection,* and *systems security.*

PART II

Overview of the High-Technology-Crime Investigations Profession and Unit

OBJECTIVE

Now that you have an understanding of the global information environment, this part will discuss the profession of the high-technology-crime investigator.[1] The objective of this part is to provide professional high-technology-crime investigators, managers, and supervisors, in the business or government agency sector, an overview of the profession and how to establish and manage a high-technology-crime investigative unit.

- Chapter 6. "Developing a Career as a High-Technology-Crime Investigator." The objective of this chapter is to provide the high-technology-crime investigator a plan to use in developing a career in that profession.
- Chapter 7. "Marketing Yourself as a Successful Investigator." The objective of this chapter is to explain some of the more unique methods to prepare for a job in high-technology-crime investigation and an "interview by portfolio" method to get the position you've been looking for.
- Chapter 8. "The Global Enterprise Corporation." This chapter describes a fictional company in which the investigator or investigative manager will work. This approach provides a practical, baseline model on which to build a company high-technology-crime prevention and investigative program.
- Chapter 9. "Understanding the Role of the High-Technology-Crime Investigator and Prevention Unit in the Business Environment." This chapter defines the role the high-technology-crime investigator plays in a corporation or government agency. In this case, the role of the high-technology-crime investigator for GEC. The duties

and responsibilities of a high-technology-crime investigator vary, depending on the place of employment. However, in this case, we assume the investigator has the "perfect" position.

- Chapter 10. "The High-Technology-Crime Investigations Unit's Strategic, Tactical, and Annual Plans." The objective of this chapter is to establish the plans for the high-technology-crime prevention organization that provide the subsets of the GEC strategic, tactical, and annual plans. These plans set the direction for GEC's high-technology-crime prevention program and play a vital role in GEC's corporate plans, indicating that the program is an integral part of GEC.
- Chapter 11. "High-Technology-Crime Prevention and Investigative Program and Organization." The objective of this chapter is to discuss the establishment and management of the organization chartered with the responsibility to lead the high-technology-crime prevention effort for GEC, including structuring and describing the organization and the job descriptions of the personnel within the organization.
- Chapter 12. "High-Technology-Crime Investigative Functions." The objective of this chapter is to discuss the major high-technology-crime investigative functions to be performed by the unit and the flow processes that can be used to establish the baseline in performing the functions.
- Chapter 13. "Sources, Networking, and Liaison." The objective of this chapter is to identify and discuss sources of various types, networking, and liaison with outside agencies.
- Chapter 14. "High-Technology-Crime Investigation Unit's Metrics Management System." The objective of this chapter is to discuss the identification, development, and use of metrics charts to assist in managing a high-technology-crime investigations unit and prevention program.
- Chapter 15. "Final Thoughts, Problems, and Issues." This chapter discusses what may happen in a dynamic, international corporation that drastically changes the high-technology-crime investigations unit, the high-technology-crime prevention program, and the unit manager's position.

NOTE

1. Much of the information contained in this part is derived from the book *Information Systems Security Officer's Guide* (Kovacich, 1998), because the information related to career development, job interviews, and the like can be applied to any profession. Furthermore, the profession of InfoSec and high-technology-crime investigations are dependent on each other and in many ways overlap both as a career and in responsibilities.

6

Developing a Career as a High-Technology-Crime Investigator

DEVELOPMENT OF THE HIGH-TECHNOLOGY-CRIME INVESTIGATOR'S CAREER

It is interesting to note that most of us go through our working lives either in a profession we love or one we got into just because it was the only one available at the time—after all a person has to eat. However you got there, you probably now are in law enforcement, security, or your current investigative position. You probably are reading this book because you want to get into high-technology-crime investigative work or maybe you are just interested in the topic.

For whatever reason, one thing is certain for most people: They work hard and hope to get promoted then retire, so they no longer must work to enjoy a good life. However, they have no formal or even semiformal game plan for accomplishing their goals. Most people just seem to work hard and hope for the best.

This is definitely the wrong approach. Although none of us can completely control our career advancements, the only real control we have is to make ourselves the most qualified candidate for that new position, promotion, or job.

Whether you want to become a high-technology-crime investigator or already are one, you should have a career development plan. The vast majority of security, law enforcement, and investigative professionals have had very little if any experience in developing project plans. However, a project plan is exactly what is needed to prepare for the position of high-technology-crime investigator.

THE CAREER DEVELOPMENT PROJECT PLAN

Currently, very few of those involved in law enforcement, security, or investigative professions are lucky enough to work full-time in high-technology-crime investigative work. The profession of a high-technology-crime investigator currently does not exist in any true, formal sense within industry. However, such work does exist in various police departments, albeit very few. It is believed that the position of high-technology-crime investigator eventually will be formalized within the private sector.

Most individuals who want to become high-technology-crime investigators seem to take the best high-technology-crime investigative position they can find (or the closest things to it) and either try to stay in that position until they retire, move to a non-high-technology-crime investigator position, or continue to move on to new high-technology-crime investigator positions without any real plan. Very often they reflect on what could have been.

So, how do you go about preparing for that next high-technology-crime investigator opportunity or *the* high-technology-crime investigator position? Let's begin with your objective. Assume you are willing to work for a company or government agency until you are 55 years old. At that time, you want to have acquired a certain salary, be in a position to manage a major international organization's, or major government agency's high-technology anti-crime program, and generally enjoy the perks that come with that type of position.

At age 55, and after an illustrious career as a well-known high-technology-crime investigator, you want to be an anti-high-technology-crime program consultant until you are 62 years old. At that time, you decide to write your memoirs, go golfing, go fishing, maybe teach a little, but generally begin enjoying the good life of retirement.

To begin, you must do research. You want to know the following:

1. What are the various high-technology-crime investigator-related positions in the business or government agency?
2. What are the minimum educational requirements of those positions?
3. What are the minimum years of experience required for each of those positions?
4. What type of agencies or businesses requires what type of high-technology-crime investigator?
5. What are the job descriptions for each of those positions?

In developing your plan, begin with your present position and use the job family described in Chapter 11 to determine your goals and the education, training, and experience you need to attain them. After determining what you need, put together a project plan with tasks and dates for accomplishment of those tasks. On completion of that project, search for the position that meets your new qualifications and begin marketing yourself for that position.

The technical skills you'll need are related to information systems, such as programming and system security; computer forensics; interview and interrogation techniques; knowledge of legal issues; and any other function that falls under the anti-high-technology-crime program category.

You'll need a general, professional education and experience related to high-technology-crime investigation, such as project management, time management, report writing, and how to develop and present briefings.

Remember that your personal career development plan is dynamic and needs constant updating and self-reevaluation. By establishing the plan using the information provided in this chapter, you could save time by focusing on specific goals and accomplishments.

CAREER AND ADVANCEMENT PROJECT PLANNING

A project plan is a structured approach to accomplishing a specific objective. Many books on the market discuss project planning in elaborate detail. Also, various project management software products are on the market as well as shareware on the Internet.

Once you have developed a career development project plan, it would be a good idea to get a project planning software program to help you maintain a current career development project plan. You do not need an expensive and elaborate software program. These are very detailed and include labor charge information, hours assigned to each task, and linking many details that may be of little use to you. Therefore, you will probably get quickly discouraged and give up on the entire project.

We suggest you first develop your plan on paper and find some simple shareware program on the Internet that will meet your needs, which is much cheaper. You have several options, depending on your knowledge of software programs: a spreadsheet software, a word processing software using the outline format, or Microsoft's PowerPoint software or similar product where again the outline form can easily be used to develop your plan.

For most people it is probably easiest to start with a blank sheet of paper, then when you are satisfied with your plan, input it onto your computer using some simple software. The key is to concentrate on the plan and not get hung up on some elaborate software input.

Actually, for our purposes, project planning is a very simple, logical approach to a problem and not all that different from conducting an investigation. When conducting an investigation, one must determine that an actual crime has been committed, determine what law was violated, determine the elements of proof, and then develop leads that prove or disprove the allegation based on the elements of proof. In other words, you use a somewhat logical, sequential approach and develop a plan (if not on paper, at least in your head) to accomplish a specific goal: to identify potential suspects and prove or disprove allegations against them.

A project plan is also developed to provide a structured, orderly approach to accomplish a specific goal or objective. The project plan should also have specific tasks and dates as to when those tasks will be accomplished. Then, it is just a matter of working the plan. The great thing about a well-thought-out, realistic plan is that it will help you focus on your goals. It is an efficient process for accomplishing your goals, for being active as opposed to passively wishing and waiting for things to change.

So, your high-technology-crime investigator's career development plan is similar to any other project plan. That is, it has stated objectives, milestones, and starting and ending dates. The starting time is now and the ending date is the date of your planned retirement. Remember, it is never too early, or too late, to begin planning your high-technology-crime investigation career and developing the career plan that will challenge you to reach your full potential. The sooner you start, the more likely you are to succeed in meeting your goals and objectives before retirement. After all, you don't want to spend your retirement regretting what might have been.

For the person putting together a personal career development program or plan, it is important to know the basic positions available within the high-technology-crime investigation career field. In most government agencies and businesses, the bureaucracy requires that there be a "job family." In both the business world and government agencies, the description for the position of high-technology-crime investigator probably does not exist. It is assumed that it would be just another investigative position. Therefore, it would fall under the investigator's job description or, in the case of business, probably under the job descriptions for security personnel.

In most businesses and government agencies, job families and their related descriptions provide a gradual progression through a specific career specialty. It is assumed that such a specialty as high-technology-crime investigator does not currently exist. However, it is believed that some day, in the not too distant future, such a specialty will be required. So, now is a great time to prepare for it.

Let us assume that there are people who want to be high-technology-crime investigators; however, they have little or no education and experience. Let us also assume that the career growth includes positions from the introductory level, through supervisory and lower-level management positions, up to the position of manager of a high-technology-crime investigative unit. Therefore, the high-technology-crime career development plan must take into account the technical positions as well as the supervisory and management ones. You may never want to do anything but investigate high-technology crimes.

In addition, the anti-high-technology-crime program management position(s) within the corporation (if there are any at all) are very limited—actually limited to one. Career growth is likely to be achieved by changing corporations or government agencies.

So, let's put together a high-technology-crime investigation career development plan outline. You can add the specifics as it applies to you. Also, assume you are new to the field, starting with no high-technology-crime investigative experience whatsoever. You may or may not even have some investigative experience.

The basic categories that are the foundation for your career development are

- Education and training required for each position.
- Experience needed for each position.
- Certifications.

EDUCATION

Education is a key factor in obtaining a professional position today, regardless of the career field. Many corporations will not even talk to a potential candidate without a college degree, regardless of the number of years of experience. In the business world, so many years of experience can be "credited" as college equivalent. For example, some corporate human resource departments use four years of experience equals one year of college as a guide.

Keep in mind the market competition. Those with more college credit or degree(s) will build up more "points." It may be a matter of a bureaucratic system where so many points are assigned for education, experience, certifications, and possibly other factors such as those having to do with affirmative action.

The only answer you normally get when not hired for a position is that the company or agency hired a more qualified candidate, but it will not provide specific information due to concerns of privacy. However, the real concerns are more about potential lawsuits. After all, we are a nation inundated by lawyers and people seem to sue for whatever reason, especially those who don't get their way. Regardless, such is life. If you prepare a great career development plan and continue to work it, your time will come.

The chance of getting a job in a corporation to fill a high-technology-crime investigator's position is dependent on qualifications, of course. So, 20 years of investigative experience and no college degree may not be good enough against a person with 10 years of experience and a college degree. Another factor to consider is the current job market. If the job market is very good, corporations have to pay more to fill their positions and they are less choosy. However, if jobs are scarce, there may be a great deal of competition. Therefore, corporations can pay less and get more qualified candidates. The potential high-technology-crime investigator must always consider the worst-case scenario. That way, he or she always is prepared for better or worse economic conditions.

Potential high-technology-crime investigators can or have used two different educational approaches: criminal justice (investigative) and high technology (technical). It is expected that most individuals will begin from security, law enforcement, or investigative positions. This is because most college students who major in high technology do so because they like working with the technology more than people, and there are more jobs at higher pay than one could find as a high-technology-crime investigator— at least today. However, in the future, it is expected that the need for high-technology-crime investigators will be such that there will be entry-level positions filled by college graduates.

As government agencies and businesses rely more and more on high technology, where losses continue to increase and where businesses are devastated by these crimes, the job prospects are expected to change. Many small businesses already have gone out of business after being devastated by a huge telephone bill from the long distance carriers because someone had attacked their PBXs and built up telephone charges over a weekend.

Criminal Justice, Security, Criminology, and Investigative College Courses, Majors, and Curriculum

In the past, degrees in criminal justice and criminology or majors under the social science degree programs were the only formal college programs available for one to get a formal education relative to investigations. Later, degrees in security management emerged as separate majors under social science or as stand-alone degrees. Not very long ago, universities began adding information systems security courses at the undergraduate and graduate levels, either as part of a computer science, information systems management, or accounting or auditing degree program. Lately, some universities have begun a series of courses that lead toward a major or degree in information systems security.

Based on this sequence of events, it is expected that at least a major in high-technology-crime investigations eventually will be a major under a criminal justice or security degree program. It is doubtful that the universities will consider, at least not in our lifetime, a high-technology-crime investigation major under a computer science or information systems management program. No matter, it is hoped that eventually the universities, driven by businesses, government agencies, and professional associations, such as the High Technology Crime Investigation Association, will begin to see the need for such a program to fulfill the needs of society.

In today's environment, a college degree with a major in computer science or telecommunications is one of the best ways to start a high-technology-crime investigation career. An alternative is to major in another high-technology program. As colleges and universities see the demand for high-technology-crime investigations-related subjects, they will offer such courses and programs.

It is interesting to note that the information systems security (InfoSec) career offers a good example of the route the high-technology-crime investigation career will follow. To this day, there is no firm agreement as to the best educational background and experience for an InfoSec professional. Many security personnel believe that the security profession is the best starting point for an InfoSec career. Others argue that a degree in computer science and experience with high technology is best.

Based on our experience, both are beneficial. It all depends on where one wants to put the emphasis. For technical InfoSec, the computer science approach is best. From an administrative, people-oriented, and management emphasis, the security background usually works best.

In the end, it boils down to the individual, and the same holds true for the high-technology-crime investigator. From a technical point of view, of course the computer science or similar technical experience and education is best. However, people commit crimes and it would seem that a knowledge of people, personalities, psychology, and the like would outweigh the technical aspects. Technical skills are great for crime scene searches, computer forensics; however, these only support the investigation. As mentioned before, after all it is a people problem.

An alternative to a college or university is a technical school that offers specialized high-technology programs in various aspects of the computer and telecommunications functions and hands-on experience, which may provide a faster avenue into the high-technology-crime investigation profession. Also, many colleges and universities offer certificates in a specialized high-technology field, such as local area networks or telecommunications. These courses also can be applied to a degree program. Those that choose the technical training path should still pursue a college degree that will enhance promotion opportunities in the high-technology-crime investigation profession.

The non-high-technology path is through security, criminal justice, psychology, or even business administration programs. These offer more information about the human elements.

Education, whether technical or academic, provides the future investigator an opportunity for a high-technology-crime investigator position. We say the *opportunity* for a position because, in today's business environment, certifications or a degree will provide you only the opportunity for a possible interview.

In today's marketplace, the need for experience coupled with advanced degrees and certifications has increased to the point where all your education, experience, and certifications get you through only the first resume-filtering process. *The interview is what will get you the job.*

Next, we offer some examples of a curriculum that, we hope, soon may become common in colleges and universities and offer the high-technology-crime investigator or potential investigator an opportunity for a formal education more related to his or her chosen profession.

Business Security Management Undergraduate Courses

- *BSA 350 Introduction to Business Security* (an overview of security). In this course the role of security within society is discussed. The functions and systems of security are examined as they apply to business, institutions, and government. Moreover, legal, organizational, and operational issues are addressed. Risk analysis and security surveys also are examined. Prerequisites: None.
- *BSA 351 Retail and Manufacturing Security* (an overview of the unique security problems associated with retail and manufacturing companies). The emphasis in this course is on establishing physical security controls, asset protection programs, and techniques used to conduct investigations relative to internal frauds, pilferage, as well as customer and supplier thefts such as shoplifting and shorting deliveries. Prerequisites: BSA 350.
- *BSA 352 Physical Security* (an examination of physical security techniques, applications, and hardware within business, industry, and government). The emphasis in this course is on environmental design, security surveys, access control and personnel identification, lighting, alarms, and closed-circuit television. Prerequisites: None.
- *BSA 450 Government Security* (an overview of security programs established for government agencies and government contractors to protect national security information and assets). This course includes general provisions and requirements, personal security clearances, security training and briefings, classification and markings, safeguarding classified information, visit procedures, subcontracting, automated information systems, special requirements, international security requirements, NATO information, assignments outside of the United States, and protection of unclassified technology. *The Industrial Security Manual* or the *National Industrial Security Program Operating Manual* will be the required text. Prerequisites: None.
- *BSA 451 Security and Law Enforcement.* The duties and responsibilities of law enforcement officers and security officers will be examined relative to crimes on business premises. The emphasis in this course is on identifying and analyzing their commonalty of functions, differences, conflicts, and drafting of policies and procedures to be used to assist in mutual assistance to mitigate against crime.

Current trends and their future roles will be explored. Prerequisites: BSA 350.

- *BSA 453 Protecting Sensitive Business Information.* The emphasis in this course is on identifying, qualifying, and quantifying the value and cost of sensitive business information as well as the threats, vulnerability, and risk associated with industrial and economic espionage. Competitive intelligence gathering also is examined. Prerequisites: BSA 350.

- *BSA 454 Principles of Investigations.* The emphasis in this course is on conducting investigations, including interviews, interrogations, crime scene searches, evidence collection, report writing, and testifying in court. Prerequisites: None.

- *BSA 455 White-Collar Crime Investigations.* The emphasis in this course is on conducting fraud investigations with emphasis on the major types of fraud, such as embezzlement, contract, procurement, identity theft, credit card, and other white-collar crimes. Prerequisites: BSA 454.

- *BSA 456 High-Technology-Crime Investigations.* This course concentrates on understanding and conducting high-technology-crime investigations with emphasis on the investigation of computer, Internet, PBX, cellular phone, and other high-technology crimes. Prerequisites: BSA 454 and 455.

- *BSA 456 National, Social, Government. and Business Ethics.* This is a basic course on the issue of ethics in all aspects of our lives, including understanding what is ethical in various cultures and working environments and interactions with others. Prerequisites: None.

Business Security Management Graduate Courses

- *BSM 500A Managing a Security Organization.* Contemporary management concepts and principals are applied to managing a security organization. This course provides the framework for the evaluation and management of a security organization. It examines organizational culture, internal operations, the budgetary process, management systems and subsystems, and internal strengths and weaknesses. Concepts discussed include mission, leadership, teambuilding, critical success factors, processes, and customers. Prerequisite: B.S. or B.A. degree in a related field.

- *BSM 500B Managing a Security Organization.* This course continues 500A and provides the framework for strategic planning and the implementation of management controls and processes. It examines organizational goals and structure, objectives, strategic planning, the implementation of management controls, process improvements, and performance management. Prerequisite: BSM 500A.

Technology Security Management Courses

- *TSM 360 Fundamentals of Technologies and Systems.* This course provides a nontechnical overview of the operations and uses of technology and systems, including private branch exchanges, micro-computers, mini and mainframe computers, networks, wireless communication, cellular phones, electronic mail, voice mail, and their related software. These technologies are discussed in terms of their hardware, software, firmware, and configurations. Prerequisite: None.
- *TSM 460 Theories and Practices of Technology Security* (introduction to the concepts, philosophies, and methods used to protect and monitor the use of technology systems). This course includes discussions concerning the technologies' key protection concepts of access control, physical security, logical security, individual accountability, and audit trails as well as personnel security, administrative security, communications security, systems security, risk analyses, and inspections. Prerequisite: TSM 360 or equivalent.
- *TSM 461 Technology and Systems Security Management.* This course is designed to provide basic guidance necessary for the development of a technology and systems security program. Using a systems approach, a technology and systems security manager is able to develop his or her own program. The course includes discussions on management techniques, leadership, and quality management techniques, followed by a discussion of strategic planning, tactical planning, metrics management, and building project teams as they relate to the protection of information, technology, and systems. Prerequisite: TSM 360 and TSM 460.
- *TSM 462 Physical Security of Technology and Facilities.* This course provides a nontechnical overview of today's physical security technologies, which can be used to protect technology facilities, systems, and information. It includes discussions on closed-circuit television, access control devices, emanations, and red/black engineering that can be applied to sensitive systems, perimeter fences, intrusion detection systems, architectural security designs, security force management, security lighting, physical security surveys, and inspections. Prerequisite: None.
- *TSM 463 Principles of Technology Investigations.* This course provides a basic overview of the techniques used to conduct investigations of technology and technology-related crime. The overview includes the different types of technology crimes at the federal and state levels, applicable laws, technology-crime indicators, categories of technology crimes, techniques used in committing technology crimes, basic investigative techniques, and prosecution as well as future projections of high-technology crime. The emphasis in this course is on those investigations related to microcomputers, mini and main-

frame computers, networks, and associated telecommunication systems. Prerequisites: TSM 360 and TSM 460.

- *TSM 464 Ethics, Privacy, and Technology.* This course discusses today's ethics and privacy issues and the impact to them caused by technology. Among the topics covered are the pros and cons of databases, which store massive amounts of personal information and processes and distributes that information in both the public and private sectors. Prerequisite: None.
- *TSM 465 Fundamentals of Network Security* (introduction to the concepts, philosophies, and methods used to protect and monitor the use of networks). This course includes discussions concerning the networks' key protection concepts of access control, physical security, logical security, individual accountability, and audit trails as well as personnel security, administrative security, communications security, systems security, risk analyses. and inspections. Prerequisites: TSM 360 and TSM 460.
- *TSM 466 Technology Crime Prevention Surveys and Risk Assessments.* This course teaches a proactive approach to deter or minimize high-technology crime by analyzing functions and processes using a total quality, continuous process improvement approach. Each major step in the processes is analyzed to determine its threats and areas of vulnerability and risk. This information is formalized into a management report with recommendations for protection improvements using a least-cost approach. Prerequisites: TSM 360 and TSM 460.
- *TSM 467 Technology Crime and the Law* (a general overview of applicable technology laws dealing with technology security and crime). This course includes a discussion of both federal and state laws, with emphasis on those affecting California law enforcement and security professionals. Case law and legal trends are discussed and analyzed. Prerequisites: TSM 360 and TSM 460.
- *TSM 468 Technology Security in a Government Environment.* This course discusses the fundamentals of protecting national security information stored, processed, and transmitted on government and contractor computing systems. The discussion focuses on the security requirements of the *Industrial Security Manual for Protecting Classified Information* and the *National Industrial Security Program Operations Manual* and how to meet those requirements. Prerequisites: TSM 360 and TSM 460.

Courses similar to some of these are available at the local colleges and universities. In addition, many universities are now beginning to offer course and degree programs through television programs and the Internet.

If you lack an associate's or higher level degree, we recommend you identify and enroll in a program that offers a certificate after completing a prerequisite number of courses approved for and directly related to a degree program.

Once the courses are completed and a certificate awarded, the next course of action would be to take those additional courses that lead to an associate's degree. After the associate's degree, go on to the bachelor's degree. Once that is completed, go on to a master's degree program. After all, your goal is knowledge, training, and those degrees that separate you from the competition. If you haven't the desire or energy to complete a master's degree program, remember that most of your competitors probably feel the same way. However, those with the desire and initiative to take on a master's degree program have the desire to be the best and stand above the crowd of other high-technology-crime investigators. They are the ones who may get the job that you wanted.

If you complete a bachelor's degree, we highly recommend that your master's degree major be an MBA in international business management. This is because you learned that "high-technology-crime investigation-related techie stuff" in your bachelor's degree program. It is extremely important that you also understand the world of business if you are to work in that environment. Even if you work for a government agency, such a degree would have much more relativity than a master's degree in public administration, for even the government agency's world revolves around a global business environment.

Such a master's degree would help give you instant credibility when talking to executive management—the people who must be your primary supporters for funding, political support, and so forth. Yes, the business world is rife with office politics, just like government and public agencies. Furthermore, understanding the world of global business provides you knowledge that will greatly enhance your high-technology-crime investigative efforts. It also gives you an appreciation for global business processes that will assist you in developing anti-high-technology-crime programs at the least cost and impact to the business or government agency.

Remember that your certificate will place you ahead of the great number of investigators with no formal training. With each additional formal educational step you take, you will have fewer and fewer competitors. So, if you are very, very serious about being the best, a doctorate or Ph.D. would come after the master's degree.

So, to develop the educational portion of your career development program (see Table 6–1), you should

- Identify the certificate, associate's, bachelor's, master's, and doctorate degree programs that provide you the technical and managerial training you will need to be a professional high-technology-crime investigator.

- On that portion of your career development plan identified as formal education, list the certificate(s) and degrees, the majors, and then the courses that you will take, filling in as many specific dates as you can.
- Enroll in the courses, learn, and enjoy.

It may seem like a huge undertaking, but remember to never lose sight of your goal and remember the old saying about eating an elephant a bite at a time.

Table 6–1 is an example of the academic portion of a career development plan with the emphasis on high technology instead of business security, using spreadsheet software. List the specific course and tentative dates of completion based on the classes in the school's catalogue.

Table 6–1   High-Technology-Crime Investigator's Career Development Plan

Formal Education	Estimated Completion Date	Actual Completion Date
Certificate Program— *Telecommunications Management*	*Jun-00*	
Course 1	May-99	Dec-98
Course 2	Aug-99	May-99
Etc.		
Associate's Degree—Information Systems	*Jun-01*	
Course 1		
Course 2		
Etc.		
Bachelor's Degree—Technology Security	*Jun-04*	
Course 1		
Course 2		
Etc.		
Master's Degree (MBA)—International *Business*	*Jun-06*	
Course 1		
Course 2		
Etc.		
Doctorate Degree—Criminology	*Jun-11*	
Course 1		
Course 2		
Etc.		*(Continued)*

Table 6–1   Continued

Certifications

CISSP	Aug-98	Feb-99
CFE	Aug-99	
CISA	Aug-00	
Etc.		

Technical Training

TCP/IP
UNIX
Firewalls
Computer Forensics
SEARCH Class
Etc.

Experience Needed

Searching Hard Drives
Interviewing Hackers
Using Computer Forensic Software
Conducting Internet Crime Cases
Coordinating with Interpol
Etc.

Conferences and Training

To prepare yourself for a position as a high-technology-crime investigator, try to complement your education with as much training as possible. Numerous associations, consultants, and companies provide training classes, workshops, and conferences that cover the entire field of high technology as well as investigations and high-technology investigations. Although none is very cheap—of course, that is relative—they provide the opportunity to gain first-hand knowledge on many high-technology-crime prevention program topics.

These topics range from the administrative, nontechnical aspects to the technical aspects. The following is a list of conference sessions and workshop from a typical high-technology-security conference, indicating courses of interest to high-technology-crime investigators.[2]

Conference sessions:

- Wireless and Cellular Phone Fraud.
- E-Cash Security.
- Developing and Implementing an Internet Security Policy.

- Controlling Dial-up Security.
- Handling Security Incidents.
- Telecommuting Security.
- Hacker Tools and Techniques.
- The Legal Aspects of Internet Connections.
- Testing Firewalls and Other Types of Barrier Security.
- Building a Security Awareness Program.
- Security and Audit Tools for Non-UNIX Systems.
- E-Mail Security.
- Security Mechanisms for Electronic Commerce.
- Navigating the Internet for Audit and Security.
- Intranet Security.
- Virus Protection.
- Information Warfare and the High-Technology-Crime Investigator.

Optional workshops:

- Disaster Recovery Planning.
- Building a Business-Oriented Anti-High-Technology-Crime Program.
- Auditing Your Internet Connection.
- Windows NT Security and Audit.

These training courses and workshops also give you the opportunity to find out what works and does not work. Furthermore, the lecturers discuss the areas of vulnerability in various types of technology and how miscreants have attacked such systems. This will come in handy when you become a high-technology-crime investigator. You won't have to learn the hard way—by experience. Don't concern yourself with the *not-invented-here syndrome*. Learn from the mistakes of others and apply what will work for you, your career, and your anti-high-technology-crime program and investigations. Remember that it's not where you get your information or methodology but whether or not you successfully apply it. Your company is interested in results. So, *be results oriented.*

Prior to attending any conference or workshop that provides a choice of courses on various topics, you should know what up-to-date information you lack. Then, be sure to attend those courses. Also, be sure to ask questions. The purpose of the courses is to exchange information and learn from each other.

To determine what relevant high-technology courses and knowledge areas you should concentrate on while at the conferences or what specialized training and knowledge you require that is available at the conference you attend,

1. Take a blank sheet of paper and identify those topics to be discussed at the conference that are most relevant to your current work.

2. Identify those about which you know nothing or very little. Rate your knowledge from 1 to 5 or high, medium, or low. Be honest and objective because, if you are not, you are cheating only yourself.
3. After you complete that section, sequentially rank the training you need and the lectures you will attend as to the priority of each. Obviously, the lower your current knowledge rating, the higher you should rank the type of training needed and vice versa.
4. Transfer that information to your spreadsheet (Table 6–1), below the formal education section.

Networking

While at a conference or training course, be sure to get a copy of the list of participants, which normally is available. Using the list of participants, make it a point to identify and seek out those who work in the government agency or business you would like to target for employment. For example, some attendees may work in the banking and finance business, others in manufacturing, some in aerospace, some in accounting firms, and so on.

During the breaks, find these people. All participants wear a badge that normally contains their name and the business or government agency for which they work. So, it won't be that difficult to find people. Go through the crowds, find the person, introduce yourself, and ask your questions. You will find that you may not be the only one puzzled by a new technology or how to apply an high-technology-crime prevention program to a particular system configuration.

Many attendees are strangers on the first day of these events but become professional friends by the time the conference ends. Then, it is a matter of continuous networking (keeping in touch by e-mail, fax, or telephone) and discussing what is going on in the profession, in industry, or whatever.

During each session, sit with someone you have not met before and learn what the person does, the company he or she works for, and so on. With each break and at each luncheon or dinner, try to meet someone new. Remember your objective is to meet people who will share high-technology-crime information with you, people you can contact later to find out about job opportunities or how to approach a particular problem or investigation.

When you attend these conferences, training sessions, and association meetings, be sure to bring plenty of business cards and don't be shy. Ask someone for his or her card. If you have no card, get some printed, even if it has only your name, home address, telephone number, fax number, and e-mail address.

If you hand out your card and someone asks what you do, be honest. If you are unemployed, employed in a non-high-technology-crime investigation position or are a student, just say so. Tell the person you really enjoy the high-technology-crime investigation profession and are trying very hard to get into it. You may be surprised at the response and how people will try to help you.

One of the greatest benefits of conferences and attending chapter meetings of law enforcement, security, audit, or investigation associations is the opportunity to network with those in the profession. This is the best way to find out what the high-technology-crime investigators in government agencies and businesses are doing. They also are some of the best sources of information on positions open at companies or government agencies.

You must remember that few of these positions are advertised in the newspapers. Those that are advertised usually are because the company did not want to hire an employment firm to fill the position or maybe the position called for $100,000 worth of experience but the company wanted to pay $25,000.

If you are new to the high-technology-crime investigator profession, you may have to apply for such a position and hope that, although you don't have all the experience and education they desire, you're the best candidate that has applied for the position. There is nothing wrong with "buying in" to the position by accepting a lower than expected salary. It is a start, and with two or three years of experience, you have a better opportunity to get a better position and command a higher salary. Who knows, your company may give you a counteroffer if you have done a great job.

Another great tool for networking is the Internet. By obtaining the names and e-mail addresses of people you meet at conferences, association meetings, and so forth, you can begin a dialogue with others in the profession.

The Internet

A rapidly growing source of information about anti-high-technology-crime programs is the Internet. Many groups on the Internet discuss both general and specific high-technology-crime and security-related issues. All these Internet sites provide information that can help you learn about high-technology-crime, investigative positions, problems, solutions to those problems, techniques for breaking into systems, and so forth. This information is available just by doing an Internet search.

If you lack Internet access, we suggest subscribing to an Internet service provider. It is almost impossible to be a high-technology-crime investigator today without an Internet account and address for electronic mail (e-mail).

You will probably find that your major problem will not be finding useful high-technology-crime and investigations-related information on the Internet but that there is so much useful information that you won't be able to keep up with all of it. Don't feel bad, no one can. Using your completed self-evaluation knowledge charts, you can concentrate your information search on those areas where you are weakest. Then, if you have time, research and review the other high-technology-crime and investigations-related documents.

A good way of ensuring that you do the research and review is to

1. Set up your Internet websites through your Internet browser's Bookmarks. That way, you won't have to continually search for the sites that have the best information relative to your high-technology-crime investigative needs.
2. Set up a specific time each day when you can commit at least one hour to reading and learning from the material in your personal library, textbooks, Internet sites, and the like.

To be successful, you must have self-discipline and good study habits, of course. However, you will find that the rewards of knowledge about new anti-high-technology-crime programs gained through such study habits, as well as successfully applying those newly learned techniques, will be well worth your effort.

Trade Journals and Magazines

Other overlooked and usually free sources of information are the technology trade journals and magazines. Such journals and magazines contain articles about the latest technologies, problems with this or that software, and more and more contain high-technology crime articles. All this information will help you stay abreast of the technology and the related issues. If you don't keep current in the technology, the technology will probably make you *obsolete* in less than five years.

EXPERIENCE

Many of the people filling high-technology-crime investigation positions today did not start out to be high-technology-crime investigators. For many, the high-technology-crime investigator did not exist when they began in their profession.

As with any person entering any profession for the first time, the challenges are many. How does one become a high-technology-crime investigator if the company or government agency wants a person with experience? Inexperienced candidates seem to never have the chance to gain that experience, the typical "catch-22" situation. However, isn't that the same for all professions?

Far too many excellent books on the market address the issues of job hunting and how to gain experience for us to address the subject in any great level of detail in this book. Suffice it to say, you can find many of these books at the local library, on-line through the Internet, and at local bookstores. The important point is to get several of these books and articles and use them to your advantage.

The best approach to take is to get experience anywhere and anyway you can. Many people fall into the trap of thinking that they can gain the high-technology-crime investigative experience they need only by being employed in the profession. If you can do it, that's great. However, what if you can't?

There are several other ways to gain related experience. Many schools, ranging from elementary and universities to senior associations, need some type of help that is information systems related—so, volunteer. It may not be an actual investigation but it is high-technology-crime related. Furthermore, one often hears of hacker kids breaking into school computer systems. Maybe you could assist in such an investigation by volunteering to help the local law enforcement investigator. Most of them may say, "thanks but no thanks"; however, others may not. This is especially true if the investigator assigned to the case has little if any knowledge of high technology, computers, and so forth.

You can volunteer to help a school or organization with its computer needs. Sometimes, the help needed may be as simple as helping to load new software on a microcomputer or installing a new piece of computer hardware.

While you are doing your volunteer work, also volunteer to set up some access controls or audits trails. Maybe, you can even volunteer to periodically review the audit trails to ensure that the system isn't being abused or used for unauthorized purposes. After all, a high-technology-crime investigator must know how systems are protected as well as their areas of vulnerability. Hands-on experience is much better than just reading about the topic.

The main point is that it is a win-win situation. The school or organization gets the help it needs while you gain the experience you need. You may be surprised to learn that many small companies also would greatly appreciate your volunteered assistance.

You can find such work by contacting charitable organizations, discussing it with members of your church, city council members, local chamber of commerce, business associations, and the like. Who knows, you may find that your volunteer work leads to consulting work or a permanent position.

CERTIFICATION

What is certification? For our purposes, *certification* means that, based on your experience, education, and successfully passing a test, generally given by some related association, you are certified to have the basic knowledge and ability that meets the criteria for certifying you as a professional or expert in a particular field.

We could find no formal, recognized high-technology-crime investigator's certification program available. If there are any, be careful that it is from a group of nonprofit associations or a consortium made up of recognized professionals in the industry and not some "consultants with a get-rich scheme" who charge an excessive amount of money for certifications unknown throughout the industry.

However, there are several related certification programs from recognized consortiums and associations. These include a certification as a

- Certified Information Systems Security Professional (CISSP; at http://www.isc_2.org).
- Certified Information Systems Auditors (CISA; at http://www.securityserver.com/company/$isaca.htm).
- Certified Protection Professional (CPP; at http://www.asisonline.org).
- Certified Fraud Examiner (CFE; at http://www.acfe.org).

ASSOCIATIONS

As a professional high-technology-crime investigator, you should become a member and take part in one or more of several associations related to high-technology security, fraud, and crime programs.

The association most relevant is the High Technology Crime Investigation Association (HTCIA), founded in the late 1980s by several economic crime detectives in Southern California and supported by members from the business community. They have local chapters in many areas and an annual conference.

The association is made up of about 75% law enforcement personnel and 25% investigators and security professionals from the business sector. At last report, qualified members paid an initial fee of $35 and an annual fee of $25.

It is highly recommended that anyone involved in high-technology-crime investigations join this association. You can find more about the HTCIA through the national and some chapter websites. Just access the Internet and search HTCIA to find more about this association.

Other relevant associations are the Information Systems Security Association (ISSA), International Computer Security Association (ICSA), Association of Certified Fraud Examiners, American Society for Industrial Security, and Institute of Internal Auditors. Another way to search for such associations is to access the Internet and search using various topics, such as crime, computer crime, security.

Like any other associations, you only get out of these what you are willing to put into them. These associations usually have local chapter meetings. You should attend these meeting, take part in them, volunteer to help, and when you are ready to lead, run for office.

Several of the associations also sponsor annual, international conferences. These conferences give the high-technology-crime investigator an opportunity to meet other such professionals and share problems and solutions on an international scale.

Joining and actively participating in your chosen professional associations not only is required of a true high-technology-crime investigation professional, but it provides you the opportunity to learn new high-technology-crime methods, new problems, and network with your peers.

You will find that, by investing your time in these associations, you will be rewarded in many ways. By supporting your chosen association(s), you are helping to support your profession and make it better.

SUMMARY

1. Career development planning helps ensure that the high-technology-crime investigator has an opportunity for a successful career.
2. Career development planning requires an understanding of high technology, crime, and investigations and the education, training, experience and certifications needed to be competitive for a high-technology-crime investigator's positions.
3. Education and training can be received from many sources: trade journals, universities, conferences, and technical schools.
4. Experience can be gained by volunteering to assist others in high-technology-crime prevention programs and information systems functions.

NOTE

1. Sessions and workshops offered at an anti-high-technology-crime program association/MIS Institute Conference.

7

Marketing Yourself as a Successful Investigator

APPLYING FOR THE POSITION OF HIGH-TECHNOLOGY-CRIME INVESTIGATOR, SUPERVISOR, OR MANAGER

Currently, very few, if any, positions in business or government agencies carry the title high-technology-crime investigator. However, positions are available for fraud examiners and investigators whose job description may include investigating high-technology violations of policies, procedures, or laws.

If you have completed your career development project plan and have begun working the plan, you will be in a better position to compare your qualifications against the job descriptions for the investigative position. This is because you would have conducted a self-analysis and an a inventory of your current education, experiences, strengths, and weaknesses.

Once you complete your plan, you may be able to begin working in the high-technology-crime investigation field. Using some of the sources and techniques explained in the previous chapter, you may find a position that you believe you are qualified to hold. There is no reason not to apply for the position. If nothing else, it will give you the experience of interviewing, thus helping you to improve your interview skills. This is especially important if you are coming from a government agency position and looking for a position in the private sector.

So, let's assume that you have found a position being advertised calling for a high-technology-crime investigator. What do you do next? Read the description of the job carefully to make sure that it is the position you really want. If you are not so much interested in fulfilling that position as getting out of the job you currently hold, you should be sure you know what you are doing. Also, be sure that the position is the one you truly want to hold before you go through the time and effort of applying for it, doing the much-needed research on the company, and going through the interview process.

If you decide that the position being advertised is the one for you, you probably will see in the advertisement that a resume is to be sent in via e-mail or fax and no telephone calls please.

Today's businesses are inundated by resumes. Many of today's businesses use a computerized scanner to scan resumes into a database. If your resume is not easily scanned into the system, it may be trashed before it ever is reviewed. Think about it. If a clerk is scanning the resumes into a computerized system—and there may be hundreds of these resumes— trashing one (the clerk will reason) would not be noticed nor will it make a big difference.

So, you have to take your chances and fax or e-mail your resume, as the business does not want you to call nor does it provide an address. Sometimes, it does not even provide its name in the advertisement. Before you submit a resume, change it. Undoubtedly, you have a resume that is generic in nature. To send in a generic resume for a investigations-related job is the wrong approach. Your resume should be specifically tailored to the position advertised. If (as we all hope) your resume is reviewed, the reviewer probably will be a human resources specialist or the manager seeking to fill the position or both. In either case, the closer your resume-identified education, experiences, and skills match those of the job description, the better are your chances to be included in the number of applicants who will be scheduled for an interview.

Your resume must give the impression that you are perfect for the job—been there and done that. Remember that out of the 50–1,000 resumes received for that position, only a handful, maybe 5–10, of the most qualified applicants will be scheduled for an initial interview.

YOUR RESUME MADE IT PAST THE INITIAL SCREENING, THE NEXT STEP IS THE INTERVIEW

Congratulations, your resume has finally made it through the filtering process and you are scheduled for an interview. Preparation is key since this is a highly competitive area.

As with most jobs these days, you will probably be subjected to a series of interviews with members of the human resources department, information systems organization, auditors, and security personnel.

Many books on the market tell you how to interview for a position. They offer advice on everything from how to dress to how to answer the "mother of all interview questions": "What are your salary expectations?"

It is not the purpose of this book to help you answer those common interview questions. We assume that you will have read those books, prepared, and practiced for the upcoming interview. The purpose here is to show you how you can distinguish yourself from your high-technology-crime investigation competition.

You probably have interviewed more times than you care to admit. In all those interviews, you, like your peers, walked in wearing conservative business attire, neatly groomed, and prepared to answer any question thrown at you. The question is, *What separates you from your competitors?* What would make the interviewers remember you and choose you above the rest?

You probably answered most questions in the most politically correct way possible; for example, "What is your major weakness?" Answer: "My major weakness is that I have very little patience for those who don't live up to their commitments. When someone agrees to complete a project by a specific date, I expect that date to be met unless the project leader comes to me in advance of the deadline and explains the reason why that date can't be met. I believe in a team effort and each of us as vital members of that team must work to provide the service and support needed to assist the company in meeting its goals."

Will that answer to that question be considered a weakness or a strength by the interviewers? Probably a strength, but that is how the game is played.

Most of us have been there, done that, and still didn't get the position. Why? The only real lasting evidence of the interview is what was written down by the interviewers and what impressions you, the prospective high-technology-crime investigator, left in their minds. Many interviewers are "screeners," human resource people who have no clue as to what high-technology-crime prevention is all about. They are there because we work in teams today. We operate by consensus. So, getting selected is much more difficult.

You need one distinguishing thing that will leave a lasting impression on the interviewers, one thing that will show them you have the talent, the *applied* education, the experience, *and* the game plan. You've done it. You've been successful in building a high-technology-crime prevention program before and you will be successful again. You can prove that you can do it because you have your high-technology-crime investigator portfolio. The next question the reader may ask is, "What the heck is my high-technology-crime investigator portfolio?"

What you must do is develop your own portfolio to take with you and leave with the interviewers, *proof* that you've been there and done that, you are the best person for the position—it's all there in the portfolio.

Your high-technology-crime investigator portfolio is something you should begin building as soon as you begin your first high-technology-crime investigation job or before. It should contain an index and identified sections that include letters of reference, letters of appreciation, copies of award certificates, project plans, and metric charts you use for measuring the success of your high-technology-crime investigations, and your high-technology-crime prevention investigative program. Probably most important are your high-technology-crime investigative philosophy and prevention plan outline that you will implement as soon as you are hired.

Develop an outline, as detailed as possible, of a high-technology-crime prevention program, processes, functions, and similar material and place it in your interview portfolio. Such an outline probably is the most important document in your portfolio and should be the first page after your table of contents. All the other documents are just proof that what you plan to do, you have done before. This is extremely important if the job you are applying for is of a supervisory or managerial nature.

If you have never been a high-technology-crime investigator, you can build the high-technology-crime prevention plan and portfolio from the information provided in this book. Build it for the Global Enterprise Corporation (GEC; see the next chapter).

The next question that may arise is, "If I never worked there, how do I know what I should do if I get hired?" Again, do some research. Your first stop should be the Internet. Find out about the company—"investigate" it. Some information you should know is

- When was it started?
- What services or products does it produce?
- How is the company stock doing?
- Where are its offices, manufacturing plants or whatever located?

Also, stop by the company and pick up an application, any company brochures available, including benefits pamphlets, annual reports, and the like.

Study the information, complete the application, and place it in your portfolio. After all, if the company decides to hire you, you'd have to fill one out anyway. Go into the interview knowing as much, if not more, about the company as the people interviewing you. This is invaluable, especially as you interview for more senior level positions. These interviews undoubtedly will include the members of executive management. Your ability to talk about the company in business terms with an understanding of it undoubtedly will impress them and indicate that you are business oriented.

All your answers to the interviewers' questions should be directed to something in your portfolio. For example, if they ask you how you would deal with downsizing in your department and what impact that would have on your ability to adequately conduct high-technology-crime investigations, try the following. Direct them to a process chart, a metric, something that indicates that you have done it before and have a business-oriented approach to dealing with the issue. Alternatively, if you have not done it before, write down how you could, how you would, do these functions.

The portfolio can work for any new high-technology-crime investigator in any company. The following sample portfolio outline can be used as a guide by a new or experienced high-technology-crime investigator. In this case, it is the high-technology-crime investigator applying for that position at GEC. It's up to you to fill in the details. Many of the ideas of what to put in your high-technology-crime investigative portfolio will be found in this book.

Note that the prospective high-technology-crime investigator applying for the GEC position has done the research necessary to tailor an high-technology-crime prevention program for GEC. The beauty of building this type of portfolio is that it seems specific and yet it is generic.

SAMPLE HIGH-TECHNOLOGY-CRIME INVESTIGATOR PORTFOLIO OUTLINE

Table of Contents

I. Introduction
II. The Position and GEC Values
III. Strategic Objective
IV. Tactical Objectives
V. Transition Plan and the Future
VI. Why I Am the Right High-Technology-Crime Investigator for the GEC Position
VII. Examples of a Proven Record in High-Technology-Crime Investigation That Will Meet GEC's Expectations and Needs

I. Introduction

A. *Purpose.* To tell you about me, my high-technology-crime prevention-related education and experience, and how I can establish and lead a high-technology-crime prevention program for GEC based on a cost-effective philosophy providing high-technology-crime prevention investigative services and support to our internal and external customers. (Note: During the interview, use the words *we* and *our* in your discussions. This will help the interviewers look at you as a GEC team member. Approach it as if you already worked at GEC and you were in a meeting discussing high-technology-crime prevention issues.)

B. *Objective.* To convince you that I am the most qualified—and best— person for the position of high-technology-crime investigator for GEC, and how we can establish a business-oriented high-technology-crime prevention program for GEC.

II. The Position and GEC Values

A. Customers
   1. Meet our customers' reasonable expectations.
   2. Show by example that we are the best in the industry in meeting any of the high-technology-crime prevention needs.
B. GEC
   1. Establish and manage a high-technology-crime prevention program that supports business needs and requirements.
   2. Strive for a high-technology-crime prevention program that adds value to GEC products and services.
C. GEC Suppliers
   1. Advise them so they can develop high-quality, high-technology-crime prevention products that meet GEC needs at a reasonable price.
   2. Assist them in understanding our high-technology-crime prevention needs.
   3. Direct them to only bring in high-technology-crime prevention products that can be integrated into the GEC high-technology-crime prevention program, cost effectively, with minimal maintenance.
D. Quality
   1. Establish and manage a high-technology-crime prevention program that provides high-quality service and support to its internal and external customers.
   2. Provide that high-quality service and support with the least impact to cost and schedules.
E. Integrity
   1. Follow the rules, both the spirit and the intent.
   2. Always be honest.
   3. Practice ethical conduct at all times.
F. Leadership
   1. Set the example.
   2. Help others along.

III. Strategic Objective

Build a comprehensive high-technology-crime prevention environment that supports the GEC's business needs at the lowest cost and least impact to schedules.

IV. Tactical Objectives

A. Define detailed milestones for GEC's comprehensive high-technology-crime prevention environment identified as the GEC strategic objective.

B. Describe the current GEC high-technology-crime prevention environment.
C. Identify the gap between A and B.
D. Establish the Master Project and Schedule to meet the strategic, tactical, and annual objectives as integral parts of GEC's business plans.

V. Transition Plan and the Future

First Month

A. Week 1
  1. Begin transition meetings with management to discuss expectations, goals, objectives, and budget.
  2. Begin familiarization with GEC processes and how systems are being used at GEC by all key departments.
  3. Begin a review of GEC policies and procedures that relate to a high-technology-crime prevention program.
  4. Establish appointments to meet with applicable department heads to discuss their ideas related to a high-technology-crime prevention program and how it may help or hinder their operations.
B. Week 2
  1. Hold one-on-one meetings with each department head.
  2. Hold in-depth interviews with peers in high-technology-crime prevention-related organizations.
  3. Begin scoping the level of effort required for high-technology-crime prevention at GEC.
C. Week 3
  1. Coordinate personnel and organizational issues with the HR staff.
  2. Coordinate identified issues with internal customers.
D. Week 4
  1. Finalize high-technology-crime prevention plans, including strategic, tactical, and annual objectives.
  2. Begin recruitment and hiring, as applicable.
  3. Continue coordination meetings with applicable peers and executive management.

Rest of the Year

A. Develop, implement, and manage high-technology-crime prevention projects.
B. Develop high-technology-crime prevention metrics and manage the high-technology-crime prevention program.
C. Continue working on high-technology-crime prevention issues with the GEC high-technology-crime prevention team.
D. Continue evaluating potential crime prevention cost reductions based on a cost–risk assessment methodology.

E. Near year-end, analyze successes and failures, validate goals and objectives, and plan projects for the next year.
F. Continue to evaluate various high-technology-crime prevention program processes and make changes where necessary to keep it a fresh, active, and viable program.

Next Year

A. Continue and refine first year's goals.
B. Increase or enhance skills of organization and staff.
C. Ensure GEC's high-technology-crime prevention program becomes an integrated, value-added program.

VI. Why I Am the Right High-Technology-Crime Investigator for the GEC Position

(This section includes the highlights of your resume; a copy of the resume should be inserted in this section. Remember, don't use a boilerplated resume; tailor the resume to fit the "advertised" GEC job.)

A. My bachelor's degree in criminal justice with a minor in information systems shows that I have the educational background to understand the academic and technical aspects of the profession.
B. My MBA shows that I have the business and management background to understand GEC from a business perspective.
C. I am experienced in supporting and providing services and support to similar customers.
D. I enjoy the trust and confidence of other professional high-technology-crime investigators in both government agencies and businesses.
E. I have detailed knowledge of all high-technology-crime prevention-related federal and state laws and regulations. (Note: The high-technology-crime investigator should identify all applicable federal and state laws.)
F. I have detailed knowledge of information systems, the threats to them, areas of vulnerability, and associated risk.
G. Wherever I have been employed I always enjoyed the trust and confidence of corporate management.
H. A proven high-technology-crime prevention plan is already prepared, tailored for GEC, and ready for implementation.
I. I have previous experience in coordinating related activities with the local district attorney and police and the FBI and Secret Service.
J. I am experienced in high-technology-crime prevention and management and played leadership roles in developing government standards and on committees, working groups, and so forth.

VII. Examples of a Proven Record in High-Technology-Crime Investigation That Will Meet GEC's Expectations and Needs

A. Functional Costs Averages (In this section, list all the information related to past budget, tracking, and so on.)
B. Project Management (In this section, list samples of project management tracking, such as Gantt charts.)
C. Metrics Management (In this section, list the metrics you have developed or would use to manage high-technology-crime prevention functions.)

SUMMARY

1. Prior to being interviewed for GEC's high-technology-crime investigator position, learn all you can about the company.
2. Read books about how to prepare and dress for interviews.
3. Prepare answers for the questions you typically will be asked and practice the interview process so your answers come across naturally and not as memorized, rehearsed answers.
4. Develop a high-technology-crime investigator portfolio to be used during the interview.
5. During the interview, refer the interviewers to the portfolio.
6. During the interview, use *we* and *our* as if you already worked at GEC.

8

The Global Enterprise Corporation

The Global Enterprise Corporation (GEC) is a fictional company in which the high-technology-crime investigator will work. It is used to present a basic, somewhat simplistic hypothetical baseline from which to go forward. You are encouraged to develop a plan, then build a high-technology-crime prevention program based on GEC. This practice not only will assist in focusing on the how-tos but can be used when building an interview portfolio. Subsequently, it can be used as a proposal for building an actual high-technology-crime prevention program.

BACKGROUND INFORMATION ON GEC

The high-technology-crime investigator must understand the business and processes of GEC if a high-quality, cost-effective, high-technology-crime prevention program is to be developed for the company. Part of that process requires the investigator to identify those key elements of GEC's history and business that must be considered in developing the GEC high-technology-crime prevention program.

The following is a summary of GEC's business environment (italics are added to identify the key phrases, important elements that the high-technology-crime investigator must take into consideration when building a crime-prevention program).

GEC is a high-technology corporation that *makes a high-technology widget.* To make these widgets, it uses a *proprietary process* that has evolved over the last seven years during which GEC has been in business.

The *proprietary process is the key to GEC's success* as a leading manufacturer of high-technology widgets. The process cost millions of dollars to develop. The protection of the high-technology widget process is *vital to company survival.*

GEC operates in an *extremely competitive business* environment. However, based on changes in technology that allow for a more efficient and effective operation through telecommunications and networks, it has found that it must *network with its customers, suppliers, and subcontractors.*

To maximize the high-technology widget process, it shares its networks with its *subcontractors, who must use GEC's proprietary process.* The subcontractors, *under contractual agreements,* have promised not to use or share GEC's proprietary information with anyone. They also have agreed to protect that information in accordance with the information systems security requirements of their contract with GEC.

GEC has a European distribution office in London, a parts manufacturing plant in Jakarta, Indonesia, and a parts manufacturing plant and Asian distribution center in Hsinchu, Taiwan.

KEY ELEMENTS FOR THE HIGH-TECHNOLOGY-CRIME INVESTIGATOR TO CONSIDER

From the background information about GEC, the high-technology-crime investigator should remember some key elements:

1. *GEC is a high-technology corporation.* This means that it uses and is dependent on state-of-the-art high-technology equipment and systems, a key factor that makes the high-technology-crime prevention program of vital importance.
2. *It uses a proprietary process.* This means that information relative to the proprietary process is the most valuable information within the GEC; and it probably resides on one or more of GEC's information systems, which are integrated and interface with the Internet, the GII, and portions of the NII, such as the telecommunications, water, power, and emergency systems.
3. *The proprietary process is the key to GEC's success and vital to company survival.* The highest priority of the high-technology-crime prevention program is to be proactive. Any breach of ethics, security, or other significant policies and procedures that adversely affect GEC's business must be quickly investigated and resolved.
4. *GEC operates in an extremely competitive business environment.* To the high-technology-crime investigator, this signals the potential for industrial and economic espionage as a factor to consider in establishing the high-technology-crime prevention program.
5. *GEC is networked with its customers, suppliers, and subcontractors and subcontractors must use GEC's proprietary process, under contractual agreements.* When the investigator builds the GEC high-technology-crime prevention program, the customers and subcontractors must be prepared to assist and support any investigation. If necessary, the high-technology-crime investigator must request additional provisions to the contract relative to liability issues and GEC's investigator's authority to conduct inquiries and investigations within customer and subcontractor facilities. This is a major challenge, but if

presented in the proper way, it could be welcomed by the subcontractors and customers.

GETTING TO KNOW GEC

Once hired, the new high-technology-crime investigator should walk around the entire company, see how widgets are made, see what processes are used to make the widgets, and watch the process from beginning to end. It is very important that the investigator understand the inner workings of the company.

It is unfortunate but many new high-technology-crime investigators sit through the general orientation given new employees and learn only general information about the company. They then start working and may not see how the company actually operates or makes widgets. They never meet the other people who play a major support role in any high-technology-crime prevention program—the employees. These people include those using automated systems on the factory floor, the human resources staff, quality control personnel, auditors, procurement personnel, contracts personnel, and in-house subcontractors and other non-GEC employees.

A high-technology-crime investigator can't provide a service- and support-oriented high-technology-crime prevention program without an understanding of the company, its culture, and how its products are made.

All the high-technology-crime prevention policies and procedures neatly typed and placed in binders will be ignored if they get in the way of employees performing their primary functions. The investigator can't see this from an office or cubicle, but can find this out only by walking around the areas where the people work and actually use the information system.

Strategic Business Plan

GEC has developed a proprietary strategic business plan. The plan describes GEC's strategy for maintaining its competitive edge in the manufacture of high-technology widgets. That plan sets the baseline and the direction that GEC will follow for the next seven years, GEC's long-range plan. Any plan longer than seven years was determined not to be feasible due to the rapidly changing environment brought on by technology and GEC's competitive business environment.

Tactical Business Plan

GEC also has a proprietary tactical business plan, a three-year plan that sets more definitive goals, objectives, and tasks. The tactical business plan is the short-range plan used to support GEC's strategic business plan. GEC's successful implementation and completion of its projects is a critical element in meeting GEC's goals and objectives.

The tactical business plan also calls for the *completion* of a high-technology-crime prevention program to help act as a deterrent. If violations occur that meet the requirements for an inquiry or investigation, then one is conducted professionally and quickly.

Annual Business Plan

GEC further has a proprietary annual plan that sets forth its goals and objectives for the year, defining the specific projects to be implemented and completed by the end of the year. The successful completion of these projects will contribute to the success of GEC's tactical and strategic business plans.

GEC's annual plan calls for hiring an investigator to establish a high-technology-crime prevention program that can provide high-technology-crime investigative support for a GEC on a global basis. The high-technology-crime investigator also will be responsible for forming and managing a high-technology-crime prevention organization. The investigator will report to the director of security, who reports to the vice president of human resources.

It should be noted that GEC's executive management agreed that the position and the investigator hired should establish and manage GEC's high-technology-crime prevention program and organization. However, no complete agreement was reached as to where in GEC the high-technology-crime investigator reported.

Some members of GEC's executive management suggested that, since the program and organization were related to high technology, the investigator should report to the vice president of information technology, while others suggested that the high-technology-crime investigator report to the vice president of the legal department.

Still other members of executive management recommended that the high-technology-crime investigator report to the director of auditing. However, the director of auditing advised that the auditing department was strictly responsible for determining GEC's compliance with applicable state, federal, and international laws and company policies and procedures. The director felt that the auditors' limited scope and functions would adversely limit the investigator in establishing and managing a high-technology-crime prevention program.

The director also argued that it may be a conflict of interest for the investigator to establish high-technology-crime prevention policies and procedures, albeit with management support and approval, while having another part of that organization (the audit group) determine not only compliance with the high-technology-crime prevention policies and procedures but also whether they were adequate.

The director of security advised that having the investigator and the high-technology-crime prevention organization in his department was the only logical choice. Eventually, a consensus was reached. It was decided that the high-technology-crime investigator's position and organization should be established within the security department.

The new high-technology-crime investigator's understanding of how this position ended up where it did provides some clues as to the feelings and inner workings of GEC's management vis-à-vis the high-technology-crime investigator and prevention program. This information will be useful when the investigator begins to establish GEC's high-technology-crime prevention program and requests support from these directors.

Furthermore, it is clear that the director of auditing would support the high-technology-crime prevention program from a compliance audit standpoint but probably would not want to join a GEC team with the responsibility for writing the new high-technology-crime prevention policies and procedures. The high-technology-crime investigator must keep this in mind when he or she decides how to establish prevention policies and procedures: what departments should be involved in some part of that development process and so forth.

HIGH-TECHNOLOGY-CRIME PREVENTION PROGRAM PLANNING

The main philosophy running through the preceding paragraphs should be obvious: As a service and support organization, the GEC high-technology-crime prevention program must include plans that support the business plans of the company.

The high-technology-crime investigator should be able to map each major business goal and objective of each plan to key high-technology-crime prevention projects and functions. When writing the applicable high-technology-crime prevention plans, the investigator will be able to see which functions are not being supported. However, the map will allow the investigator to identify areas where required support to the plans has not been identified in the crime-prevention plans. The investigator then can add tasks where increased high-technology-crime prevention program support is needed. An additional benefit of following this procedure is to be able to show management how the high-technology-crime prevention program supports the business.

When mapping the crime-prevention plans to the business plans, summarize the goals, as they will be easier to map.

SUMMARY

You can use GEC, a fictitious corporation, to build an high-technology-crime prevention program that later can be used as part of an interview portfolio and to build or improve an high-technology-crime prevention program for a corporation.

Most corporations set their goals and objectives in planning documents like strategic, tactical, and annual business plans. These plans are key documents for the high-technology-crime investigator to read to determine the corporation's future directions.

The plans also are key documents that the investigator can use to determine what is expected from him or her and a high-technology-crime prevention program. The plans should be used as the basis for writing service and support high-technology-crime prevention plans, as separate documents or sections integrated into the identified corporate planning documents.

The decision process of the GEC executive management in determining in which department the investigator and the high-technology-crime prevention organization belong provides some key information, which should be used by the investigator in establishing the high-technology-crime prevention program and organization.

9

Understanding the Role of the High-Technology-Crime Investigator and Prevention Unit in the Business Environment

THE POSITION OF HIGH-TECHNOLOGY-CRIME INVESTIGATOR

The position of high-technology-crime investigator is extremely important, as that person is the in-house consultant on high-technology-crime prevention matters. The investigator also represents GEC to the *outside world* on high-technology-crime prevention matters.

If you are chosen as the new high-technology-crime investigator, you should have determined the history of that position:

- When was it established?
- Why?
- What is expected of the high-technology-crime investigator?
- What happened to the last one? (You want to know so you can understand the political environment in which you will work.)

Those questions should have been asked and answered during the interview process. If not, get them answered now.

As you begin your new job with GEC, you must clearly determine what is expected of you. What are your responsibilities and duties? For what are you accountable? Again, this information should have been asked during your interview process for two reasons: (1) so you know what you are getting into by accepting the position and (2) so you can better prepare for the position with a more-detailed high-technology-crime prevention program prior to your first day at work. The high-technology-crime investigator's biggest challenge is not being looked upon as the "cop."

Those retiring from law enforcement or the military may have to change how they conduct themselves and investigations. They no longer have a position of authority backed by the law, a badge, and a gun. They have authority just as long as the management and the employees are willing to give it to them, and that can change quickly. It is a different world with different attitudes. There are no interrogations as they may have come to know them. In addition, if they are dealing in a company with a strong "rights-oriented" human resources group or unions, they most definitely must change their tactics.

In the new position, you also must determine how many high-technology-crime investigators, if any, you will need, the qualifications for each position, the tasks to be performed—and the list goes on. On top of that are learning about GEC—its culture, normal corporate policies and procedures—and all the learning that comes with just joining a company.

As the new GEC high-technology-crime investigator, you can't afford to waste any time in your 12- to 14-hour, time-consuming days. You must understand and learn your new environment, the key players, and the issues that must be addressed first.

The GEC high-technology-crime investigator must eventually get into a proactive mode to be successful; that is, identifying problems and solutions *before* they come to the attention of management. This will happen when the problem has an adverse impact on costs or schedules. As you remember, adverse impacts to costs and schedules run contrary to the high-technology-crime prevention program's goals, objectives, and so on.

When an investigator is in the position of constantly *putting out fires*, the proactive high-technology-crime prevention battle is lost. If that battle is lost, the results are adverse impacts to costs and schedules and cost-effective programs are not enforced.

WHAT IS EXPECTED OF YOU?

You have been told that you are expected to establish and manage a high-technology-crime prevention program that works and is no burden to GEC. You are told to establish the program you believe is necessary to get the job done. You have the full support of management because it has come to realize how important its information and systems are to GEC maintaining its competitive advantage in the marketplace. This *honeymoon* will last about six months. So, take advantage of it.

Based on management's "blank check" and your prior experience (or for the inexperienced investigator, the information gained reading this book), you have evaluated the GEC environment and decided that the overall goal of GEC's high-technology-crime prevention program is to "administer an innovative high-technology-crime prevention program that mitigates crime with the least impact on costs and schedules, while meeting all of GEC's and customers' reasonable expectations."

Everything you do as the GEC high-technology-crime investigator should be directed toward meeting that goal. This includes

- The high-technology-crime prevention strategic plan.
- The high-technology-crime prevention tactical plan.
- The high-technology-crime prevention annual plan.
- How the high-technology-crime prevention unit is organized.
- What functions are to be established.
- The process flow of those functions.

THE RESPONSIBILITIES OF GEC'S HIGH-TECHNOLOGY-CRIME INVESTIGATOR

As GEC's high-technology-crime investigator, you have certain duties and responsibilities:

1. Managing people, which includes building a reputation of professional integrity, maintaining excellent business relationships, dealing with changes, communicating, helping your staff in developing their careers, influencing people in a positive way, and building a teamwork environment through performance management, such as directing and helping the high-technology-crime prevention staff to be results oriented.
2. Managing the business of high-technology-crime prevention, which consists of a commitment to results, being customer and supplier focused, taking responsibility for making decisions, developing and managing resource allocations, planning and organizing, solving problems, thinking strategically, using sound business judgment, and accepting personal accountability and ownership.
3. Managing high-technology-crime prevention processes, which includes project planning and implementation, maintaining a persistently high quality in everything, maintaining a systems perspective, and maintaining current job knowledge.

GOALS AND OBJECTIVES

At a minimum, the following must be your objectives:

1. Enhance the quality, efficiency, and effectiveness of the high-technology-crime prevention organization.
2. Identify potential problem areas and strive to mitigate them before GEC management or customers identify them.
3. Enhance the company's ability to attract customers because of the ability to efficiently, effectively, and discreetly conduct high-technology-crime investigations and inquiries.
4. Establish an organization that is the high-technology-crime prevention leader in the widget industry.

LEADERSHIP

As the high-technology-crime investigator and manager, you will be a leader. In that position, it is extremely important that you understand what a leader is and how a leader is to act.

According to the definition of *leadership* found in numerous dictionaries and management books, it is the position or guidance of a leader, the ability to lead, the leader of a group; a person that leads; the directing, commanding, or guiding head, as of a group or activity.

As a *leader*, you must set an example, create and foster an ethical and crime prevention conscienceness within the company.

As a *corporate leader* you must communicate the company's community involvement, eliminate unnecessary expenses, inspire corporate pride, and find ways to increase profitability.

As a *team leader* you must encourage teamwork, communicate a clear direction, create a high-technology-crime prevention environment conducive to working as a team, and treat others as peers and team members not as competitors or, worse yet, suspects.

As a *personal leader* you must improve your leadership skills, accept and learn from constructive criticism, take ownership and responsibility for your decisions, make decisions in a timely manner, and demonstrate self-confidence.

PROVIDING HIGH-TECHNOLOGY-CRIME PREVENTION SERVICE AND SUPPORT

As the high-technology-crime investigator and leader of a service and support organization, you must be especially tuned to the needs, wants, and desires of your customers, both those within the company (your internal customers) and those outside the company, usually the company's customers (your external customers).

To provide service and support to your *external* customers, you must

- Identify their high-technology-crime prevention needs.
- Meet their reasonable expectations.
- Show by example that you can meet their expectations.
- Treat customer satisfaction as your highest priority.
- Encourage feedback and listen.
- Understand their needs and expectations.
- Treat customer requirements as an important part of the job.
- Establish measures to ensure customer satisfaction.
- Provide honest feedback to customers.

To provide service and support to your internal customers, you must

- Support their business needs.
- Add value to their services.
- Minimize the impact of the investigative and crime-prevention program on current processes.
- Follow the same guidelines as for external customers.

The GEC investigator also will be dealing with suppliers of high-technology-crime prevention products. These suppliers are valuable allies because they can alert you to what's new in the area of high-technology crimes, how their products mitigate against those crimes, and generally keep you up-to-date on the latest news within the high-technology-crime investigation profession.

In dealing with suppliers of high-technology-crime prevention-related products, you should[1]

- Advise them of your needs and what types of products that can help you.
- Assist them in understanding your requirements and the products you want from them, including what modifications they must make to products before you are willing to purchase them.
- Direct them in the support and assistance they are to provide you.
- Respect them as team members.
- Value their contributions.
- Require high-quality products and high standards of performance from them.
- Recognize their needs, too.

USING TEAM CONCEPTS

It is important that the investigator understand that GEC's high-technology-crime prevention program is a company program. To be successful, the investigator cannot operate independently but as a team leader, with a team of others who share a vested interest in the mitigation against high-technology crime through an excellent prevention program.

It is important to remember that a good high-technology-crime prevention program will require the investigator to emphasize constant communication as a means of ensuring support from others within the company. The investigator must be sensitive to the division of functions, "turfs," office politics, and must ensure that even more communication and coordination occur between all the departments concerned.

The program must be sold to the management and staff of GEC. Everyone must be willing and see a personal need to support the high-technology-crime prevention program because all know it is the best way and in their own interests as well as in the interest of GEC.

In GEC, as in many companies today, success can be achieved only through continuous interdepartmental communication, cooperation, and specialists from various organizations formed into integrated project teams to solve company problems. The high-technology-crime investigator should keep that in mind: Teamwork and success go together in today's corporation.

VISION, MISSION, AND QUALITY STATEMENTS

Many of today's modern corporations have developed vision, mission, and quality statements using a hierarchical process. The statements, if used, should link all levels in the management and organizational chain. The statements of the lower levels should be written and used to support the upper levels and vice versa.

Most employees seem to look on such statements as just another management task that somehow is supposed to help all employees understand their jobs—or whatever. However, they often are developed in employee team meetings, get printed, placed on walls, and soon are forgotten. Confidentially, many managers feel the same way, and that is probably why they are presented by managers as another task to be performed by or with employees.

This is unfortunate, as the idea is a good one if it is presented with the right attitude and used to focus the employees as a team on objectives and a better understanding of why they are there doing what they are doing.

If at all possible, judge the attitude within GEC before getting involved. If they appear to be something accepted and supported by the employees, then try to get some aspects of your high-technology-crime prevention program into the higher-level statements. If such statements do not appear to be something well supported by the employees, it may be better to not get any portions of your program into them. That way, the program won't be "tainted" by the employees' perception of the statements and the statement development process.

Vision Statements

In many of today's businesses, management develops a vision statement. The vision statement usually is a short paragraph that attempts to set the strategic goal, objective, or direction of the company. GEC has a vision statement and requires all organizations within the corporation to have statements based on the GEC corporate statements.

What Is a Vision Statement?

A vision statement is

- A short statement.
- That is clear, concise, and understandable by the employees.
- That is connected to ethics, values, and behavior.
- That states where the company wants to be (long term).
- Meant to set the tone and direction for the company.

GEC's Corporate Vision Statement

GEC will design, produce, and sell a high-quality widget and thereby expand market shares while continuing to improve processes to meet customers' expectations.

The GEC Security Department's[2] Vision Statement

In partnership with our customers, we will provide a competitive advantage for the GEC widget by continuous protection of all GEC's assets without hindering productivity and cost-effectively support increased production of GEC's widgets.

The High-Technology-Crime Prevention Vision Statement

The organization will provide the most efficient and effective high-technology-crime prevention program for GEC, which adds value to GEC's products and services, as a recognized leader in the widget industry.

Mission Statements

Mission statements are declarations as to the purpose of a business or government agency.

The GEC Mission Statement

GEC's mission is to maintain its competitive advantage in the marketplace by providing the best widgets to its customers when they want them, where they want them, and at a fair price.

The GEC Security Department's Mission Statement

The mission of GEC's security department is to provide low-cost, productivity-enhanced, technology-based assets protection services and support that will assist GEC in maintaining its competitive advantage in the marketplace.

The High-Technology-Crime Prevention Mission Statement

The organization will administer an innovative high-technology-crime prevention program that assists in deterring or minimizing high-technology crime risks with the least impact on costs and schedules, while meeting all of the company's and customers' high-technology-crime prevention requirements.

Quality

Quality is what adds value to a company's products and services. It is what internal and external customers expect from the company.

The GEC Quality Statement

GEC will provide high-quality widgets to its customers with no defects by building them right the first time.

The GEC Security Department's Quality Statement

The department will provide high-quality security support and services while enhancing the productivity opportunities of the GEC workforce.

The High-Technology-Crime Prevention Quality Statement

The organization will consistently provide high-quality high-technology-crime prevention and investigative services and support that meet the customers' requirements and reasonable expectations, in concert with good business practices and company guidelines.[3]

HIGH-TECHNOLOGY-CRIME PREVENTION PRINCIPLES

As the GEC high-technology-crime investigator, you must never lose sight of the three basic high-technology-crime prevention principles:

1. Develop and support the development of policies, procedures, and processes that mitigate against the motive, rationalization, and opportunity to violate GEC rules, policies, procedures, and controls as well as local, state, and federal laws.

2. Conduct statistical analyses and provide feedback to management relative to high-technology-crime prevention investigations, threats, areas of vulnerability, profiles of offenders, and preventive measures.
3. Conduct professional, efficient, and discreet high-technology-crime investigations, inquiries, and surveys and provide investigative reports to management.

These three principles must be incorporated into the GEC high-technology-crime prevention program.

PROJECT AND RISK MANAGEMENT PROCESSES

Two basic processes are an integral part of a high-technology-crime prevention program: project management and risk management.

Project Management

As the high-technology-crime prevention manager and leader for GEC you provide oversight on high-technology-crime prevention projects worked on by members of your staff.

The criteria for a project is as follows. Formal projects, along with project management charts, are initiated where improvements or other changes will be accomplished and where that effort has an objective, beginning and ending dates, and will take longer than 30 days to complete.

If the project will be accomplished in less than 30 days, a formal project management process is not needed. The rationale for this is that projects of short duration are not worth the effort (cost in terms of hours to complete the project plan, charts, and so forth) of such a formal process.

Risk Management

To be cost effective, the high-technology-crime investigator must apply risk management concepts and identify

- Threats to GEC's assets, including those by its personnel.
- Areas of vulnerability that some internal or external threat may use to its advantage.
- Risks to GEC's assets through analyses of the results of inquiries, investigations, and surveys.
- The appropriate department countermeasures to mitigate against those risks in a cost-effective way.

ORGANIZATIONAL RESPONSIBILITIES OF THE
HIGH-TECHNOLOGY-CRIME INVESTIGATOR

As the GEC high-technology-crime investigator, you will manage and lead a high-technology-crime prevention organization. You are responsible for developing, implementing, maintaining, and administering a company-wide high-technology-crime prevention program.

You have evaluated the GEC environment and found that a centralized high-technology-crime prevention program would not work at the corporation. However, you believe that leading a team of representatives from selected departments can cost-effectively *jump-start* the high-technology-crime prevention program and its associated processes. Your evaluation of what is needed led you to consider the following high-technology-crime prevention functions for development.[4]

The GEC High-Technology-Crime Investigator's
Formal Duties and Responsibilities

Based on the preceding and in concert with the executive management of GEC, the high-technology-crime investigator developed and received approval for formally establishing the following charter of GEC high-technology-crime investigator responsibilities.

The GEC high-technology-crime investigator will lead the development, implementation, maintenance, and administration of an overall, GEC-wide high-technology-crime prevention program including all plans, policies, procedures, and processes necessary to mitigate against high-technology crime and effectively, efficiently, and discreetly conduct applicable inquiries, surveys, and investigations. To that end the GEC high-technology-crime investigator will be accountable for the following:

- Identifying all government, customer, and GEC high-technology-crime prevention requirements necessary for the mitigation against high-technology crime; interpreting those requirements; and developing and leading implementation and administration of GEC plans, policies, and procedures necessary to ensure compliance.
- Identifying high-technology business practices and possible security violations or infractions; conducting inquiries; assessing potential damage; directing and monitoring GEC management's corrective action; and implementing or recommending corrective and preventive action.
- Establishing and directing a GEC-wide high-technology-crime prevention program.
- Developing, implementing, and administering a proactive crime survey and inquiry program; providing analyses to management; modi-

fying GEC and subcontractor requirements accordingly to ensure a lowest-cost high-technology-crime prevention program.

- Establishing and administering a high-technology-crime prevention awareness program for all GEC employees, customers, and subcontractors, as appropriate, as part of the security department's security awareness program; ensuring they are cognizant of the high-technology-crime threats and preventive measures.
- Directing the development, acquisition, implementation, and administration of high-technology-crime prevention software systems.
- Representing GEC on all high-technology-crime prevention matters with customers, government agencies, suppliers, and other outside entities.
- Providing advice, guidance, and assistance to GEC management relative to high-technology-crime prevention.
- Performing common management responsibilities in accordance with GEC's management policies and procedures.

SUMMARY[5]

The high-technology-crime investigator holds a leadership position within a company. The recently hired investigator must know what is expected as the company's new high-technology-crime investigator and have a clear understanding of those expectations before taking the position.

The three primary responsibilities of a high-technology-crime investigator are managing people, managing the business of high-technology-crime prevention organization, and managing the processes of high-technology-crime prevention. To fulfill these responsibilities, the high-technology-crime investigator must

- Set forth clear goals and objectives.
- Be a company leader, team leader, and personal leader.
- Provide high-technology-crime prevention service and support using team concepts.
- Develop vision, mission, and quality statements as guides to developing a successful high-technology-crime prevention program.
- Strive to lead the administration of a high-technology-crime prevention program.

NOTES

1. If you recall, we discussed cost-effective ways to keep current in the high-technology-crime investigation profession. This is another way of doing it.

2. If you recall, the high-technology-crime investigator reports to the director of the security department.
3. You will find that the same themes of service, support, cost-effectiveness, customer expectations, and so on run continuously through this book. We hope that the constant reinforcement will cause you to always think of these themes when establishing and managing an high-technology-crime prevention program.
4. As previously mentioned, GEC is the ideal company for a high-technology-crime investigator, and therefore, we are developing an ideal high-technology-crime prevention program and organization.
5. Much of the information in this chapter provides information that could be used to fill in the details of the high-technology-crime investigator's portfolio as noted in the portfolio sample outline presented in Chapter 7.

10

The High-Technology-Crime Investigations Unit's Strategic, Tactical, and Annual Plans

GEC'S HIGH-TECHNOLOGY-CRIME PREVENTION UNIT'S STRATEGIC PLAN

To be successful, the GEC high-technology-crime investigator must have a high-technology-crime prevention strategic plan (HTCP-SP). That plan should be integrated, or at least compatible, with GEC's strategic business (seven-year) plan, which sets the long-term direction, goals, and objectives for the high-technology-crime prevention program.

The GEC HTCP-SP is the basic document on which to build the GEC high-technology-crime prevention program with the goal of building a comprehensive high-technology-crime prevention environment with the least cost and impact to the company.

When developing the HTCP-SP, the investigator must ensure that the following basic, high-technology-crime prevention principles are included, either specifically or in principle (since it is part of the high-technology-crime prevention strategy):

1. Minimize the probability of a high-technology crime.
2. Conduct professional, effective, efficient, and discreet investigations.
3. Report the investigative findings to management to include an analysis of investigations and recommendations to minimize the probability of recurrence. (Note: Never recommend disciplinary action as that is the employee's manager's job and it also takes away your objectivity in conducting these investigations.)

The High-Technology-Crime Prevention Strategic Plan's Objective

The objectives of the HTCP-SP are to

1. Minimize the probability of a high-technology crime.
2. Minimize the impact of the crime on costs.

3. Minimize the impact of the crime on schedules.
4. Assist in meeting GEC's contractual requirements.
5. Assist in meeting GEC's noncontractual requirements.
6. Build a comprehensive high-technology-crime prevention environment.
7. Maintain the flexibility to respond to changing needs.
8. Support customers' high-technology-crime investigative needs.
9. Incorporate new high-technology and investigative techniques related to crime involving that technology as soon as needed.
10. Assist in attracting new customers.
11. Maximize the use of available resources.

HTCP-SP and Team Concepts, Communication, and Coordination

To have a successful high-technology-crime prevention program, the strategy calls for dealing with the office politics' aspects of the GEC environment. A key element is to remember that the GEC information and high-technology equipment (e.g., computers, cellular phones, etc.) belong to GEC and not the high-technology-crime investigator. Therefore, cooperation and coordination are a must.

Many functional organizations have an interest in the HTCP-SP and other high-technology-crime prevention plans; therefore, the plans should be discussed with other team members, such as the auditors, security personnel, human resources personnel, and legal staff. The HTCP-SP should also be discussed with and input requested from employees such as union representatives and GEC managers. After all, what you do affects what they do. It is a great way to get communication and interaction going. This will lead to a better plan and one that has a broad base of support. Their input and understanding of what the GEC high-technology-crime investigator is trying to accomplish will assist in ensuring GEC-wide support for the high-technology-crime prevention plans.

HTCP-SP Planning Considerations

The HTCP-SP planning considerations must also include

1. Good business practices.
2. High-quality management.
3. Innovative ideas.
4. A high-technology-crime prevention vision statement.
5. A high-technology-crime prevention mission statement.
6. A high-technology-crime prevention quality statement.

7. Providing channels of open communications with others such as the employees, auditors, systems personnel, security personnel, users, and managers.

All these factors must be considered when developing a high-technology-crime prevention strategy and documenting that strategy in the GEC HTCP-SP.

The GEC process flow of plans begins with the GEC strategic business plan through the GEC annual business plan. Each plan's goals and objectives must be able to support the others, top down and bottom up.

The next step is to map the GEC HTCP-SP into the GEC strategic business plan's goals and objectives, mapping GEC's high-technology-crime prevention strategic plan to the GEC strategic business plan.

GEC's strategic business plan identified the goals for annual earnings over the next seven years as well as market-share percentage. This clearly underscores the need for a high-technology-crime prevention program to be cost effective. Furthermore, any high-technology-crime investigations also must have as a goal the recuperation of any financial losses. This could be accomplished through such processes as recovery or supporting legal action against the violators and miscreants.

Any overhead program (one that is not directly related to building the widget, e.g. high-technology-crime prevention program) is a "parasite" on the profits of GEC if it cannot be shown to be a value-added (needed to support the "bottom line") function. Therefore, the high-technology-crime prevention strategy must be efficient (cheap) and effective (good). If that can be accomplished, then the high-technology-crime prevention program will be in a position to support the GEC's strategy relative to earnings and market share. Mapping these points can help the investigator visualize a strategy prior to documenting it in the HTCP-SP.

For example, if GEC Strategic Goal 1 is to "increase employee's productivity," then the HTCP-SP Goal 1 should be to "coordinate with the employee's manager prior to interviewing an employee and establish a time for the interview that will not adversely affect or will minimize the impact on an employee's work schedule."

Writing the High-Technology-Crime Prevention Strategic Plan

Writing the HTCP-SP will be much easier once the mapping is completed. At that time, the high-technology-crime investigator will write the HTCP-SP following the standard GEC format for plan writing. The GEC format was determined to be as follows:

1. Executive Summary
2. Table of Contents

3. Introduction
4. Vision Statement
5. Mission Statement
6. Quality Statement
7. High-Technology-Crime Prevention Strategic Goals
8. How the High-Technology-Crime Prevention Strategies Support GEC Strategies
9. Mapping Charts
10. Conclusion

GEC'S HIGH-TECHNOLOGY-CRIME PREVENTION TACTICAL PLAN

A tactical plan is a short-range (three-year) plan that supports the GEC HTCP-SP goals and objectives. The high-technology-crime prevention tactical plan (HTCP-TP) should

1. Identify and define, in more detail, the vision of a comprehensive high-technology-crime prevention environment, as stated in the HTCP-SP.
2. Identify and define the current GEC high-technology-crime prevention environment.
3. Identify the process to be used to determine the differences between the two.

Once that is accomplished, the investigator can identify projects to progress from the current GEC high-technology-crime prevention environment to where it should be, as stated in the HTCP-SP. In the HTCP-TP, it is also important to keep in mind

1. The company's business direction.
2. The customers' direction.
3. The direction and pace of technology development.

When these are established, the individual projects can be identified and implemented, beginning with the high-technology-crime prevention annual plan (HTCP-AP).

The GEC tactical business plan stated that "In addition, it is expected to be able to integrate new hardware, software, networks, etc. with a *minimum* impact on schedules or costs." Therefore, it will be necessary to establish a project with the objective of getting trained and training all high-technology-crime investigators on new high technology prior to or soon after its arrival. After all, this will be the potential new crime scene.

The high-technology-crime investigator then also must consider that the GEC high-technology-crime prevention program must contain processes to upgrade investigative methodologies that will be used in conducting investigations into high-technology crime in the new environment. Therefore, a project must be established to accomplish that goal.

The GEC tactical business plan also called for the *completion* of a high-technology-crime prevention program within three years. Therefore, another project must be developed to accomplish this goal.

Writing the High-Technology-Crime Prevention Tactical Plan

Writing the HTCP-TP should be somewhat easier, based on the experience gained in mapping the goals for the HTCP-SP, HTCP-TP, and writing the HTCP-SP. With these accomplished, the high-technology-crime investigator will write the HTCP-TP following the standard GEC format for plan writing.

The GEC format was determined to be as follows:

1. Executive Summary
2. Table of Contents
3. Introduction
4. The High-Technology-Crime Prevention Strategic Goals
5. How the High-Technology-Crime Prevention Tactics Support the HTCP-SP
6. How the High-Technology-Crime Prevention Tactics Support GEC Tactics
6. Mapping Charts
7. Conclusion

GEC'S HIGH-TECHNOLOGY-CRIME PREVENTION ANNUAL PLAN

The high-technology-crime investigator must also develop a high-technology-crime prevention annual plan to support the GEC HTCP-SP and HTCP-TP. The plan must include goals, objectives, and projects that support those of GEC's annual business plan.

GEC's HTCP-AP is to be used to identify and implement projects to accomplish the annual goals and objectives as stated in the HTCP-SP and HTCP-TP. These accomplishments are the building blocks of the HTCP program.

Remember, the high-technology-crime prevention program requires the following:

1. Project management techniques.
2. Gantt charts (schedule).
3. Identified beginning date for each project.
4. Identified ending date for each project.
5. An objective for each project.
6. Costs tracking and budget.
7. Identification of the project leader responsible.

High-Technology-Crime Prevention Annual Plan Projects

The initial and major project of the GEC high-technology-crime investigator's first HTCP-AP is to identify the current GEC high-technology-crime prevention environment. To gain an understanding of the current GEC environment, culture, and philosophy, the following projects are to be established:

- Project title: GEC high-technology-crime prevention organization

  Project leader: High-technology-crime investigator

  Objective: Establish a high-technology-crime prevention organization

  Starting date: December 1, 1999

  Ending date: December 1, 2000

- Project title: High-technology-crime prevention policies and procedures review

  Project leader: High-technology-crime investigator

  Objective: Identify and review all high-technology-crime prevention-related GEC documentation and establish a process to ensure applicability and currency

  Starting date: February 1, 2000

  Ending date: April 1, 2000

- Project title: High-technology-crime prevention team

  Project leader: High-technology-crime investigator

  Objective: Establish a GEC high-technology-crime prevention working group to assist in establishing and supporting a high-technology-crime prevention program

  Starting date: June 1, 2000

  Ending date: July 1, 2000

- Project title: High-technology-crime prevention organizational functions

  Project leader: High-technology-crime investigator

  Objective: Identify and establish the high-technology-crime organization's functions, processes, and work instructions

  Starting date: June 15, 2000

  Ending date: December 15, 2000

Mapping the GEC HTCP-AP to the GEC Annual Business Plan

As previously shown, mapping the GEC HTCP-AP to the GEC annual business plan can be accomplished easily. However, in this case, the GEC annual plan objectives are not indicated or used to map the HTCP-AP. (By now, you should understand the process and have no trouble with the mapping method.)

Writing the High-Technology-Crime Prevention Annual Plan

As noted, writing the plan must follow the GEC format. The GEC HTCP-AP is no exception and the following format is required:

1. Executive Summary
2. Table of Contents
3. Introduction
4. The High-Technology-Crime Prevention Annual Goals
5. The High-Technology-Crime Prevention Projects
6. How the High-Technology-Crime Prevention Projects Support GEC's Annual Plan Goals
7. Mapping Charts
8. Conclusion

11

High-Technology-Crime Prevention and Investigative Program and Organization

THE INVESTIGATOR'S THOUGHT PROCESS IN ESTABLISHING THE HIGH-TECHNOLOGY-CRIME PREVENTION AND INVESTIGATION ORGANIZATION

The GEC investigator must now begin the arduous task of establishing a high-technology-crime prevention and investigation program and organization. In doing so, the investigator must understand:

- The limits of his or her authority.
- The budget available.
- The impact of establishing a high-technology-crime prevention program on GEC, the cultural change.

The investigator also must find qualified people who can build and maintain a cost-effective high-technology-crime prevention program. The staff must be able to develop into a high-technology-crime prevention team where everyone acts and is treated as a professional.

The high-technology-crime investigator/organizational manager must consider that building an *empire* and a massive bureaucratic organization not only will give the wrong impression to GEC management but it will also be costly. Furthermore, the manager must build an efficient and effective high-technology-crime prevention organization, as required by GEC and stated in the numerous plans.

In developing the high-technology-crime prevention organization, the manager must bear in mind all that has been discussed with GEC management and what was promised:

- GEC's history, business, and the competitive environment.
- The mission, vision, and quality statements.
- The need to develop a high-technology-crime prevention program as quickly as possible, for the work will not wait until the manager is fully prepared.

THE HIGH-TECHNOLOGY-CRIME INVESTIGATIVE ORGANIZATION

The high-technology-crime investigator was hired as investigator and manager of a new organization that is to be formed. However, little did the manager know that the only guidance given was to first follow the GEC format and develop a charter that would be approved through the GEC process for approving new organizations. The manager quickly found that the paperwork, meetings, and various bureaucratic requirements not only were more than expected, they were taking up the majority of the working day. After studying the GEC files and reviewing other organizational charters, talking to other managers, human resources personnel, the legal staff, security personnel, audit managers, and of course, the director of security, the following charter was submitted for approval.

High-Technology-Crime Prevention and Investigations Organization Charter

Purpose of the Organization: Lead a GEC-wide effort to mitigate against high-technology criminal activities and, where identified, to thoroughly investigate such incidents.

Responsibilities:

- Develop and manage a high-technology-crime prevention program as an integral part of the security department's asset protection program.
- Conduct high-technology-crime investigations and report the results to applicable management when there are allegations of unlawful activity.
- Conduct high-technology-crime inquiries and report the results to appropriate management when there are indications of violations of GEC policies or procedures that adversely affect GEC.
- Conduct proactive high-technology-crime prevention surveys on management request and report the results to management.
- Represent GEC as the focal point for all applicable high-technology-crime investigations' coordination with local, state, and federal investigative agencies; other members of the criminal justice systems; and other authorities, as required.
- Serve as GEC liaison with customers, subcontractors, government agencies, suppliers, and other non-GEC agencies relative to high-technology-crime prevention and investigation.

After gaining the approval of the director of security, the manager submitted the document to the person in charge of organizational development in the human resources department and hoped for the best. After all, nothing really should go wrong, since the director of security already signed off on it.

DETERMINING THE NEED FOR A HIGH-TECHNOLOGY-CRIME INVESTIGATION SUBORDINATE ORGANIZATIONS

The investigator/manager reviewed the draft organizational charter. The High-Tecnology-Crime Investigative Organization (HTCIO) manager was told by the human resources department that all charters were considered in draft stage and stamped accordingly until they had been approved through the formal approval process—estimated time until completion unknown, of course. However, the HTCIO manager could not wait until final approval was given, so assuming approval, it was important to put together an organizational structure.

The HTCIO manager had to determine whether subordinate organizations are needed. If so, a functional work breakdown structure must be developed to determine how many subordinate organizations are needed and what functions should be integrated into each subordinate organization.

The HTCIO manager discussed the current and potential workload with the director of security, audit manager, and legal staff. The HTCIO manager subsequently determined that neither the budget nor workload warranted developing subordinate organizations at this time.

HIGH-TECHNOLOGY-CRIME INVESTIGATIVE ORGANIZATION JOB DESCRIPTIONS

The following detailed high-technology-crime investigations job family functional descriptions were developed and approved by the applicable GEC departments:

- High-Technology-Crime Investigative Administrative Assistant

  Position summary: Provide all technical administrative support for the high-technology-crime investigations organization, including filing, typing reports, word processing, developing related spreadsheets, databases, and text and graphic presentations.

  Qualifications: High school diploma, one year of security administration or two years of clerical experience, must type at least 60 words per minute.

- High-Technology-Crime Associate Investigator

  Position summary: Assist and support high-technology-crime investigative staff in conducting administrative inquiries and surveys.

Duties and responsibilities:

1. Support the implementation and administration of high-technology-crime investigations software support systems.
2. Provide advice, guidance, and assistance to employees relative to high-technology-crime prevention.
3. Identify current high-technology-crime prevention functional processes and assist in the development of automated tools to support those functions.
4. Assist in the analysis of manual high-technology-crime prevention functions and provide input to recommendations and reports of the analyses to high-technology-crime investigative management.
5. Collect, compile, and generate high-technology-crime functional informational reports and briefing packages for presentation to customers and management.
6. Perform other functions as assigned by high-technology-crime investigations management.

Qualifications: This position normally requires a bachelor's degree in a high technology, business, security, criminal justice, or social science profession.

- High-Technology-Crime Analyst

Position summary: Identify, schedule, administer, and perform assigned technical high-technology-crime analyses functions.

Duties and responsibilities:

1. Represent the investigative organization to other organizations on select high-technology-crime and crime-prevention matters.
2. Provide advice, guidance, and assistance to managers, employees, and guests relative to high-technology-crime and crime-prevention matters.
3. Provide general advice and assistance in the interpretation of high-technology-crime prevention requirements.
4. Identify high-technology-crime prevention requirements necessary for mitigation against and deterrence of unlawful conduct.
5. Identify current high-technology-crime prevention functional processes and develop automated tools to support those functions.
6. Analyze manual high-technology-crime prevention functions, and provide recommendations and reports of the analyses to high-technology-crime prevention management.
7. Maintain, modify, and enhance automated high-technology-crime prevention functional systems and processes.
8. Collect, compile, and generate high-technology-crime and crime-prevention functional informational reports and briefing packages for presentation to customers and management.
9. Perform other functions as assigned by high-technology-crime investigations management.

10. Conduct noncompliance inquiries: Identify and analyze high-technology-crime prevention business practice irregularities and violations or infractions; conduct detailed inquiries; assess potential damage; monitor corrective action; and recommend preventive, cost-effective measures to preclude recurrences.
11. Assess potential risks: Perform limited risk assessments of high-technology-crime prevention systems and processes; determine their threats, areas of vulnerability, and risk; and recommend cost-effective solutions.
12. Plan, conduct and lead high-technology-crime surveys.

Qualifications: This classification normally requires a bachelor's degree in a high technology, business, social science, security, or criminal justice profession and at least two years of practical experience.

- High-Technology-Crime Senior Analyst

Position summary: Identify, evaluate, conduct, schedule, and lead technical high-technology-crime and crime-prevention analyses functions, inquiries, surveys, and investigations.

Duties and responsibilities:

1. Provide technical analysis of the crime-prevention requirements necessary for the protection of all high-technology assets, interpret those requirements, and implement and administer GEC plans, policies, and procedures.
2. Represent high-technology-crime and crime-prevention investigative matters with other entities as assigned.
3. Provide advice, guidance, and assistance to senior management, systems' managers and users, and custodians relative to high-technology-crime and crime-prevention matters.
4. Perform other functions as assigned by high-technology-crime investigations management.
5. Conduct noncompliance inquiries: Identify and conduct technical analyses of high-technology-crime prevention business practice irregularities, violations and infractions; plan, coordinate, and conduct detailed inquiries; assess potential damage; and develop and implement corrective action plans.
6. Conduct proactive high-technology-crime surveys and investigations and prepare reports of the results for presentation to management.
7. Support high-technology-crime investigations through the use of high-technology devices and equipment.

Qualifications: This classification normally requires a bachelor's degree in a high technology, business, criminal justice, security, or social science profession and four years of practical, related experience.

- High Technology Analyst Specialist

  Position summary: Act as technical high-technology-crime prevention advisor and ensure all high-technology-crime prevention functions and investigations meet GEC requirements.

  Duties and responsibilities:

  1. Act as technical advisor for complex high-technology-crime investigations.
  2. Represent the high-technology-crime investigative organization with other entities as assigned.
  3. Provide advice, guidance, and assistance to senior management, IT managers, and system users and custodians relative to high-technology-crime and crime-prevention matters.
  4. Perform other functions as assigned by high-technology-crime prevention management.

  Qualifications: This classification normally requires a bachelor's degree in a high-technology profession, and six years of high-technology-crime prevention experience.

- System Security Engineer

  Position summary: Act as a technical systems management consultant and project leader for high-technology-crime investigative and crime-prevention functions and programs developed to ensure GEC requirements are met.

  Duties and responsibilities:

  1. Act as a leader in the identification of government, customers, and GEC high-technology-crime investigations and ensure crime-prevention requirements are met; interpret those requirements; and develop, implement, and administer GEC high-technology-crime prevention plans, policies, and procedures.
  2. Represent the high-technology-crime investigative organization, when applicable, on high-technology-crime and crime-prevention matters as well as serve as GEC's liaison with customers, government agencies, suppliers, and other outside entities.
  3. Provide advice, guidance, and assistance to senior and executive management, GEC's subcontractors, and government entities relative to high-technology-crime and crime-prevention matters.
  4. Provide technical consultation, guidance, and assistance to management and systems users and maintain high-technology-crime prevention software systems by providing controls, processes and procedures.
  5. Establish, direct, coordinate, and maintain the high-technology-crime investigative and crime-prevention processes.
  6. Act as a leader for the technical evaluation and testing of crime-prevention and investigative hardware, firmware, and software.

7. Develop or direct the development of original techniques, procedures, and utilities for conducting high-technology-crime prevention risk assessments and schedules.
8. Direct or lead others in conducting technical high-technology-crime investigations and crime-prevention countermeasure surveys to support high-technology-crime prevention requirements and report findings.
9. Investigate methods and procedures related to the prevention of high-technology crime involving microcomputers, local area networks, wide area networks, the Internet, GII and NII networks, mainframes, and their associated connectivity and communications.
10. Design, develop, and maintain high-technology-crime prevention-related databases.
11. Recommend and obtain approval for procedural changes to effect high-technology-crime prevention implementations with emphasis on lowest cost and minimal risk.
12. Lead and direct high-technology-crime investigative and prevention personnel in the conduct of investigations, surveys, and inquiries.
13. Participate in the development and promulgation of high-technology-crime prevention information for general awareness.
14. Perform other functions as assigned by the high-technology-crime prevention manager.

Qualifications: This classification normally requires a bachelor's degree in a high-technology, security, criminal justice, social science, or psychology profession and a minimum of ten years high-technology-crime prevention-related experience.

RECRUITING HIGH-TECHNOLOGY-CRIME PREVENTION PROFESSIONALS

Once both the high-technology-crime investigation and crime-prevention organizational structure and the job family functional descriptions have been approved through the human resources' process, the next task is to begin recruiting and hiring qualified high-technology-crime prevention professionals.

To do so, the manager should first determine the following:

1. How many high-technology-crime investigators are needed?
2. What functions will they perform?
3. How many are needed in each function?
4. How many are needed in what pay grade?

The high-technology-crime investigator must plan for the gradual hiring of personnel to meet investigations' needs based on a ranked listing of functions. One or two high-level personnel should be hired to begin establishing the basic high-technology-crime investigations. In addition, these more experienced investigators can handle a greater range of functions and investigations.

At least two people who meet the qualifications of a high-technology-crime investigator and system engineer should be hired immediately. One would be the project leader, to begin the process of assisting the manager in establishing the formal functions of one of the high-technology-crime prevention programs. The other would begin the process of assisting the manager in formalizing the high-technology-crime investigative processes.

For the high-technology-crime investigator who is trying quickly to build a high-technology-crime prevention program and organization, compromises on staff selection may come in to play, as very few ideal candidates usually are found. In either case, it is important to quickly begin the hiring process.

Identifying In-House Candidates for High-Technology-Crime Investigator

Those individuals within GEC organizations who have been providing the audit, security, or information systems security functions may be good candidates because they know the GEC culture, processes, and people and have talents that, with some training, probably can make them into good or excellent investigators. The information technology department also may be a place to recruit high-technology-crime investigators.

In addition, since these potential candidates already work for GEC, their transfer to the new organization would be faster than locating and hiring candidates from outside GEC. Furthermore, the in-house training time would be faster, since the outsiders would have to learn the GEC processes, culture, contacts, and the like.

However, the high-technology-crime investigator/manager should beware of individuals who the managers recommend. These may just be the people that the manager has been trying to find some way to get rid of for some time. The high-technology-crime investigator/manager has enough problems—building a high-technology-crime investigation unit and crime-prevention program, handling the day-to-day crime prevention problems, attending endless meetings, trying to hire a professional staff, and having to transfer personnel who don't meet the investigator's expectations—to be saddled with someone recommended by another manager who turns out to be a *difficult* employee.

Identifying Outside Candidates for High-Technology-Crime Investigator

Many sources can be used to recruit talented high-technology-crime investigators, the number limited only by imagination and budget (especially budget). Regardless of how or where you recruit, the recruitment must be coordinated with the human resources staff.

Recruitment of high-technology-crime investigators involves a process, validating the position opening, budget, and so forth; and this process normally does not work quickly. The manager must be prepared for the gap between identification of a candidate, interview, selection, approval, and hiring and starting date. It is not unusual for such recruitment to take several months, sometimes six or more months.

The usual way to recruit high-technology-crime investigators is with the support and leadership of the employment personnel assigned to the human resources department and/or:

- Advertise in trade journals, local newspapers, and the like.
- Hire a recruitment firm to find the right people.
- Pass the word among colleagues. Ask people in the High Technology Crime Investigation Association to *pass the word*, use your own network of friends and associates, and advise the local law enforcement agencies, since they may have investigators who soon will retire and have done some high-technology-crime investigations.
- Use the Internet to advertise the position.

One alternative, if adequate staff are not readily available, may be to use consultants to outsource some aspects of investigations. With a few high-technology-crime investigators on board, the manager and staff can begin to work on establishing the high-technology-crime investigative processes; conducting inquiries, investigations, and surveys; and begin the process of establishing a high-technology-crime prevention program.

12

High-Technology-Crime Investigative Functions

DETERMINING MAJOR HIGH-TECHNOLOGY-CRIME INVESTIGATIVE FUNCTIONS

High-technology-crime investigative functions may be defined in numerous ways. However, the manager of the high-technology-crime investigations unit, after careful analysis and coordination, established five basic functions to be performed by the unit. The high-technology-crime investigation unit manager coordinated this functional breakdown with the head of security, audit manager, information systems security manager, and the legal staff. This was done because the manager knew that their support would be needed if the unit was to be successful. Furthermore, it was another indication of the manager trying to do the right thing and be a team player.

The basic five functions that the high-technology-crime unit was to perform were (1) support the security department in high-technology-crime prevention, (2) conduct high-technology-crime investigations, (3) conduct inquiries regarding noncompliance with anti-high-technology-crime policies at the request of management, (4) conduct high-technology-crime prevention surveys, and (5) establish and lead a high-technology-crime prevention program.

Support the Security Department

The director of security recommended that the high-technology-crime investigations and prevention unit would help by integrating anti-high-technology-crime policies, procedures, and awareness information into those processes already established and operated by the security department. The HTCIO manager enthusiastically agreed with this approach because it saved the unit budget and other resources since it was easier to add documents, slides, and other high-technology-crime and anti-crime media to the security department's existing program than to establish an entire program.

Conduct High-Technology-Crime Investigations

The high-technology-crime investigations would only be conducted relative to violations of local, state, federal, or international laws. The allegations of criminal conduct by an employee were to be evaluated as to their merit, then coordinated with the legal staff and others as appropriate. A decision would be reached as whether to conduct the investigation, refer it immediately to the appropriate law enforcement office, or classify it as an inquiry to determine if evidence was sufficient to refer it to a law enforcement agency, something GEC management was loathe to do for the following reasons:

- Such allegations normally caused the employee(s) in question to sue GEC, costing a great deal of money in legal fees, whether the case was won or lost.
- The bad publicity and poor public image caused by allegations of high-technology fraud and other crimes by employees always caused a concern to stockholders, the general public, and was bad for business.
- Law enforcement investigators often were not skilled in handling such investigations, consuming a lot of the other employees' time, and even if it did go to trial, the verdict very often would be "not guilty."

Conduct Noncompliance Inquiries at the Request of Management

The noncompliance inquiry (NCI) would be either a preliminary high-technology-crime investigation or an inquiry into a violation of GEC policies, procedures, or rules. However, it was decided to differentiate between a criminal investigation and an NCI because, even if the allegations were of a criminal nature, obviously some GEC policy or procedures would have been violated. Therefore, these investigations were considered to be violations of GEC rules. If the NCI determined that a criminal act had occurred, then management would be in a better position to look at the options of internal, non-job-termination disciplinary action against the employee, termination of employment for cause, allowing the employee to resign, or referring the matter to law enforcement authorities. In other words, the NCI approach gave GEC management options.

Conduct Crime-Prevention Surveys

The purpose of crime-prevention surveys was to look into areas where the potential for high-technology crime may be high and determine if any indications suggested that crimes were being committed. They also were a form of risk management to determine if any external or internal threats or areas of vulnerability would cause GEC to take unacceptable risks.

Establish and Lead an Anti-High-Technology-Crime (or Crime-Prevention) Program

The objective of the anti-high-technology-crime (or crime-prevention) program was to be a deterrent, especially within GEC, to those who would contemplate committing a high-technology crime either against GEC or through the use of GEC resources. It was hoped that this program would lessen the motivation of employees to commit such a crime as well as eliminate the opportunity. Thus, the opportunity portion of the triad of opportunity, motive, and rationale would "prevent" a crime from occurring.

HIGH-TECHNOLOGY-CRIME INVESTIGATIONS POLICY

Based on the requirements and factors driving high-technology-crime investigations, the investigator/manager must take the next step, which is to develop a high-technology-crime investigations policy, coordinate that policy with applicable department managers, and gain executive management approval for the policy to be incorporated into the GEC security policy.

The manager reasoned that the policy should be clear, concise, and written at somewhat of a high level. It must conform to the GEC policy format, of course. The GEC high-technology-crime investigations policy should not get bogged down in details but set the high-technology-crime investigations guidelines for the corporation.

Once integrated in the GEC security policy document, the high-technology-crime investigations policy should be distributed to all department managers and that distribution should be done through a cover letter signed by the CEO, president, or chairman of the board. The letter should basically state the following:

To: All GEC Employees
Subject: Protecting GEC's Information, High Technology, and Competitive Edge

The advances in the technology of computers and telecommunications and our use of them has provided us with the opportunity to gain a competitive advantage. Therefore, aside from you, they are our most vital assets. They are a vital asset because they are used to run our business by transmitting, processing, and storing our vital information.

All of us at GEC have derived great benefit from being able to use our state-of-the-art high-technology equipment and devices, not the least of which is our access to our systems and ability to communicate across the corporation as well as with our customers, suppliers, and subcontractors. At the same time, the GEC systems contain vital information that if destroyed, modified, or disclosed to outsiders would be harmful to the corporation and adversely affect our competitive edge. Therefore, it is in the interest of all of us to report such incidents to the security department's high-technology-crime investigations unit.

We must be able to use our high technology, our systems and information, in a secure manner. It is imperative that these vital GEC resources be protected to the maximum extent possible but consistent with cost-effective operations.

This directive is the roadmap to our high-technology protection and anticrime programs. They are needed to help ensure the continued success of GEC. For these programs to be successful, you must give it your full support. Your support is vital to ensure that GEC continues to grow and maintain its leadership role in the global widget industry.

(Signed by the GEC president and CEO)

GEC'S HIGH-TECHNOLOGY-CRIME INVESTIGATIONS REQUIREMENTS AND POLICY DIRECTIVE

The GEC high-technology-crime investigations policy is set forth in the high-technology-crime investigations requirements and policy directive (IRPD; GEC high-technology-crime investigations-P-001). This directive follows the standard format for GEC policies and includes the following:

1. Introduction, which includes some history as to the need for a high-technology-crime investigations unit at GEC.
2. Purpose of the Directive, which describes why the document exists.
3. Scope of the Directive, which defines the directive's breadth.
4. Responsibilities, which defines and identifies the responsibilities at all levels, including executive managers, organizational managers, and all users of high-technology equipment and devices. The directive also includes the requirements for customers', subcontractors' and vendors' access to GEC's high-technology equipment, such as systems and information.
5. Requirements, which include the requirements for

   Identifying the value of the high technology.

   Access to the GEC systems.

   Access to specific applications and files.

   Audit trails and their review.

   Reporting responsibilities and action to be taken in the event of an indication of a possible violation.

Minimum protection requirements for the hardware, firmware. and software.[1]

Requirements for reporting high-technology crimes and policy violations at the GEC department level and lower levels.

HIGH-TECHNOLOGY-CRIME INVESTIGATION PROCEDURES

Based on the GEC high-technology-crime investigations policy and stated in the IRPD, each department must establish procedures for reporting indications of high-technology crime and related incidents to the high-technology-crime investigations unit.

The GEC culture is such that the protection of high-technology, e.g., the information systems and the information they store, process, and transmit, is the obligation of every GEC employee. The managers of GEC are required, based on their management position, to protect the assets of GEC. Therefore, the high-technology-crime investigator reasoned, and executive management agreed, that each department should comply with the IRPD based on its unique position with GEC. The departments were to document the procedures and processes they would use to comply with the reporting and other requirements of the high-technology-crime investigations procedural directive.

This had several advantages:

- The GEC department managers were in a better position to write the document and develop cost-effective procedures that worked for them.
- It made the department, especially the managers, responsible for compliance with the IRPD.
- It negated the managers' complaints that their situation was unique and so they could not comply with all aspects of an high-technology-crime investigations procedure (that written by the high-technology-crime investigator), as written.
- It took this level of detailed high-technology-crime investigative responsibility off the shoulders of the investigator and placed it squarely where it belonged—on the managers.

AWARENESS PROGRAM

The GEC high-technology-crime investigator decided to concentrate, as a high priority, on incorporating the high-technology-crime awareness information into the security department's security awareness program. This was done to "get the word out" and quickly gain the managers' and employees' support in identifying and reporting incidents that fell under the purview of the high-technology-crime investigations unit.

The high-technology-crime investigator/manager reasoned that, once the GEC high-technology-crime investigation policies and baseline procedures were developed and published, the employees must be made aware of them and why they were necessary. Only with the full support and co-operation of the GEC employees could a successful high-technology-crime prevention and investigation program be established and maintained.

The high-technology-crime prevention and investigation portion of the security department's awareness program was patterned and developed in accordance with the format being used by that department. This would ensure a smooth, quick integration of the material. The awareness program was broken into two, major parts: awareness briefings and continuous awareness material.

Awareness Briefings

The awareness briefings included the security department's information relative to the need for high-technology protection and controls; for reporting violations of rules, policies, procedures, and laws; the impact of not doing so; and an explanation of the GEC security program that included that high-technology-crime prevention and investigations program.

The high-technology-crime investigator/manager was informed by the security manager responsible for the awareness program that the awareness material and briefings, when given as a general briefing, could be used only for new employees. The general briefings failed to provide the specific information required by various groups. Therefore, the awareness briefings were subsequently tailored to several specific audiences:

- All new hires, whether or not they used high-technology systems (the rationale was that they all handle information and come in contact with computer and telecommunication systems in one form or another).
- Managers.
- System users.
- Information technology department personnel.
- Engineers.
- Manufacturers.
- Accounting and finance department personnel.
- Procurement personnel.
- Human resources department personnel.
- Security and auditing department personnel.
- The system security custodians (those that would be given day-to-day responsibility to ensure that the systems and information were pro-

tected in accordance with the information systems security policy and procedures).

A process was established to identify these personnel, add their profile information into a database, and using a standard format, track their awareness briefing attendance, both to initial briefings and annual rebriefings. The information would be used also to provide them, through the GEC internal mail and e-mail systems, awareness material.

The high-technology-crime investigator/manager determined that the current awareness program met the needs of the unit. Therefore, the unit's staff would provide specific information concerning high-technology crime and its prevention to the awareness program manager for incorporation into the current program. This is another example of saving budget resources, not reinventing the wheel, and using another organizations' resources to meet the goals of the unit.

Awareness Material

The high-technology-crime investigator/manager, in concert with the staffs of the human resources and training departments, decided that ensuring that employees were aware of their high-technology-crime reporting responsibilities and prevention techniques would require constant reminders. After all, high-technology-crime prevention is not the major function of most of the GEC employees; however, a way must be found to remind the employees that it is a *part* of their major function.

It was decided that awareness material could be cost-effectively provided the employees. This was accomplished through providing high-technology-crime investigation material to the employees through annual calendars, posters, labels for systems and diskettes, articles published in GEC publications such as the weekly newsletter, and logon notices and e-mail system broadcast messages, especially of high-technology-crime investigations changes. Although not all inclusive, the investigator/manager believed this was a good start that could be analyzed for cost-effective improvements at the end of the calendar year.

PROACTIVE HIGH-TECHNOLOGY-CRIME PREVENTION SURVEYS AND THE MANAGEMENT OF RISK

The investigator/manager believed that an integral part of a high-technology-crime prevention program, in addition to the policies, procedures, and awareness program, was the need to assess the threats, areas of vulnerability, and risk that affect the potential for high-technology crime.

The manager reasoned that it always was more cost effective to prevent crimes than investigate them. Furthermore, an aggressive proactive position always is more effective than reacting to crimes after they occurred.

The manager coordinated the survey process with the audit manager to ensure that there was no duplication of effort. The audit manager advised that the department's audits focused primarily on compliance with GEC internal controls through the GEC policies and procedures as well as government rules and regulations. Therefore, the audit manager saw no redundancy or conflict with audit processes and goals.

To ensure that everyone was working together in the best interest of GEC, communicating, and sharing information, the investigations unit manager advised that a copy of each survey would be forwarded to the audit manager for that department's use. The audit manager thought such information would be very beneficial and advised that the annual audit schedule would be provided to the unit manager to avoid a scheduling conflict, where both organizations would have staff in an organization at the same time.

The two department managers discussed each other's work and decided to establish a process to share information, including

- Planned and postaudit meetings to discuss targets and results.
- Current investigations.
- Deficiencies and findings uncovered during investigations that point to a lack of controls or inadequate procedures.
- Audit findings that may be indicators of fraud, waste, abuse, some type of GEC violations, or other forms of criminal activity.

Both managers believed that, by working together, they could work "smarter" and maximize the use of the resources with the least impact on their budgets, thus meeting their charter obligations and benefiting GEC. In addition, they agreed that the investigations unit manager would conduct a series of fraud, waste, and abuse awareness briefings at the auditor's staff meetings, so the staff members would be more knowledgeable concerning fraud indicators when they conducted their audits.

What Is Risk Management?

Risk management is defined as the total process of identifying, controlling, eliminating, and minimizing uncertain events that may affect system resources. It includes risk assessments; risk analyses, including cost-benefit analyses; target selection; implementation and testing; security evaluation of safeguards; and overall high-technology-crime investigation reviews.

Risk Assessment

The process of identifying the risk of high-technology crime, determining their magnitude, and identifying areas needing safeguards is called *risk assessment*. In other words, you assess the risk of a particular target, such as the potential for overhearing cellular phone conversations of GEC's CEO. The risk assessment process is subdivided into threats, areas of vulnerability, and risk.

Threats

Threats are human-made or natural occurrences that can cause adverse effects to systems and information when combined with specific vulnerabilities; for example,

- Natural threats include such things as fire, floods, hurricanes, and earthquakes.
- Human-made threats and related matters include unauthorized system access; hacker, cracker, or phreaker programs; the perpetrators themselves; theft of systems or services; denial of services; and destruction of systems or information.

Areas of Vulnerability

Weaknesses can allow specific threats to cause adverse effects to systems and information; for example,

- Lack of audit trails.
- Lack of information backups.
- Lack of access controls.
- Anything that weakens the security of GEC's high technology, the systems, or the information they process, store, or transmit.

Risk

Risk is the chance that a specific threat can take advantage of a specific area of vulnerability to cause adverse effects to systems and information; for example,

- Systems located in a strong earthquake area are likely to be damaged in the event of a strong earthquake.
- Without audit trails on a system that contains company information of value to others, someone might try to steal that information. The lack of audit trail logs would make it difficult to know if someone had tried to penetrate the system and, worse yet, whether the penetration succeeded.

The Assessment Process

Assessments are an evaluation of the threats and areas of vulnerability to determine the level of risk to systems or the information they store, process, or transmit. Assessments are usually done through a qualitative or quantitative analysis or a combination of the two.

Qualitative analyses usually determine the chance of risk as high, medium, or low. It is an "educated best guess," based primarily on the opinions of knowledgeable others gathered through interviews, history, tests, and the experience of the person doing the assessment.

Quantitative analyses usually use statistical sampling, based on mathematical computations, to determine the probability of an adverse occurrence based on historical data. It still is an "educated best guess" but is based primarily on statistical results.

Risk analysis assesses the chance of each type of risk, the countermeasures to mitigate against the risk, and the costs and benefits associated with those risks and countermeasures—these make up the risk analysis process. Basically, it is risk assessment with the cost and benefit factors added.

The Risk Management Process

The goal of the risk management process, of course, is to provide the best protection of the high technology and the information it stores, processes, or transmits at the lowest cost consistent with the value of the devices and the information. High-technology-crime prevention surveys are a form of risk assessment and are used to identify the threats, areas of vulnerability, and risk that would allow the commission of a high-technology crime.

Remember that the high-technology-crime investigations program is a company program made up of professionals who provide service and support to the company. Therefore, the combination of proactive surveys and risk management processes must be based on the needs of GEC customers.

Also, be sure that the survey and risk management concepts, programs, and processes are informally and formally used in all aspects of the high-technology-crime prevention and investigation program.

The following items should be considered in the high-technology-crime prevention program:

- *Management interest.* Identify areas of major interest to executive management and customers, approach this issue from a business point of view. The process should begin with interviews of your internal customers to determine what high-technology areas can be adversely affected by noncompliance and crime. Then, target those areas first as the starting point for the surveys.

- *Targets.* Identify specific targets, such as the private branch exchange (PBX).
- *Input sources.* Users, system administrators, auditors, security officers, managers, technical journals, technical bulletins, CERT alerts (Internet), risk assessment application programs—these are just some of the sources of information on high-technology crime and noncompliance.
- *Survey.* Conduct the high-technology-crime prevention survey using a standard survey format.
- *Recommendations to management.* When the high-technology-crime prevention survey is completed, the investigator/manager must make recommendations to management. Remember in making recommendations to think from a business point of view: cost, benefits, profits, public relations, and so forth.
- *Risk management reports.* A briefing that includes a formal, written report is the vehicle to bring the results of the survey to management's attention. The report should identify areas that need improvement and those performing well and recommended actions for improvement, with costs and benefits, as applicable.

Remember management will decide either to accept the risk or mitigate against the risk and how much to spend to do so. The high-technology-crime investigator is the specialist, the in-house consultant on high-technology crime and crime prevention. Management holds the responsibility to decide what to do. It may follow your recommendations, ignore them, or take some other action. In any case, the high-technology-crime investigator has provided the service and support required.

HIGH-TECHNOLOGY-CRIME PREVENTION SURVEYS

The following standard survey was developed to assist in successfully meeting the goals and objectives of GEC's and the high-technology-crime investigative unit's strategic, tactical, and annual plans.

The high-technology-crime prevention surveys are designed to proactively determine the potential for an individual or individuals to attack or otherwise take advantage of a GEC high-technology area of vulnerability for unauthorized or illegal purposes. The survey is to provide information necessary to assist management in deciding the potential for unauthorized conduct or criminal risk within the company's high-technology environment and organizations and to assist in making cost-effective decisions to mitigate the risks.

Survey Report Format

The following standard format was developed to meet the needs of the GEC management:

- Title page.
- Table of contents.
- Executive summary (a clear and concise summary of the report, not more than one page long).
- Body of the report (consists of the following five sections).
  - Purpose (a sentence or two describe the reason or objective of the survey, such as "This high-technology-crime prevention survey was conducted to determine the potential misuse, abuse, and theft of hardware, software, and information possible by the introduction of notebook computers into the workforce.").
  - Background information (not more than one page of information explaining the rationale for the survey).
  - Methodology (the philosophy and approach used in conducting the survey, not more than one page long).
  - Findings (the discrepancies, deficiencies, or noteworthy—good—items discovered during the survey, not more than two pages long).
  - Recommendations (all findings must include recommendations for corrective action to mitigate against the potential for crime or violations of GEC rules; these must be clear, concise, and written based on the professional expertise of the investigator, concurred with by the manager; they also must include considerations of their impact on costs and productivity).
- Appreciation (a list of the people, with their titles, and organizations that assisted in accomplishing the survey).
- Attachments (these are appended to the report as applicable: a glossary, the operational plan used to conduct the survey, and any supporting documents deemed appropriate, such as audit reports, prior investigations related to that high technology, news items relative to the high technology in question, hacker site comments, or CERT announcements).

The report must be clear, concise, and written with GEC management as the audience. The investigator is to assume that the reader has no knowledge of surveys, high-technology crimes, or crime prevention.

Cellular Telephones High-Technology-Crime Prevention Survey

Once the investigator/manager was prepared, the manager sent e-mail to the GEC managers advising them of the unit's capability to conduct surveys.

The manager responsible for the GEC cellular telephones immediately contacted the unit manager over concerns about cellular phone fraud. The manager had read about recent cellular phone fraud in the newspapers and was concerned about the over 200 GEC cellular phones being used by GEC employees that could become "victims" of fraudsters.

A survey was conducted using the following operational plan:

1. *Introduction.* Cellular phones have become an object for furthering fraud and other crimes. GEC has procured cellular phones for company personnel to use in the furtherance of GEC business. The potential for exploitation of GEC cellular phones by unauthorized users is no less than that for other corporations.
2. *Purpose.* The purpose of the cellular phone crime prevention survey is to determine if any GEC cellular phones or related services are being misused, abused, or used for criminal or other unauthorized activities.
3. *Objective.* The survey's objective is to identify the processes being used to procure, distribute, use, and control GEC cellular phones that may lead to their theft or use for criminal or unauthorized activities.
4. *Resources.* One senior high-technology-crime investigator to be used for 32 hours per week for a period of five weeks.
5. *Target.* GEC cellular phones' use and processes.
6. *Target plan.*

   Identify the process used to request a cellular phone.

   Identify the process to monitor cellular phone usage.

   Identify the individuals responsible for the processes.

   Identify the cellular phone tracking processes.

   Identify the processes used by the provider to bill and safeguard GEC cellular phones.

   Identify the process used to install cellular phones in GEC vehicles.

   Identify all directives and rules that apply to the cellular phone processes.

   Locate and interview the GEC cellular phone individuals responsible for processing requests, installing and maintaining the phones, and key players in the entire process.

   Conduct applicable interviews.

   Interview a statistical sampling of GEC cellular phone users.

   Review and analyze a statistical sampling of cellular phone bills.

   Compare the cellular phone database inventory files with the current record of employees.

   Set up a controlled test of the processes by making up a nonexistent person and, using the current process, requesting a cellular phone. If it is received, make several calls that should stand out, such as to a foreign country. Then, report the cellular phone missing, by memo, to the person responsible in the process for taking stolen or missing reports for cellular phones.

Document the results.

The survey determined that

- Monthly billing statements were paid without verification by those responsible for the individual cellular phones that the charges were for valid GEC business.
- The cellular phone database was out of date.
- Some employees had taken the GEC cellular phones with them when they left GEC's employment and GEC continued paying for their monthly calls.
- The policy and procedures governing the entire cellular phone process were over six years old and outdated.
- All cellular phones included call features such as call forwarding, three-way conference calling, Star* services (STAR JAM, STAR FIND, STAR SORT, and STAR WAITING) at additional cost although no justification was required for these features.
- Anyone could request a cellular phone as long as any level of management approved it; however, no one questioned the justification, use, or even the manager's signature on the requests.

Recommendations included

- The GEC employee records should be cross-referenced against those in receipt of cellular phones.
- Those cellular phones that could not be identified to a current employee should have their services terminated immediately.
- Those individuals no longer employed at GEC should be sent a registered letter, billing them for past calls and requesting an appointment to pick up the phone. If that went unanswered, a second registered letter would be sent, advising the former employee that further use of the phone could constitute fraudulent, criminal conduct. Further pursuance and confiscation of the cellular phones from former employees was determined not to be cost effective based on the price of replacements.
- All call features should be eliminated on all cellular phones until such features could be shown and endorsed by *executive* management to be in the best interest of GEC.
- All cellular phone users were to receive an acknowledgment statement to sign and return stating they would safeguard the cellular phone, use it only for GEC business, and reimburse GEC for any unauthorized (e.g., personal, nonemergency) calls. Furthermore, they

were responsible for reimbursing GEC in the event the phone was stolen.

- The cellular phone policy should be updated immediately.
- The monthly bills should be sent to the manager of the employee's organization and the employee and the manager both sign and date the bill, verifying its accuracy and that the calls were in furtherance of GEC business.

Executive management and others were extremely pleased with the results of this "quick and dirty" survey because it

- Pointed to potential cellular fraud problems.
- Helped to prevent future occurrences.
- Saved GEC hundreds of thousands of "future" dollars through closer monitoring of the monthly bills, elimination of a nonjustified need for some phones, and the elimination of most of the STAR features.
- GEC also recouped thousands of dollars from present and some former employees for unauthorized calls.

Such surveys can have a positive effect on profits and costs, and it is an excellent public relations tool for the high-technology-crime investigator.

PRIVATE BRANCH EXCHANGE SURVEY

The following is a "sanitized" version of a survey operations plan and operation developed and used by Dr. Kovacich and an associate to conduct high-technology-crime surveys. It can be used as a baseline by high-technology-crime investigators for conducting PBX high-technology-crime prevention surveys.

I. Introduction

1. Purpose

The purpose of this survey is to identify the process of maintaining, configuring, receiving, storing, and transmitting phone calls using the Site A telephone switch (also referred to as the *private branch exchange*, or PBX) and the threats, areas of vulnerability, and risk associated with that process and to recommend changes to mitigate against the risk. The survey will concentrate on external attempts to penetrate the Southern Phonecom Telecom Global system telephone switch and use it to perpetrate toll fraud or to damage, destroy, modify, or read the switch or voice mail of others.

1.1. PBX penetration and long distance toll fraud are increasing dramatically in both the number of occurrences and dollars lost. Toll fraud is a highly charged issue because long distance carriers contend customers should pay for fraudulent calls.[2]

1.2. The U.S. Secret Service estimates companies in the United States lose about $2.23 billion each year in charges for fraudulent calls. Other experts claim the total probably is closer to $4 billion. In any case, the typical average "hit" today is worth $40,000.[3]

1.3. How do they do it? Phone phreaks and hackers gain access to company telephone systems in a variety of ways: by accessing the direct inward system access (DISA) function; by obtaining remote-access telecom codes; by using "demon attack dialers" to penetrate a system; through underground "call-sell" operations, "shoulder surfers," "dumpster divers," and "phone phreakers"; or finally, just by asking for it (social engineering).

2. Scope

The scope of this survey will address common penetration techniques used by phreakers to gain access to company phone systems. Select use of certain techniques will determine our areas of vulnerability. It also will identify the telephone system service process, from initial installation and user training to the termination of user service. Each step in this process will be analyzed to determine threat, areas of vulnerability, and risk potential. After the survey results are analyzed, recommendations will be made to mitigate against risk. Recommendations will be based on a "least-cost" approach.

3. Target

For the purposes of this survey, the target will be the Southern Phonecom Global system presently in use at the XYZ Company's manufacturing facility, located at Site A, Anytown, USA. The survey also will include the Global voice mail messaging option also in use at Site A.

II. Objective(s)

1. Identify the common penetration techniques used by phreakers to gain access to company phone systems.
2. Under controlled test conditions, determine how vulnerable the Site A Global system (with the Global mail option) is to penetration attempts by phreakers from outside the facility.
3. Ascertain what preventive steps can be taken to lessen exposure to this type of activity.
4. Make recommendations to management.

III. Operational Steps

1. Phase I (Covert)

1.1. Initially coordinate the survey with the system integrity (security) staff of NDI, a long distance service provider. (Note: NDI offered its expertise in identify system weaknesses and areas of vulnerability, as well as techniques used to exploit them.)

1.2. Perform the following tests on the indicated systems to determine if they can be penetrated from the outside. (Note: These tests may be performed off-site to preclude the compromise of any test that, if done at the office, may result in using an extension on the Global switch.)

On the switch (Global PBX):

1.2.1. Is a remote maintenance access port available on the system? Can it be accessed (i.e., no password protection, use of a common number string such as 1111, 9999, 1234, 1993)? Is it adequately protected from outside penetration?

1.2.2. Can it be determined if the modem supporting the remote maintenance access port uses an unpublished number with a prefix different from the system's voice telephones?

1.2.3. Can the system be penetrated through direct inward system access?

1.2.4. Can any unused DISA numbers or unauthorized codes be located in the system?

1.2.5. Can it be determined if DISA numbers have unrestricted or restricted trunk group access?

1.2.6. Are system administration accounts still in the original default condition or have they been customized by the administrator(s)?

1.2.7. Can system administrator or user passwords be accessed and compromised through outside penetration?

1.2.8. Are vendor maintenance accounts in a default condition or have they been customized for specific system use?

1.2.9. Can installation codes be determined? If so, are they in a default condition or have they been customized?

1.2.10. Can it be determined if trunk tie-lines are configured for restricted or unrestricted use?

1.2.11. Are tie-lines protected by a class of service (COS) configuration?

1.2.12. Is the external access parameter set to disallow caller transfers to an outside line?

1.2.13. Is the system's international calling capability in use? Can it be accessed through penetration attempts?

1.2.14. Using social engineering techniques, can any restricted number be compromised by telecommunications or help desk personnel?

On voice mail (Global mail):

1.2.15. Has the voice-mail capability been configured to facilitate trunk access? (This permits access to long distance calling or through-dial capability.)

1.2.16. Are any controls in place to protect trunk access (i.e., voice mail software or PBX operating system)?

1.2.17. Can outbound international dialing be accessed or is it restricted in voice mail?

1.2.18. Can it be determined if call blocking is in use through voice mail?

1.2.19. Have the restricted extension dialing access codes been adjusted to block dialing access to trunk lines from within the voice-mail system?

1.3. Utilize techniques and support provided by NDI security representatives in testing the Site A Global system against outside penetration.

1.4. Document test results.

1.5. Develop a countermeasures matrix by listing each vulnerability in a column and in an adjacent column, list what would mitigate that vulnerability.

2. Phase II (Overt)

2.1. Identify the processes for (a) acquiring and installing system hardware, (b) installing and maintaining software, (c) making system software modifications, (d) handling internal and external maintenance, (e) providing system physical security, (f) establishing and maintaining system operational safeguards, (g) maintaining and reviewing audit trails, (h) reporting lost or stolen company telephone credit cards, and (i) terminating user features and services.

2.2. Identify the requirements and directives that govern telephone operation at Site A; obtain and review copies of pertinent documentation.

2.3. Identify key vendor representatives (i.e., Telecom) and players who make up the overall Site A telecommunication environment.

2.4. Locate and interview key vendor and Telecom personnel who have functional responsibility for (a) Global switch operations, (b) telephone installation and maintenance, (c) Global switch maintenance, and (d) telephone customer service. Locate and interview the Site A telecommunications management representative.

2.5. Key personnel should be interviewed to (a) develop a good understanding of the processes and system used to provide telecommunications support and (b) identify the various features and functions of the switch that may be susceptible to break-in or fraudulent use of the system. A partial list of questions follows.

On the switch (Global PBX):

2.5.1. Are system administration accounts still in the original default condition or have they been customized by the administrator(s)?

2.5.2. Can system administrator or user passwords be accessed and compromised through outside penetration?

2.5.3. Are vendor maintenance accounts in a default condition or have they been customized for specific system use?

2.5.4. How easy can system features be activated or disabled (especially at night and over weekends)? Are those features denied or disabled by default?

2.5.5. Are user-assigned features (e.g., remote access, weekend remote access, inbound 800 calls, outbound dialing, remote originating and call forwarding) disabled when not required by a particular user?

2.5.6. Are default remote access codes limited to one per person?

2.5.7. Are trunk tie-lines configured for restricted or unrestricted use?

2.5.8. Are tie-lines protected by class of service (configuration)?

2.5.9. Can the system be penetrated through direct inward system access?

2.5.10. Are unauthorized DISA numbers and codes disabled?

2.5.11. Is call blocking in use?

2.5.12. Can system be penetrated through use of the system's 800 number?

2.5.13. Are calls to area codes 900 and 976 restricted?

2.5.14. Can area code 809 be accessed?

2.5.15. Is the external access parameter set to disallow caller transfers to an outside line?

2.5.16. Are credit cards used to facilitate long distance calls? (The law limits victim liability to $50 per card for losses due to fraud.)

2.5.17. Is the system's international calling capability in use?

2.5.18. Have controls been established on remote maintenance access?

2.5.19. Is an unpublished number used for the modem port with a prefix different from those used for voice phone numbers?

On voice mail (Global mail):

2.5.20. Has the voice-mail capability been configured to facilitate trunk access? (This permits access to long distance calling or through-dial capability.)

2.5.21. Are any controls in place to protect trunk access (e.g., voice-mail software or PBX operating system)?

2.5.22. Has outbound international dialing been restricted in voice mail?

2.5.23. Can it be determined if call blocking is in use through voice mail?

2.5.24. Have the restricted extension dialing access codes been adjusted to block dialing access to trunk lines from within the voice-mail system?

2.6. Document interview results.

3. Phase III, Report Writing

3.1. Compile survey and test data.
3.2. Prepare draft report.
3.3. Management review; determine addressees.
3.4. Finalize survey report; disseminate to addressees.

IV. Resources

1. Labor

1.1. The services of the project leader part time (four hours a day) for a period of ten nonconsecutive days to (a) read and digest survey training material, (b) develop a security assessment survey operation plan and associated charts, (c) coordinate the plan with and seek approval from investigations manager, (d) coordinate with and obtain training from long distance carrier's security personnel, and (e) briefly survey personnel on operation plan. *Subtotal*: 40 hours.

1.2. The services of the project leader and one investigator full time (eight hours a day) for a period of five days will be needed when identifying processes, requirements, and directives (see Section III, Operational Steps, paragraphs 1 and 2). *Subtotal*: 80 hours.

1.3. The services of the project leader and one investigator full time (eight hours per day) for a period of five days will be required when identifying key players, developing questions, interviewing personnel, and documenting results (see Section III, paragraphs 3–6). *Subtotal*: 80 hours.

1.4. The periodic, nonconsecutive support of key telecommunications personnel in identifying and providing copies of applicable processes, requirements, and directives (see Section III, paragraphs 1–6). Additionally, approximately one hour of interview time for each key representative. *Subtotal*: 15 hours.

1.5. The services of the long distance carrier (NDI) security representatives in providing training and technical assistance in support of this survey (see Section III, paragraph 7). *Subtotal*: 10 hours.

1.6. The services of the project leader and one investigator part time (five hours a day) for a period of two nonconsecutive days to conduct penetration testing and document results (see Section III, paragraphs 8 and 9). *Subtotal*: 40 hours.

1.7. The services of the project leader and one investigator part time (four hours a day) for a period of five nonconsecutive days to analyze all accumulated data in determining specific threats, areas of vulnerability, and risk before documenting findings and recommendations (see Section III, paragraph 10, and Section VI, Analyses). *Subtotal*: 40 hours.

1.8. The services of the project leader full time (six hours a day) and one investigator part time (two hours a day) for a period of seven nonconsecutive days to draft, coordinate, finalize, and disseminate the survey report. *Subtotal*: 56 hours.

Grand total

Local investigative staff time:	336 hours
Local Telecom staff time:	15 hours
NDI representative time:	10 hours
Total:	361 hours

2. Equipment

XYZ Company Security: Use of off-site telephones, two personal computer systems (one system on-site and one off-site) equipped with modem and printer, specialized software.

XYZ Telecom Staff: None.

NDI: Unknown.

3. Monetary Contingency

Company reimbursement for long distance phone calls made from off-site location during test periods and incidental expenses (e.g., purchase of special connectors, cabling).

V. Charts

Project management charts depict the plan schedule.

VI. Analyses

Analyses of general threats, areas of vulnerability, and risk criteria to be used for this survey.

1. Threats

The Global system used at Site A can be penetrated from the outside employing a variety of previously proven phreakers methods, some of which follow.

1.1. Using a compromised direct inward system access number to gain PBX access.

1.2. Obtaining and using compromised user, system, and system administrator passwords exchanged through phreakers bulletin boards.

1.3. Using a stolen or illegally acquired company phone credit card or credit card information, including unique access code information.

1.4. Using illegally acquired remote-access telecom codes.

1.5. Dialing 800 numbers to gain access to PBX-attached voice mail.

1.6. Taking advantage of special phone system features to penetrate or manipulate the system.

1.7. Using a "demon" or "war dialer" (automated attack dialer) that repeatedly calls a system and pumps in access codes until a valid one is found, allowing system penetration.

1.8. Giving up company information to "dumpster divers" (people who dig through trash cans for discarded information).

1.9. Using a cover story to request system information from company employees, switchboard operators, switch maintenance personnel, management, and the like (social engineering).

2. Areas of Vulnerability

The following are general system areas of vulnerability previously identified in other surveys, investigations, and audits.

2.1. DISA number is listed, is in the incoming service group (ISG), is not deactivated when not in use or not required, and account codes are not changed on a regular basis.

2.2. User and system passwords not adequately protected; they do not meet acceptable criteria for selection, minimum password length, or invalid password attempts. Allowable user access is not periodically reviewed and revalidated. Information regarding configuration, modem numbers, and passwords is not adequately safeguarded.

2.3. Procedures not in effect to immediately notify phone company of lost, misplaced, or stolen company telephone credit, access, or calling cards. Cards may contain an access telephone number. Employees are not security conscious when using calling cards in public places.

2.4. Employees are not instructed to adequately protect phone access numbers; authorization codes are changed infrequently.

2.5. Special parameters are not placed on the company 800 numbers (e.g., dialed from only those calling areas specified).

2.6. International calling (011) and area code 809 (Caribbean) is accessible to all system users. Calls to the 900 and 976 prefixes are not restricted.

2.7. PBX remote maintenance ports are not disabled when service is not needed. System physical dial-in ports and DISA ports are not monitored regularly.

2.8. Company phone books and system administrator manuals are not treated as sensitive material when discarded.

2.9. Switchboard operators, master console operators, system administrators, maintenance personnel, and other system support employees are not trained to be suspicious of telephonic requests for system information, maintenance work, execution of programs, and so forth.

3. Risk

Risk will be classified as High, Medium, or Low, based on severity of the threat or vulnerability. Recommendations will be developed using a "least-cost" approach.

SL -1 Switch (PBX) Tests

Test 1

Attempt to identify any 800 numbers used by the company at all locations.

Test 2

Using phreaker social engineering techniques, attempt to gain access to the Global switch using a suitable ruse.

Test 3

Using a telephone, blindly hack at the XYZ Company system in an attempt to determine type of system, size, features, and so forth.

Test 4

Using phreaker techniques, attempt to identify all lines equipped with modems attached to the system as a potential means of external penetration.

Test 5

Using phreaker techniques, attempt to identify authorization (authcodes) on those lines equipped with modems as a potential means of system penetration from the outside.

Voice-Mail Tests

Test 1

Attempt to access an outside line using the "dial thru" feature on voice mail.

Test 2

Attempt to access an outside line through voice mail by dialing a voice-mail extension and transferring to outside line (9) or Site B tie-line (42).

Test 3

Determine process for issuing, monitoring, and terminating voice mailboxes.

Test 4

Determine if voice mailboxes could be penetrated from the outside by compromising the user's individual password.

SUMMARY

Establishing the proper high-technology-crime investigative functions set with the right priority is vital to establishing the high-technology-crime investigations program baseline. Generally, these functional processes should follow the function descriptions noted in the high-technology-crime investigator's charter of responsibilities. Those functions and processes that should be developed first are the investigative policies and procedures documentation, the establishment of a high-technology-crime investigations and prevention awareness function, investigative function, and noncompliance inquiry function.

High-technology-crime prevention surveys are much like risk assessments. However, the surveys concentrate exclusively on potential criminal activities.

NOTES

1. The physical security aspects of the requirements will have been coordinated with the applicable security department and information systems security managers, since they have the responsibility for the security of GEC assets. The high-technology-crime investigator's rationale was that security should be addressed in this document since it a basic protection process. The director of security agreed and approved the process.
2. Annabel Dodd, "When Going the Extra Mile Is Not Enough," *Network World* (April 12, 1993).
3. Brian Quinn, "Dialing for Dollars," *Corporate Computing* (May 1993).

Thanks to Investigator Jerry Swick for his input to the PBX section.

13

Sources, Networking, and Liaisons

Contacting sources of all types, networking, and forming liaisons with outside groups and government agencies are all excellent ways to

- Help solve crime cases.
- Obtain necessary information to keep up with the latest events in the profession.
- Share information with peers.
- Provide a community service by supporting the local law enforcement agencies and others.

Caution should be used in dealing with sources due to adverse political and legal ramifications. If done properly, a database is an excellent method of maintaining a "source file."

COLLECTING INFORMATION

As any good investigator knows, when it comes to getting information you usually are only as good as your sources. In government agencies at the local, state, and federal levels, the use of sources (also known by some as spies, informants, rats, finks) is not only practiced, it usually is encouraged. Law enforcement officers and investigators often receive extensive training in handling sources. The sources that work for local, state, or federal government agencies usually can be "leveraged" to assist investigators by providing information relevant to an ongoing investigation.

In the business world, the use of sources (covert) within a corporation generally not only is not condoned, it may be prohibited. However, some corporations require that all employees always cooperate and be truthful to those individuals conducting an inquiry or investigation. The high-technology-crime investigator/manager found that this was the policy at GEC.

The manager also determined the following other "pro-investigation" policies were in effect at GEC:

- Refusal to cooperate usually is grounds for immediate termination of employment.
- Lying to an investigator conducting a formal corporate investigation, if those lies are subsequently verified, also is grounds for immediate termination of employment.
- All GEC property, high technology, and other assets to be used only for corporate business. Therefore, GEC advises all new employees in writing that their e-mail, desks, and office areas are subject to search. The employee must acknowledge this in writing on a document maintained in each employee's personnel records. A main reason for security officers to conduct such searches is to help ensure that sensitive corporate documents are locked up.

Another advantage the high-technology investigators have at GEC, and in most businesses, is that the investigators do not have police powers. Therefore, no employee or any other person being interviewed by the investigator has any Fifth Amendment rights to self-incrimination. So, the investigator does not have to inform the interviewee or suspect that he or she may retain a lawyer, may refuse to answer if that answer may incriminate him or her, and so forth.

However, once a public law enforcement officer is involved in the investigation and that person asks you to find out certain information from a suspect or others, you may be considered by the courts as acting on behalf of the law enforcement officer; therefore, the interviewee's Fifth Amendment rights would apply.[1]

However, as good as that sounds to an investigator, in most corporations the human relations personnel or union representatives also may "impede" the conduct of your investigation as they often tend to side with the employees and not the best interests of the GEC. In fact they sometimes take on the attitude of a defense lawyer!

SOURCES

The word *sources* has a more "politically correct" connotation than the word *informants* or other similar words one can think of to describe someone who provides information. There are two primary types of sources: overt and covert. Overt sources are people who openly provide information to an investigator, newspapers, journals, radio, television, or generally any source of information that is available to the public. Covert sources are those people who provide information or other sources (spy satellites) whose identity is protected.

In GEC and most corporations, the use of people as covert sources generally is either prohibited or not condoned except under special circumstances. This also applies to the use of hidden cameras and microphones.

Internal Sources

Internal sources at GEC must be overt unless someone contacts a member of the high-technology-crime investigations unit and requests that his or her name not be used.

Those GEC overt sources that would be of use should first be identified by that person's position. This is because, no matter who holds that position, the person has access to information beneficial in conducting high-technology-crime investigations, noncompliance inquiries, and surveys. The positions would include at least the following:

- Manager of the audit organization.
- Manager of the employment organization.
- Manager of each major security organization.
- Security guards at specific posts.
- Manager of employee relations.
- Manager of the legal department.
- Manager of the accounting and finance organization.
- Manager of the procurement and purchasing organization.
- Manager of each information technology organization and specifically the manager of the information systems security organization.

You probably can add others to this list. As the manager of the high-technology-crime investigations unit, you should make it a point to

- Meet these people.
- Get to know them.
- Become familiar with their duties and responsibilities; for example, obtain copies of their organization charters.
- Identify how they can help your unit.
- Identify ways that your unit can help them.

As your unit matures and you have a few more high-technology-crime investigators, each should be assigned specific organizations to visit regularly when they are not conducting investigations, inquiries, briefings, surveys, and the like.

At the same time, as the unit manager, some overt sources must be handled personally because of their positions. In fact, some managers who have high opinions of themselves may not have time in their schedules for one of your investigators but always seem to find time for you. If that occurs, then maybe bringing a specific investigator along for several visits will help build a relationship between the two and your visits can then be reduced although never eliminated. That may be too obvious and adversely affect any relationship that you have built over the past months or years, but it may be worth a try.

As you receive information from other individuals who appear to be helpful and willing to assist at times, you would want to determine what type of information this person could have access to. Again, one must be careful to not appear to be recruiting informants.

When someone does contact, or has been contacted by, the investigator and does not want his or her name used for fear of reprisal, there should be a process to accommodate that. However, the accommodation should be coordinated with a member of the legal staff so that this protection can be handled properly. The process should be developed at one of the first coordination meetings held between the unit manager and the manager of the legal department. In that way, the investigator would be able to immediately explain to the source exactly what protection can be assured under what circumstances.

External Sources

External sources may be anyone outside GEC or anyone in GEC who is not considered a GEC employee, such as a consultant or subcontractor employee working in a GEC facility.

One should be very cautious in dealing with such sources. If the sources are overt, then there is less concern that someone may look on your activities as covertly recruiting informants. If the sources want their identify protected, one should be more cautious to not get tainted with accusations of source recruitment against employees of another company. Again, a process for handling these sources should already have been developed with the coordination of the legal department manager.

"Carding" Sources

Those individuals who provide high-technology-crime related information should be identified for future reference. In the "old days," source information was kept on index cards. In the information age, this information is better kept on the unit's source database, where searches and queries easily can be conducted to find sources that provided information in the past and work in the organization or may have knowledge of an incident being investigated. These sources also are good contacts to talk to before conducting a survey, as they can provide information as to the processes in place, how information flows, and so on.

Some of the basic information that should be placed in the database on a source is

- Name.
- Employee number or other identification numbers.
- Organization.
- Address.
- Telephone number.
- Fax number.
- E-mail address.
- Time, date, and location of first contact.
- Purpose of the contact.
- Results of the first contact.
- Name of investigator providing this input.

The information can be expanded and include more detail, such as social security number, date and place of birth, home address, and the like. However, caution must be used to ensure that this information can be shown to be necessary, in the event it becomes known to others outside the unit. Additionally, such information should have a short expiration date. If there is no contact with the source in a year, then the information should be deleted. However, such decisions are based on the culture and working environment within a business. It is a judgment call by the unit manager.

The database should also have fields for input each time source contact is made and information is provided. The fields should include basically the same information as noted above (e.g., time, date, and place of contact, information provided, and what investigator was contacted).

Also, all inquiries and high-technology-crime investigation suspects, crimes, and the like should be entered in the database. Later, this will provide an excellent tool for doing searches relative to unsolved crimes where the commonalties, patterns, and trends can be seen.

Classifying Reliability of Sources and the Accuracy of Their Information

Different sources have different motives for providing information and cooperating with investigators. A track record of source contacts maintained in the database provides that information; however, what is lacking is anything indicating the importance and validity of the information and the ability of the source to provide reliable information.

At GEC, the unit manager decided to include two fields in the record of each database that would assist in evaluating the source and the information provided. The unit manager devised the following two fields: the reliability of the source and the reliability of the source's information.

Each investigator who had significant contact (when a source provided meaningful information) with a source would be required to update the database with reliability information and code the source and information. The following codes were used for source reliability:

- Code 1: Always reliable.
- Code 2: Usually reliable.
- Code 3: Sometimes reliable.
- Code 4: Questionable reliability.
- Code 5: Has never been reliable.
- Code 6: Reliability unknown at this time.

Information provided by the source has proven to be

- Code A: Always accurate.
- Code B: Usually accurate.
- Code C: Sometimes accurate.
- Code D: Accuracy is always questionable.
- Code E: Never accurate.
- Code F: Accuracy of the information is unknown at this time.

By keeping the source database up to date, the investigators have a ready reference to reliable sources and are in a better position to judge the accuracy of the information they provide, based on past information. Although caution must be used in talking to sources and constant questioning of their motives is necessary, such a database will be a good reference point for investigators. The database should be checked prior to any interview with an individual to determine if he or she previously has provided information and whether the information was useful.

An example of ulterior motives is as follows. During a period of downsizing at GEC, several individuals made anonymous calls to the investigations unit and advised that an employee in a certain department was using the computer to operate a personal tax service.

Should an investigator, having received such information, immediately open an investigation? It is a difficult decision. If ignored, it may continue indefinitely—if the allegations are true. If an investigation is opened, it may be based on a false accusation. The person calling may have done so to make a peer look bad so that the person under investigation would be a more likely candidate for layoff than one who was not under investigation. Remember that, during downsizing, desperate measures sometimes are taken by desperate people.

NETWORKING

As discussed in a previous chapter but worth mentioning again, it is imperative that the investigator continuously network with peers met at conferences, association meetings, or even talking to someone while on a plane. These individuals also should be identified in a database or just by placing their business cards in a file and categorizing them by line of business, such as computer consultant, vendor, or government employee. In today's information environment, one can obtain a great deal of free information, advice, and warnings of high-technology crimes and criminals through these contacts.

Most of these individuals will have e-mail addresses. Contacting them periodically via e-mail and telephone calls is a very cost-effective way to gather information and keep abreast in your profession.

We recommend contacting these individuals periodically to determine "what's new." It is surprising how much relative information can be gathered using this cost-effective method. Often, the information gathered could provide the source and information that may call for a high-technology-crime prevention survey targeting a particular process or high-technology device or other actions.

For example, if a new social engineering technique were being use by phreakers to gain access to a corporation's PBX, that information could be sent out immediately in a GEC e-mail message. The message would warn the employees of such a technique and advise them to report any such attempts but not to provide the information or action that the phreaker has requested.

In fact, this happened at GEC and was the basis for a new checklist given to employees. The unit investigators devised a short checklist, similar to the one provided by the Security Department and used in the event a caller made a bomb threat. The checklist included similar information as on the bomb checklist about the person calling being male, female, background noises, so forth. This one provided not only a list of some of the social engineering techniques used to obtain user IDs, passwords, and PBX access but also reporting procedures. It called for the person receiving the call to transfer the call to the high-technology-crime investigations unit under one of several ruses, so the phreaker would think that the call was being transferred to allow access per the phreaker's request. The high-technology-crime investigator then had several options, such as gather more details to identify the phreaker and determine the phreaker's objective.

This checklist and the information provided were expanded and included in the updated awareness briefings given employees. Subsequently, the investigators conducted a survey by making social engineering calls to selected organizations as a quality check. When conducting such a test, the objective is not to embarrass anyone but to ensure that a high-technology-crime prevention process was in place and working. Therefore, any report should not include the names of individuals contacted. One of the fastest ways to lose the respect and support of employees is to conduct such a covert test and then place the names of those that fail into a report. The manager would then in all probability contact that employee and counsel him or her.

However, if this survey was done again after six months or a year and the same person provides the information in violation of the policy, then the employee should be contacted. The employee's manager should be advised, and with the employee's manager present, the issue should be discussed using a briefing and teaching method in lieu of a counseling method. For those who object to this "soft" approach, remember in the business world you succeed by gaining the trust and support of the employees. After all, you don't have a badge and a gun to provide that support.

LIAISON

According to one dictionary, the word *liaison* means "close bond; communication between groups." For GEC's high-technology-crime investigations unit it means just that: communicating between the unit and local, state, and federal criminal justice agencies.

Such liaison always is in the best interest of GEC as part of its involvement in the community. In addition, sharing information with law enforcement agencies on high-technology-crime and crime-prevention matters will be of mutual benefit to both groups. Again, membership and active support of your local High Technology Crime Investigation Association will provide the opportunity to build that relationship of trust and support.

As with other sources of information, the individuals with whom you come in contact should be entered into the database. Another advantage of such a database is that the source is not lost if an investigator leaves the unit.

NOTE

1. It is recommended that the corporate investigator check with the company's legal staff, since a court decision could change this process.

14

High-Technology-Crime Investigation Unit's Metrics Management System

INTRODUCTION TO METRICS

This chapter is designed to provide basic guidance necessary for the development of a metrics methodology to understand what, why, when, and how the high-technology-crime investigation workload can be measured. Using the fictitious company (GEC) and functions previously described, a metrics system will be developed. The chapter includes a discussion of how to use the metrics to brief management, justify budget expenses, and use trend analyses to develop a more efficient and effective high-technology-crime investigations program. Metrics management is a useful process for managing any organization. The information can be analyzed and used for resource allocation decisions, determining the success of the high-technology-crime prevention program, justifying budgets, and marketing the unit's success in meeting objectives.

To begin to understand how to use metrics to support management of a high-technology-crime investigations program, it is important to understand what is meant by *metrics*.

WHAT IS A HIGH-TECHNOLOGY-CRIME INVESTIGATION METRIC?

For our purposes, a *metric* is defined as a standard of measurement using quantitative, statistical, or mathematical analyses. A high-technology-crime investigation metric is the application of quantitative, statistical, or mathematical analyses to measure the high-technology-crime investigation unit's functional trends and workload.

WHAT IS HIGH-TECHNOLOGY-CRIME INVESTIGATION METRICS MANAGEMENT?

In this case, metrics management is the use of metrics in managing of a high-technology-crime investigations unit and crime-prevention program. Metrics are used to support managerial tasks such as justifying the unit's position on budget matters, demonstrating the cost effectiveness of decisions, determining the impact of downsizing on providing service and support to customers, and so forth.

The primary process to collect metrics is as follows:

1. Identify each high-technology-crime investigation function.[1]
2. Determine what drives that function, such as labor (number of people or hours used), policies, procedures, or systems.
3. Establish a metrics collection process, which could be as simple as filling out a log for later summary and analysis. Using a spreadsheet that can automatically incorporate high-technology-crime investigation statistics into graphs is the preferred method. The graphs make it easier for the manager to use the metrics to support management decisions, for briefings, and the like.

The decision whether to collect statistics on a particular high-technology-crime investigation function should be decided by answering the following questions:

- Why should these statistics be collected?
- What specific statistics will be collected?
- How will these statistics be collected?
- When will these statistics be collected?
- Who will collect these statistics?
- Where (at what point in the function's process) will these statistics be collected?

By answering these questions, the manager can better determine whether a metrics collection process should be established for a particular function. This thought-out process will be useful in helping explain the need for collecting these statistics to the investigations staff or management, if necessary. It also helps the manager decide whether to maintain those metrics after a specific period of time.

All metrics should be reviewed, evaluated, and reconsidered for continuation at the end of each year. Remember that, although the collection of the metrics information will help the manager better manage the investigation responsibilities, a cost is incurred in the collection and maintenance of them, in terms of resources (people who collect, enter, process, print, and maintain the metrics as well as the hardware and software used to support that effort).

The chart format and colors sometimes are dictated by management; however, the options of what type of chart is best for analysis or presentation to management is probably up to the unit manager.

The manager should experiment with various types of line, bar, and pie charts. We recommend keeping the charts simple and easy to understand. Remember the old saying: A picture is worth a thousand words. The charts should need very little explanation.

If the charts will be used for briefings, the briefing should only comment on the different trends. The reasons for this are to present the material clearly and concisely and not get bogged down in details that distract from the objective of the charts.

One way to determine if the message the charts are trying to portray is clear is to have someone look at them and describe what the chart "says." If that is what the chart is suppose to portray, then no changes are needed. If not, the manager should ask what the chart seems to represent and what leads the person to that conclusion. The manager then can rework the chart until the message is clear and exactly what the manager wants it to show.

HIGH-TECHNOLOGY-CRIME INVESTIGATIONS DRIVERS

An organization has three major high-technology-crime investigation drivers; that is, those things that increase or decrease the workload:

1. The number of high-technology devices that fall under the unit's investigative purview. The more high-technology equipment and devices support GEC, the higher is the probability that someone will use one as a tool to violate rules or laws.
2. The number of GEC employees. The more employees at GEC, statistically more employees will violate GEC rules or laws.
3. The number of customer requests for crime-prevention surveys.

These metrics are worth tracking because they drive the number of hours that the high-technology-crime investigations staff must expend in meeting their responsibilities.

As the workload fluctuates so does the number of staff members and amount of budget required. For example, assume that GEC is downsizing—not an unusual occurrence, which all managers eventually will face in their careers. If the manager knows that GEC will downsize its workforce by 10%, assuming that all members of the workforce use high-technology equipment, again not an unusual occurrence, the workload also should decrease by about 10%. This may cause the manager to also downsize (lay-off staff members) by approximately 10%.

However, the downsizing, whether it is more or less than the GEC average, should be based on the related high-technology-crime investigations workload. The investigations drivers are metrics that can help the manager estimate the impact of the GEC downsizing on the high-technology-crime investigations budget and organization. The metrics associated with that effort also can justify downsizing decisions to GEC management, including possibly downsizing by 5% instead of 10%.

In the case of downsizing, more employees probably will be frustrated and angry and may want to hurt GEC or in some way use the high technology available to violate policy or to perpetrate a crime. Therefore, it is quite possible that the workload will increase for some time period. The metrics-based charts could show upper management that downsizing within the unit was not the best decision to make at this time. However, after the current downsizing efforts were concluded, the workload should then level off at (ideally) a lower level. At that time, downsizing within the unit could take place.

The manager must remember that, even though metrics are a tool to support many of the manager's decisions and actions, they are not perfect. Therefore, the manager must make some assumptions relative to the statistical data to be collected. That is fine. The manager must remember that metrics is not rocket science, only a tool to help take better-informed actions and make better-informed decisions. So never get carried away with the hunt for "perfect metrics."

The spreadsheets and graphs used for metrics management can become very complicated with links to other spreadsheets, elaborate three-D graphics, and the like. That may work for some, but the manager should consider the KISS (Keep it simple, Stupid) principle when collecting and maintaining metrics. This is especially true if the manager is just getting started and has no or very little experience with metrics.

One may find that the unit's project leaders, who are developing the "automated statistical collection" application, are spending more hours developing an application that never seems to work just quite right than it takes to calculate the statistics by hand. Automation for the sake of automation is not a good idea.

Also important from a managerial viewpoint is that all charts, statistics, and spreadsheets be done in a standard format. This is necessary so that they can be ready at all times for reviews and briefings to upper management. The standard is indicative of a professional organization and one that operates as a focused team.

Those managers who are new to the management position or management in general may think that this is somewhat ridiculous. In the business environment, standards, consistency, and indications of teamwork always are a concern of management. Just grin and bear it. Pick your "fights" for something more important.

The job of getting and maintaining management support is hard enough. Another negative impact concerning nonconformance of format will be that the charts will be the focus of attention and not the information on them. By the time the nonconformance to briefing charts' standards is discussed, management already will have formed a negative bias.

Of course, the number, type, collection methods, and so on that the manager uses will depend on the environment and the manager's ability to cost-effectively collect and maintain the metrics. The following example shows general metrics that may be used, based on the duties, responsibilities, and functions of the GEC high-technology-crime investigations unit manager.

EXAMPLE

As an manager, you decided that it would be a good idea to use metrics to track the number of employees, the number of inquiries, and the number of investigations conducted over time. You have gone through the analytical process to make that decision based on answering the how, what, why, when, who, and where questions noted previously:

- Why should these statistics be collected? To determine the ratio of employees to the workload, so personnel requirements could be forecasted over time.
- What specific statistics will be collected? Total number of GEC employees, noncompliance inquiries, and investigations.
- How will these statistics be collected? The total number of paid employees will be taken from the human resources department's master personnel database file. The total number of noncompliance inquiries (NCI) and total number of investigations will be gathered by the unit coordinator from the unit's NCI database file.
- When will these statistics be collected? The statistics will be compiled on the first business day of each month and incorporated into the high-technology-crime investigation-drivers' graph, maintained on the unit's administrative microcomputer.
- Who will collect these statistics? The statistics will be collected, entered, and maintained by the unit's coordinator.
- Where (at what point in the function's process) will these statistics be collected? The collection of statistics will be based on the information available and on file in the high-technology-crime investigations unit's database at close of business on the last business day of the month.

The figures that follow are samples of various high-technology-crime metrics charts, shown in various formats, covering various time periods. On occasion, we have used more than 40 different metrics charts to track and analyze NCIs and investigations by organization, type of incident, losses, patterns, and trends by time and date, and other metric charts specifically requested by executive management.

Figure 14–1 shows the drivers for the unit. However, something is wrong with the chart. Do you know what it is? All the information was properly entered. The problem with using a bar graph for this chart is that the number of employees is very high compared to the number of NCIs and investigations. Therefore, the two bars are so small that they are almost impossible to view. The solution is to use a line chart and a ratio of employees to NCIs and investigations. That way the trend lines can be clearly visible. After all, trend lines usually are more important, not the daily, weekly, or monthly numbers.

Figure 14–2 provides the unit manager with trend indicators. When looking at these trends, the manager must question why the NCIs continue

- The number of GEC employees have increased based on GEC's need to rapidly build up the work force to handle the new contract work.
- The number of noncompliance inquiries have increased during that same time period.
- The number of crime investigations have increased during that same period of time.
- This increased workload has caused some delays in completing the inquiries and investigations in the 30-day period that was set as the goal.
- The ratio of incidents compared to the total number of employees indicates:
  – Personnel may not be getting sufficient information during their new-hire briefings
  – The personnel being hired are not being thoroughly screened priot to hiring

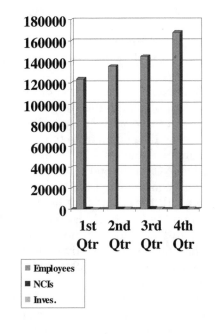

Figure 14–1　The drivers for the unit.

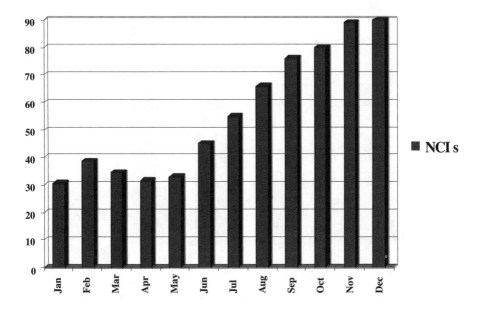

Figure 14–2   The total number of NCIs completed during 1998.

to increase? Is the ratio to employees still the same? If so, there may be systemic causes for the NCIs. The goal would be to eliminate these causes. A project plan could be developed and a team effort between the training, awareness, and human resources/security orientation personnel could try to determine if the information provided the new employees is adequate. The NCIs would be analyzed to determine

- The reason for each employee's noncompliance.
- The position and organization of the employee.
- The employee's seniority date.
- Identification of the patterns.
- Main offenses.

This information would be provided to the project team. Based on that information, the briefings would be updated and more emphasis placed on those areas that caused the majority of problems.

The information in Figure 14–3 can be used to establish another project, similar to that on the NCIs, assuming that the chart shows a lower ratio of investigations to employees.

The numerous types of charts can be a great tool for management (see Figures 14–4 through 14–6). They include the bar charts, pie charts, and line charts. The charts can be monthly, quarterly, weekly, or annually. The timeliness of the charts should depend on the manager's need

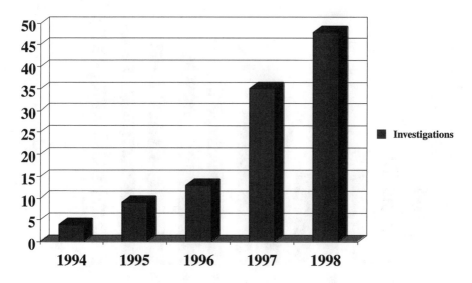

Figure 14–3   The number of investigations over a five-year period.

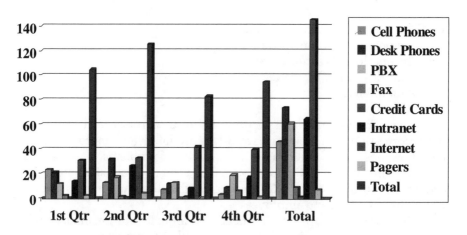

Figure 14–4   The number of investigations by type of high technology.

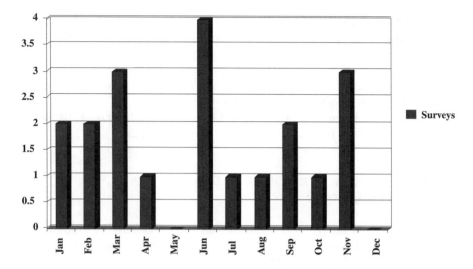

Figure 14–5   The number of crime-prevention surveys conducted each month in 1998.

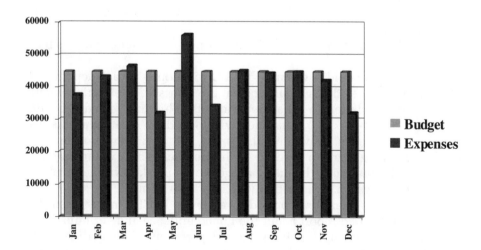

Figure 14–6   Expenses versus budget.

for the information. The key to the charts is to look more at trends than monthly numbers. The goal is to continue to maintain and improve on good trends. Negative trends should be analyzed for systemic causes and plans implemented to reverse the trends. The charts then could be monitored to determine if the changes caused the reversal of the negative trend. If not, new analyses and rethinking are called for.

At the end of the year, don't forget to reevaluate the charts to make sure they are useful. If not, don't hesitate to delete them.

REPORTS TO GEC MANAGEMENT BASED ON THE METRICS

The metrics charts can be used to develop an executive briefing to show the "status of GEC" from a high-technology-crime investigations and crime-prevention viewpoint. For example,

- The total number of surveys conducted, broken down by department.
- The total number of noncompliance inquiries conducted, broken down by department.
- The total number of investigations conducted, broken down by department.
- A profile of the employees (no personal identification for privacy reasons) involved, including job title, age, seniority date. and other meaningful information.
- The amount of high technology and information lost, stolen, or not accounted for, in terms of dollar value and amounts.
- The number of high-technology equipment, devices, and the like recovered.
- The dollar amount of recoveries from fines, confiscation, and the like.

This report would be given to the CEO with copies to each department head. The vice presidents would look at the charts and determine where they stood in relation to other departments. This undoubtedly would cause the "worst-looking" department vice president to gather all the department's managers, show them the report, and advise them of the goal for the upcoming year—to have the lowest number in each of the negative categories. Furthermore, the unit manager could breakdown the numbers further, to show each organization within a department.

This is one example of providing a service to GEC management by providing a detailed report about the noncompliance and "criminal" investigations conducted involving their departments. The analyses will include the estimated losses in time, money, and productivity and recommendations as to what management can do to eliminate or minimize the problems. The vice presidents are not investigators, they need your expert advice and assistance. The public relations benefits of such annual reports are tremendous, if properly done.

NOTE

1. Each function is assumed to cost time, money, and equipment to perform.

15

Final Thoughts, Problems, and Issues

High-technology-crime investigators usually come from a security, police investigator, or law enforcement background. Working in the world of private industry or, to a great extent, in a government or public agency, as stated more than once in this book, one must understand that the badge and gun are not available to assist you to get the information you want. In addition, you must think from a business perspective when working for a corporation. What you do or don't do, can affect the bottom line—profits. So, keep that in mind if you are entering the private sector from the public sector.

When you do something the wrong way, the profession suffers and whoever replaces you will suffer. Whether you remain or are replaced, consider this: Yours is a service and support job. You are there to support the needs of GEC or whatever business you work for. The high technology, information, and processes are there to support that business. They belong to the owners of the business: the private individuals, consortium, holding company, or stockholders.

Regardless of ownership, the owners have entrusted executive management and delegated to other management the decisions on how that business will be run. Decisions related to security, controls, investigations, inquiries, and disciplinary actions to be taken against violators of the law or business policy are theirs to make. You serve at their request and you are the specialist, their in-house consultant. They have gotten along without you before your employment and can get along without you again. The business is there to make a profit for its owners—*increase stockholder value* is the term coined today for such objectives.

If you recall. earlier in this book, GEC was identified as a global corporation with plants and offices in Jakarta, Indonesia, Hsinchu, Taiwan, and London, England. You are in charge of the high-technology-crime investigations unit and lead GEC's high-technology-crime prevention program.

On Wednesday, you are called to a meeting with your boss, the director of security, and asked, "Now that you have been here for a few weeks, how do you like your job?" You think it is a great opportunity and tell the director how much you enjoy the position.

Then the director asks you, "What are you going to do to handle investigations, incidents, and surveys at those overseas locations?" You probably have not thought about this because you are too busy developing the processes, putting together a unit, recruiting investigators, writing the unit charters, identifying functions, coordinating your paperwork through the bureaucratic maze, attending meetings, and performing hundreds of other tasks that you never dreamed of when you were hired.

The director tells you that a tour is being put together for the CEO and all directors to visit the overseas facilities, to "show the flag," so to speak. The CEO had asked the director of security how the new unit was shaping up and planned to handle the international facilities. The director said that he (the CEO) would like a briefing on the new unit, its processes, and its goals, including the international facilities. You are directed to prepare a briefing to show the director on Friday morning. The director reasoned that together you can "work the bugs out" since you are new at this and would be giving the briefing to the CEO and the GEC board of directors at 9 o'clock Monday morning—and, by the way, "Pack your bags because you're coming along. We leave next Wednesday, first to Taiwan. Sorry for the late notice. I just found out myself. See my secretary about your reservations, and the travel plans on your way out."

The director then said that another issue had to be dealt with as soon as you return from the trip, if not before. The director advised that, when talking to the CEO, the name of the unit—using the *investigations, crime prevention*, and similar words—gave the impression, according to the CEO and the board of directors, that crime was rampant and GEC had a bunch of criminals working for it. Also, from a public relations (i.e., the general public and stockholders) viewpoint, it was probably not the right name for the unit. The board agreed on the concept of an investigations unit but left the details (e.g., the name of the unit and its charter) to lower management.

The CEO and the board of directors agree that GEC needs such a unit, but the image issue must be resolved. They decided that the entire program boiled down to ethical behavior on the part of GEC employees. Therefore, the unit would be called the *ethics office* and you the *ethics office manager*. You would wear "two hats." As ethics office manager, you would report to the vice president of human resources for all ethics-related issues and matters involving noncompliance inquiries. However, in all investigative matters and the crime-prevention program, you would continue to report to the director of security.

As the newly appointed ethics manager, you are directed to redo the charter, review outstanding hiring advertisements, and hire from inside GEC someone to concentrate solely on ethics issues. You are to provide a short-term project to accomplish that objective within 30 days of return from the trip. "And, by the way," the director went on to say, "be sure that the ethics process includes an ethics hot line, which can be used by employees to call in anonymously, if they so desire, and provide information about unethical conduct. Also, be sure to get with the training folks and the awareness program people to change the briefings and also develop an ethics-training program. We can discuss the details on the 15-hour flight to Taiwan. Thanks for coming in. See you at the airport."

How would you handle such a challenge? If you never have been involved in the field of ethics programs, the first place to start would be e-mailing your contacts and networking with those who have such programs. Ask them to send you all they can on the topic, such as their training material, briefings, and everything else on the subject—plus as much advice as possible. If the networking peers do not do the ethics work themselves, ask them for the name, phone number, and e-mail address of their ethics person, plus an introduction to them for you. This is a perfect example of the usefulness of networking. Of course, you must promise to provide them a copy of everything you develop. Be sure to keep that promise, as you never know when you will need additional help.

Also, on your Internet search engine, type in the word *ethics* and start collecting information. Download the information to your notebook computer for reading on the trip. After all, it will be a long trip and, if properly used, traveling on the plane can give you enough uninterrupted time not only for reading the material you collected but also for reengineering your organization. Be sure to consider outsourcing some of the work and purchasing some of the training documentation (after coordination with the training and awareness program personnel, of course). It may be cheaper. For example, the Association of Certified Fraud Examiners (ACFE) (at http://www.acfe.org) can provide the ethics hot line service for GEC at a reasonable cost.

SUMMARY

Always be flexible, be prepared for change, welcome it as a new challenge and an opportunity to expand your experiences and knowledge. If you cannot adapt, your career not only will be short-lived but also a disappointment. One never knows when opportunity knocks. You now also report to the vice president of human resources. The restructure of the unit opens up the possibility of a promotion to the position of *director* of ethics. Remember the old sayings, "Every dark cloud has a silver lining" and "If you can't stand the heat, get out of the kitchen."

PART III

High-Technology Crimes and Investigations

OBJECTIVE

The objective of this part is to provide a sampling of actual high-technology crime. These crimes happen daily around the world. Although the purpose of this book is to provide a basic overview of the profession of high-technology-crime investigator and an overview of the global information environment in which the investigator will work, it would not be complete without at least an overview of investigating high-technology crime.

- Chapter 16. "High-Technology Crime: Case Summaries." The purpose of this chapter is to provide a range of cases that illustrate types of incidents that may be encountered under the general grouping of high-technology crimes. Although not exhaustive, the cases provide a sense of the many challenges that face high-technology-crime investigators in both the public and private sectors.
- Chapter 17. "Investigating High-Technology Crime." This chapter provides an overview of important concepts associated with "computer forensics." It describes the potential sources of evidence available on the typical microcomputer, how to conduct a search for evidence, and how to conduct the search in a systematic and effective manner.

16

High-Technology Crime
Case Summaries

WHAT CONSTITUTES HIGH-TECHNOLOGY CRIME?

The range of offenses that may be investigated under the general umbrella of high-technology crime is very wide. The following examples are actual high-technology-crime and -fraud cases that have taken place in the United States and other countries. They are provided to show the broad spectrum of high-technology crime vis-à-vis types of criminals, damage, dollar value, and other factors.

As you examine the synopses of these cases, consider the implications for the design and operation of the specific high-technology-crime investigation unit and prevention program:

- Which local, federal, or state agency should lead the investigation in each case?
- Which enforcement agencies have dealt effectively with the specific type of crime or offense?
- What laws apply to the proscribed activities?
- What specific elements of the crime must be proven to use those statutes?
- What investigative strategies, tools, and techniques will be necessary to successfully investigate and prosecute through the criminal justice system today and in the future?

PROPERTY CRIME

Citibank Attacked by Russian Hacker

In 1994, a Russian successfully penetrated the systems of Citibank and allegedly stole $10 million. Citibank subsequently admitted to a loss of less than $1 million (*The Business Journal of Charlotte*, October 13, 1998).

Comments

In what many see as the prototypical high-technology crime of the coming millennium, a small team of Russians, under the leadership of mathematician Andre Levin, systematically penetrated a number of Citibank computer systems in ways that allowed them to transfer out almost $11 million over the course of nearly a year. However, Citibank was able to recover all but $400,000 of the stolen loot. Many aspects of this incident are troubling: The attacks lasted almost a year and were initiated from St. Petersburg (formerly Leningrad), Russia, probably at the instigation of a Russian Mafia (organized crime group), by a computer-savvy member of that nation's impoverished intelligentsia—all these are disturbing elements. Although Russian police agencies and U.S. law enforcement cooperated in this case, Levin was "apprehended" in the United Kingdom, not in Russia. One can only speculate as to whether law enforcement globally will enjoy future success against other sophisticated cyberthieves if Russia fails to sustain its current experiment in democracy or if rogue states (such as North Korea, Iraq, or Libya) sanction such crimes.

Counterfeit Computer Cards

Federal agents arrested two Southern California residents for allegedly producing and selling counterfeit versions of Adaptec Inc.'s computer boards. The federal investigations and subsequent arrests followed a lawsuit filed by Adaptec in 1996, which claimed that a company known as Nitro Link Corp. had been counterfeiting their computer boards in 1995 and 1996.

Comments

Counterfeiting and knockoffs are common in the garment and toy industries, but even in high technology, the enterprising criminal may find a niche. The potential to manufacture counterfeits offshore and distribute in-country at a lower cost can be an attractive combination. The popular "computer swap meets" and flea markets in many large urban areas provide a convenient vehicle for distribution of such goods as "discounted" originals. In such locations, the buyers' primary motivation is likely to be price, and they may have little or no knowledge of the identifying characteristics of the original manufactured devices. The investigation unit should consider the elements of the offense to be proven and structure its efforts accordingly. Surveillance, arranged buys, and other techniques may prove useful to counter efforts to feed the marketplace inferior copies of original devices.

China's First Cyber Bank Robbers

China arrested its first suspected cyber bank robbers in late October 1998 after two brothers allegedly hacked into a bank network system and stole 260,000 yuan ($31,000) in the eastern province of Jiangsu. The older brother, an accountant at the bank, had mastered the entire computer network (Reuters, October 22, 1998).

Comments

Even China, which had less that 1 million Internet users in 1998, reported over 200 cases of cybercrime over the preceding two years. To head off what could be dangerous precedent, China has apparently decided to deal very harshly with cybercriminals. Subsequent information (Reuters, "Chinese Hackers Get Death," December 28, 1998) indicates that these two criminals were sentenced to be executed for their efforts. Well, at least that solves the recidivism issue!

Computer Bank Hacker Arrested in South Russia

A bank employee was arrested in a southern Russian city in the first reported attempt in the Rostov region to rob a bank by penetrating its computer network. The network penetration could have cost the bank tens of thousands of dollars, but security experts noticed the hacker's program and blocked him (Itar-Tass, October 29, 1998).

Comments

Many, if not most, cybercrimes tend to be "inside jobs," as the employees working with the systems are well positioned to learn and exploit areas of vulnerability in applications and networked systems. When developing an investigation plan for similar incidents, it tends to be very productive to start with insiders who have motive and access to the environment and, only after eliminating them, consider outsiders, who may include former employees or those with a close relationship to knowledgeable insiders.

Truckers Use Internet Crime Reporting System
to Combat Cargo Thieves

To combat sophisticated thieves, the trucking industry has introduced "Cargo Tips," a World Wide Web-based cargo theft reporting system, providing theft reports, trends and investigative reports, bulletin boards, lists of stolen goods, and e-mail alerts. Law enforcement agencies are given full access to the system at no charge (*Nando Times*, December 1, 1998).

Comments

Proper and creative use of the Internet and modern databases can help even the odds for law enforcement and private sector investigators. In addition to information sharing, the application of various new technologies, including real-time global positioning system tracking of vehicles and satellite communications can reduce the vulnerability of expensive shipments. Food presently is the most popular target for cargo thieves, since it is easy to resell and difficult to trace the origin of many commodities. Consumer electronics, expensive clothing, computers and computer parts, and perfumes and cosmetics also are very popular targets. According to the Transportation Loss Prevention and Security Council of the American Trucking Associations, the hottest regions for cargo theft are the New York–New Jersey corridor, Southern California, and Southern Florida. Both Memphis and Chicago are becoming increasingly popular. An international airport and ports, which allow stolen products to quickly leave the country, are key factors in the popularity of these regions. Other factors that encourage the cargo thieves are the low priority these crimes enjoy for police investigation and the foreign origin of many of the criminals.

Since most police departments put violent crimes ahead of property theft, cargo thieves rarely are caught and even more rarely severely punished. Since many of the most successful thieves are foreigners, it is a simple matter of returning to their homeland if the environment gets too "hot" for them in the United States. Often the thieves belong to organized crime groups, typically from South or Central America. The work is highly profitable, since the gangs are often able to obtain 90% or more of the retail price of the items. Some organized crime groups actually go so far as to provide drivers to trucking companies, especially during the Christmas holiday season, when drivers are in short supply. One clue to this is when the same driver is involved in multiple trucks that are robbed. Diligent preemployment screening of personnel is a "low-tech" measure that may reduce the potential for repeat offenders working at multiple companies.

COPYRIGHT AND TRADEMARK CASES

Judge Blocks PC Recording Device

A federal judge temporarily banned production of a handheld device that can download and play pirated computer music files. The company is prohibited from producing the portable MP3 player until the judge decides whether the device violates the 1992 federal Audio Home Recording Act, which is designed to prevent piracy (*San Jose Mercury News*, October 18, 1998).

Comments

The competition between owners of intellectual property rights and digital technology that promises to abuse those rights will continue. If devices such as the MP3 players are ruled illegal in the United States, the demand for black-market copies imported from overseas likely will increase the customs' caseload. If the devices are found not to be in violation of the relevant laws, then controlling the distribution of pirated audio files via the "warez" network of underground crackers will challenge corporate and industry association intellectual property protection departments.

INFORMATION CRIME

The *New York Times* Suffers a Website Hack

The worst hack in the history of the *New York Times* disrupted service for over nine hours. The group Hacking for Girlies claimed responsibility for the incident, which was aimed at writer John Markoff, coauthor of a book about Kevin Mitnick, and Carolyn Meinel, the author of a book on hacking (CNET News.com. September 16, 1998).

Mexican Hackers Speak Out

A trio of Mexican computer hackers declared electronic war on the Mexican state. They have hacked the Finance Ministry's website and vowed to publicize bank accounts, cellular phone conversations, and e-mail addresses. "We protest with the weapons we have and those weapons are computers," said LoTek, one of the hackers (Reuters, August 5, 1998).

Comments

The websites of companies and government organizations are tempting targets for activists, as well as criminals, for their particular political, economic, or social agenda. Investigating incidents is becoming more difficult as the criminals make improved use of the global network to screen their physical identities and locations. Computer and network security measures may not be rigorous enough to prevent or detect such activities, which can make efforts to investigate cybercrimes, whether committed for profit or politics, nearly impossible. This is especially true when forced to seek assistance in other nations, where computer-literate law enforcement resources may be nonexistent.

Hackers Get 5,000 Accounts

Computer specialists at Stanford University are investigating the theft of 5,000 passwords, most from student accounts, which occurred in mid-October 1998. The hackers logged on through Sweden and Canada but may have been based in other countries. The hackers planted a "sniffer" program to steal the logon passwords.

Comments

First, note that the assessed point of origination of the intrusion is outside the United States. Whether the intruders were American nationals or foreigners, they used cyberspace to cover their tracks and protect their identities. Second, at the time of the incident, President Clinton's daughter was a student at Stanford University, so a possible motive could have been to learn about her for nefarious purposes. More likely though is that the intruders intended to give or sell the accounts to other criminal users, who could then use them to commit other crimes. Stolen accounts often are used as a channel to dispense pirated software, or other criminal digital "warez," such as child pornography. Universities are an attractive target for these purposes because, by nature, they are a very open environment.

Airport Hack Raises Flags

A Massachusetts teenage hacker, who penetrated a local telephone service, temporarily disabled a regional airport's telecommunication links, cut vital services to the airport's control tower, and prevented incoming planes from turning on runway lights. The hacker confessed and obtained a plea bargain from the U.S. Justice Department (http://www.news.com/News/Item, March 19, 1998).

Comments

Although the case was settled quickly, the limited punishment meted out to the youth in this matter likely will do little to deter others. Loss of landing lights at night or during bad weather could induce pilot error and a subsequent crash. It seems that the young hacker did not deliberately target the airport, but the results of his hacking had potential consequences well beyond his intent. Similarly, investigators dealing with denial of services or other computer or networking crimes must consider that the target so affected, which triggered their investigative activities, may have been an unintentional rather than deliberate target.

Hacker Jailed for Three Years

The man who pleaded guilty to hacking Internet service provider AusNet, stealing, and publishing subscriber credit card numbers was sentenced to three years in prison, the harshest sentence ever for a federal hacking crime in Australia. AusNet lost $9.5 million in revenue as customers fled after the incident (*The Australian Financial Review*, March 28, 1998)

Comments

The consequences of this incident were even more serious than the direct revenues lost. AusNet had expected to raise at least $200 million in an initial public offering on the NASDAQ stock exchange, but after this incident, the offer became impossible and AusNet eventually went bankrupt. The perpetrator claimed to be operating out of "perverse altruism" in an effort to publicize the weaknesses and failures of the service provider. As customers lost confidence, they fled the service to competitors. In this case, it does not appear that competitors directly encouraged or supported the intrusions; however, in future incidents, "hired hackers" may attempt to discredit or disrupt commercial rivals to the benefit of their employers.

'Net Called a Boon to Hate Groups

The number of hate groups in the United States rose by 20% in 1997. According to the Southern Poverty Law Center, the Internet makes it easier to preach intolerance and recruit new members. There now are 474 hate groups in the country (Courtney Macavinta, CNET News.com, March 3, 1998).

Comments

Investigators should keep in mind the unfortunate significance of the Internet as a breeding ground for racist and other hateful groups. Many groups at every end of the political spectrum are adept at leveraging the communication potential of the new medium to their objectives. Searching a suspect's microcomputer and reviewing the browser cache and history files may reveal a pattern of access to such locations that can be very useful in establishing motive for racially directed threats or actions.

Government Employees Selling Private Information

Poor computer security allowed a ring of West African credit card thieves working with Social Security Administration employees to steal records on 20,000 Americans. The thieves stole credit cards and then obtained the person's Social Security number, date of birth, and mother's maiden name to activate the card (Scripps-Howard News, http://www.freecongress.org/cfcl/latest.htm).

Comments

The government employees involved in this scheme, which occurred in 1996, were paid only about $10–50 for each file. However, for that relatively low cost, thieves were able to obtain more than $70 million using the stolen credit cards before the scheme was ended. Twenty-seven people were charged in 1996 and 1997 in this case. The computer systems exploited provided excellent audit trails and documented all access to the records. However, managers were too busy to check the audit logs until after the scam was discovered by other means. Few organizations today have effective programs for dealing with infiltration or exploitation by organized criminal gangs, especially those with a transnational base of operation. Audit trails and other activity logs may be essential to prove the involvement of the insiders working in collusion with outsiders but should not be the only method to alert management to the existence of possible abuse.

INFORMATION ESPIONAGE

CIA Uses Hacker Technology

It has been reported that the U.S. CIA has used hacker technology to disrupt international money transfers and other forms of financial activities of Arab businessmen who support the activities of alleged terrorists (*The Washington Post*, September 14, 1997).

Comments

Other reports subsequently identified the target of this "cyberwar" attack as the Saudi terrorist Osama bin Laden. The danger from an investigation perspective is that "innocent" bystanders may get caught in the crossfire between the national intelligence services and their opponents. Many national intelligence services and even some military forces allegedly have begun "practicing" for the next major war by using technology and tools originally developed by the hackers and crackers of the computer underground. With the resources of such powerful organizations behind them, it is likely that the attack tools have been substantially improved. As with any weapon, there will be pressure to use the information weapon when, as it seems in this case, national policy objectives may be achieved by their use. However, as their use becomes more common, we can expect a small number of those trained in national services and military techniques to "cross over" to work for criminal gain, either personally or as "mercenaries" on behalf of well-financed transnational organized crime groups.

TELECOMMUNICATIONS FRAUD

Phone Scam Against Police Departments

A police department was victimized by a phone scam when it received calls in which the caller, claiming to be a phone company employee testing lines, requested that the person receiving the call transfer the person by dialing 9-0-#. Unsuspecting staff members transferred the calls, which incurred long distance charges ("POLICE-L: The Police Discussion List," posting by Sgt. J. J. DeStefano, Suffolk, Virginia, Police Department).

Comments

Theft of long distance and cellular telecommunication services is a huge and thriving black market. Even police departments have been duped into providing long distance services to criminals. Corporations and large companies are at high risk of this same scam and consistently lose to the con artists who prey on gullible telephone users. Organizations should establish a system for tracking and responding to incidents of telecommunication abuse. The company security or telecommunications department should review all call accounting records, especially long distance international calls and cellular phone calls to ensure that patterns of abuse are quickly detected. Close cooperation between company investigators, telephone company security departments, and law enforcement agencies will sometimes, but not often, result in successful prosecution of such cases. In this area, prevention generally is a more productive strategy.

COUNTERFEIT SOFTWARE AND HARDWARE

On April 30, 1997, a federal grand jury in San Jose returned an indictment charging criminal copyright violations. The defendants were indicted for their role in selling counterfeit Microsoft computer software to owners of a Canadian computer software outlet. Between January 1994 and October 1995, the defendants allegedly sold counterfeit Microsoft software totaling more than $500,000. The San Francisco Field Office of the FBI investigated this case with the cooperation of the U.S. Customs Service and the Royal Canadian Mounted Police.

On April 24, 1997, a federal grand jury in Seattle returned a three-count indictment charging a defendant with trafficking in copyright infringing CD-ROMs containing computer software. More than $50,000 worth of merchandise was seized. This case was investigated by the FBI's Seattle Field Office and will be prosecuted by the U.S. Attorney.

On April 10, 1997, the FBI executed a search warrant on a Dallas-area local computer distributor and seized pirated Microsoft software valued at $88,500 and remarked (counterfeit) Intel Corporation central processing units (CPUs) valued at more than $94,000. On April 25, 1997, the FBI seized 1,200 remarked Intel Corp. CPUs valued at more than $500,000. This case was investigated by the Dallas Field Office of the FBI and will be prosecuted by the U.S. Attorney. (The source for the preceding three cases is the U.S. Department of Justice website.)

Comments

These three cases show why software piracy and counterfeit hardware is a popular offense. The value of the materials seized represents a minuscule fraction of the $12 billion in annual software losses and billions in counterfeited products, but they provide a sense of the amount of money that criminals can obtain through their schemes.

17

Investigating High-Technology Crime

THE SIGNIFICANCE OF COMPUTERS IN CRIME AND INVESTIGATIONS

This chapter provides an overview[1] of the important concepts associated with "computer forensics." Because computers have become ubiquitous, they often are a highly productive source of evidence and intelligence that may be obtained by a properly trained and equipped investigative unit. Creating and equipping the high-technology-crime investigations unit to competently search the most commonly used microcomputers is essential. In many cases, a suspect will use a computer to plan the crime, keep diaries or records of acts in furtherance of a conspiracy, or communicate with confederates about details via electronic mail. In other schemes, the computer will play a more central role, perhaps serving as the vehicle for an unauthorized intrusion into a larger system from which valuable files or other information is downloaded or tampered with.

Surprisingly, even many sophisticated criminals who are highly computer literate remain unaware of the software utilities available that allow evidence to be scavenged from various storage media, including hard drives, random access memory, and other locations in the operating system environment, such as file slack space, swap space, and temporary files. Therefore, every investigation of crime or unauthorized activities should assume that some effort will be invested in examining computers and computer records to locate relevant evidence to prove or disprove allegations or suspicion of wrongdoing.

Webster's Collegiate Dictionary defines *forensics* as "belonging to, used in, or suitable to courts of judicature or to public discussion and debate." Therefore, we define *computer forensics* as describing the application of legally sufficient methods, protocols, and techniques to gather, analyze, and preserve computer information relevant to a matter under investigation. Operationally, *computer forensics* encompasses using appropriate software tools and protocols to efficiently search the contents of magnetic and other storage media and identify relevant evidence in files, fragments of files, and deleted files, as well as file slack and swap space. Each of these areas merits some discussion.

- *File slack space.* Most computer disk operating systems divide up the available storage media into "chunks" called *clusters.* For most micro-computers, clusters come in various sizes, ranging from 12K to 16K to 32K. When an application creates a new file, a minimum number of clusters is assigned to it. However, if the file doesn't completely fill the cluster with data, there will be an area *between* the last byte of file data and the "physical" end of the assigned cluster size, which contains no file data. The operating system fills this space with random data taken from the swap space. In some computers, as much as 20–30% of the total space allocated to files actually may be slack space. Searching so much space can be very tedious, but with the proper software utilities, it sometimes can be a very productive source of information.
- *Swap files.* To operate more efficiently, many operating systems create a data cache or buffer in the random access memory (RAM) to speed up processing. The computer does not need to access the hard drive to read data, it merely restores it from the RAM cache. This cache or buffer area is called the *swap file* in Windows (from the concept that the file is "swapped" in or out of RAM as needed). When Windows is open, the dynamic swap file changes constantly as new files are opened and closed. When Windows closes normally, these files are written out to the hard drive, stored into the file slack space, and unallocated "free" space. In most desktop computers, the swap files may be as large as 100 megabytes, which means that a great deal of information may be stored in the swap file. If Windows has been improperly shut down (e.g., the power was terminated), then the entire swap file may be recoverable from the hard disk drive of the microcomputer, in the file 386.swp.
- *Temporary files.* Many applications create temporary "working" copies of the files created by users. These files typically are "deleted" by the operating system when the user closes the application or exits the program. Many common tasks also create temporary files. For example, when a document or file is printed, the operating system typically creates a print spool file that also is deleted when the print operation is completed. These temporary files are created using "free" or "unallocated" space on the attached storage media, and then "deleted" when no longer needed. However, "deleted" files are *not physically eliminated* from the storage media. There is a very good chance that evidence may be recovered from these areas through a careful search with disk editing software or by using customized forensic search utilities.
- *Deleted files.* Many investigators and sophisticated computer users understand that files are not physically removed from storage media

when they are "deleted" or "erased." Rather, the operating system flags the files (and thus the associated storage space allocated to that file by the file allocation table) as "open" or "available for use." This means that, when the system needs to store a new file, the space may or may not be used, depending on a number of variables. If the file has been "deleted" very recently, it may be fully recoverable through the use of file recovery utilities. Less well understood is that, when a file consists of multiple clusters (i.e., a big file!), it's possible that significant "chunks" of relevant evidence or data still may be discoverable through the use of disk editing tools or specialized computer forensic software. Also important to consider is that the huge number of temporary files generated by Windows and applications may be fully or partially recoverable and thus could provide important evidence if properly searched.

- *Free or unallocated space.* As noted previously, the portion of the storage media (the hard, floppy, or other drive) that has not been assigned or allocated to existing files and documents is called *unallocated* or *free space.* Even though it appears empty to the casual user, it may contain a wealth of material that could be relevant to the investigation. Although it is possible to search the unallocated space using a disk editor, given the rapidly increasing size of hard drives (often 10 gigabytes or more), the task could be compared to draining a swimming pool using a bucket: It can be done but it takes a very, very long time. As a practical matter it has become very important to use specialized search utilities to filter the vast holdings and find the character strings that indicate useful evidence.

RETRIEVING AND PRESERVING ELECTRONIC EVIDENCE

The remainder of this chapter includes a systematic approach to retrieving and preserving "electronic" evidence: how to recover deleted information, identify and recover hidden password data, and avoid inadvertently destroying evidence. It is divided into several sections:

- A general discussion of computer crimes and the laws that apply.
- How to prepare for a search.
- How to search computers and storage media.
- How to read media containing evidence.
- How to collect, transport, and store evidence.
- A sense of the future of computer-related investigations and some difficulties that await investigators (see Part IV).

LEGAL REQUIREMENTS FOR COMPUTER-RELATED CRIME

Computer Crime

The legal definition of *computer crime* varies widely from state to state. In some states, using a computer to defraud or commit other crimes may make it a special type of violation. Some forms of computer crime are specified by federal legislation, such as attacks on or misuse of federal government-owned systems: Computer crime is "Any illegal act for which knowledge of computer technology is used to commit the offense" (National Institute of Justice, Issues and Practices, Dedicated Computer Crime Units). Computers can be used as the tool of the crime, or the computer can be the object of the crime.

There are many and varied statutes (various federal and at least 49 different state statutes) relative to computer crime. Each statute has different *elements of proof*. It is vital that the investigator be familiar with the language and elements of the relevant statutes, which would include federal laws as well as state laws, in which the organization has offices and conducts operations.

Computer fraud is defined as the use of a computer with the intent to commit a fraudulent act: "Any defalcation or embezzlement accomplished by tampering with computer programs, data files, operations, equipment, or media, and resulting in losses sustained by the organization whose computer system was manipulated" (defined in Association of Certified Fraud Examiners' Computer Fraud course). Elements of proof of computer fraud include knowingly accessing or otherwise using a computer, without authorization or exceeding authorization limits, with the intent to commit a fraudulent act.

Violations of Organization Policies

In most North American organizations, every staff member has one or more individually assigned microcomputers, perhaps including a designated laptop for travel, desktop workstation for in-office work, and a palm-size PDA (personal digital assistant). These systems may be used to commit acts that are not crimes but violate the organization's policy or procedures, such as downloading or viewing pornography on company computers or sending harassing or sexually explicit e-mail messages to coworkers. When an employee is known or suspected to have engaged in such activities, the evidence to prove these or other serious policy violations may exist on the hard disk drive or other media.

Although policy violations are less serious than crime, organizations now often are held to a very high standard of proof in situations in which employment is terminated for violating a policy. Given the increased volume of wrongful termination lawsuits, evidence recovered from computers may be essential both to prove the violation as well as shield the organization against trivial wrongful termination suits.

PRESEARCH PREPARATION

Prior to conducting a search of any computer, it is important to obtain as much information as possible about the system(s) to be examined. The more that's known about the system and its configuration, the better prepared the investigator will be to conduct an effective search. At a minimum, the following information is required:

1. System configuration: stand-alone, LAN connection, WAN connection, other connection (e.g., dial-up modem lines).
2. Type of hardware (CPU), memory, and storage capacity (hard drive(s), other media).
3. Type and versions of application software, brand names.
4. External or internal modem: Brand and type, speed, and so forth.
5. Security system (access controls, encryption). If the computer is password protected, can it be accessed without the suspect's knowledge?
6. Are there booby traps that destroy information if "unauthorized" access is attempted? (An example is given later of a crude but effective device for this purpose.)
7. Where exactly is the system physically located?

Expert Assistance

Many alternative sources can be used to compensate for any lack of technical knowledge by an investigator. These range from trustworthy members of the organization's systems technical staff, to computer systems auditors working for the organization or available from the "Big 5" professional service organizations, to computer consultants from the hardware or software vendors or manufacturers.

As a last resort, and only after consultation with the prosecuting attorney or members of the company's legal department, the suspect may be able to help. The best option, of course, depends on the specific situation, but never assume that an "expert" in one hardware/operating systems/application combination will be able to translate that skill to another environment.

The high-technology-crime investigator should be experienced in rules of evidence and the interpretation of investigative leads. If the person is not knowledgeable about a specific system, assign someone who is to assist the team. When in doubt, find a consultant with the relevant expertise, but always remember that the investigator must remain in charge of the investigation.

SEARCHING THE COMPUTER: WARRANTS AND POLICY ISSUES

Law enforcement investigators most likely will need a search warrant to obtain evidence from a personally owned computer unless it has been seized at a crime scene under pertinent authority. Under exceptional circumstances it's possible that the system owner may indulge a request for a consent search, but it's not very likely that any criminal or anyone involved with any serious offense will be so cooperative.

In the private sector, obtaining *physical* access to a target computer may be simple. However, the investigative unit manager must ensure that the company policy framework supports a legal search, so that any evidence discovered will be usable. Employee handbooks and other policy pronouncements should contain language that explicitly states that the company owns the microcomputers used by the staff.

These management communications also should reserve the company's right to inspect the computer at any time for any legitimate business purpose, including investigating known or suspected violations of company policy or relevant laws. The language should advise employees that they have no reasonable expectation of privacy in using the machine and that, if they choose to use the computer for personal communications or other purposes, they do so at their own risk.

If the company has no such policy and procedure foundation, the employee may be able to sue the organization for violation of privacy, especially in states like California, where there is an explicit state constitutional right to privacy. Some of the issues to consider in planning a computer search are

- Exactly why is the system being searched?
- What evidence is expected to be recovered?
- Is there a specific time period that is likely to be most productive?
- How long should the investigators wait before telling the suspect?

Crime Scene Tool Kit

Whether searching a system in place or moving it to another location, it is important to have a portable tool kit consisting of at least the following for typical microcomputers: the operating system software, applications software, and hardware.

Operating System Software

Current microcomputer operating system (OS) software should include, at least, MS Windows, MS-DOS, and the latest OS software for IBM and Apple computers. Software for minicomputers and local area networks should be included as well but usually are too expensive to maintain unless actually needed for the assignment. Therefore, it is very important to know where you can get original software when needed for these other environments.

Applications Software

Plan on current microcomputer software, including utility software that runs on both MS-DOS and Apple systems. The utility software should provide disk editing, data recovery, diagnostics, and virus scanning, at a minimum. A typical example of this type of tool is the Norton Utilities. QuickView or equivalent file viewers can save time in examining contents of unusual file formats.

In addition, the most commonly used word-processing, spreadsheet, graphics, and database software as well as tools that may allow you to crack the common application-specific password systems should be available.

Hardware

Your hardware should include, ideally, notebook systems that are MS-DOS compatible as well as Apple compatible. Those systems should provide the power and flexibility you need to conduct your search. You should have a "clean" system on which you can recreate the system that is the subject of the search.

Some of the hardware to consider are cables, disk drives, tape drives, power supplies, dialed number recorders (DNR), printer, surge protectors, and a wrist strap for grounding. If you think that a simple wrist strap is not needed, try explaining to a victim how the evidence on a diskette was zapped through static electricity, and why prosecution may no longer be possible because the best evidence is now defunct.

In addition, a set of computer maintenance tools, such as Phillips-head screwdrivers and pliers, should be included. After all, you may have to dismantle the system to transport it to the evidence room or to install a SCSI card to run a tape backup system on the target.

Operations Plan

In any serious effort, remember the five *P*s: proper planning prevents poor performance. As with any other search, a computer search requires careful planning. The bigger the system(s), the more important it is to plan.

The following sections should be considered for inclusion in a written computer search or investigative plan (items with a star are relevant to the private sector or corporate organizations):

1. Objective.*
2. Jurisdiction.
3. Call signs.
4. Frequencies.
5. Investigative agencies.
6. Command post.
7. Communications.*
8. Logistics.
9. Assignments.
10. Hospitals.
11. Locations.*
12. Floor plans.*
13. Maps.
14. Assembly area.
15. Team(s).
16. Resources, such as personnel, budget, equipment.*
17. Surveillance options, such as type of business, public access, hours of operation, number of employees.

Planning for the search should include specific information to cover most search aspects and contingencies:

- Who will bring the warrant?
- Who will bring the tool kit?
- Who will make out the evidence tags?
- Who will search the systems? Do you want to print out a hard copy of the contents of the hard drive? (Remember, a 4-gigabyte drive could hold approximately 1 million printed pages or enough hardcopy documents to fill over 400 drawers of filing cabinet space.)

SEARCH PROCEDURES

Prior to searching a computer for evidence, it is important to know the violation of law or company policy on which you are going to base your search warrant and associated effort. Once that is done, and the plan is developed and briefed, you are prepared to conduct the search. It is important to remember that each search must be addressed individually.

Entering the Search Scene

When entering the facility where the computer is located, it is important to treat it as a real or potential crime scene. Overall, generally accepted procedures should apply for most of these types of searches. Remember that electronic evidence is very fragile, it may be disguised, the suspect can quickly destroy it through deliberate measures, and the investigator may destroy it through improper handling.

Determine early in the search whether or not the system will be searched on the premises or in another location. This decision determines how to conduct the on-site search. Generally, it will be more convenient to remove the system to a laboratory location for more detailed examination, but this may not be possible or desirable, depending on the facts of the case.

Be aware that the system should be examined slowly and meticulously, as if the investigator were about to dismantle a ticking bomb. Keep that analogy in mind, because any mishandling or wrong movement on the system could damage or destroy your computer crime scene evidence. Depending on the suspect, the computer actually could contain an explosive device set to destroy the system and the unwary investigator! As the following examples demonstrate, even if there is no bomb, suspects can take steps that could negate the search of their systems.

Destroying Information on a Storage Media

Use an AC current bulk VCR tape eraser from Radio Shack. Just lay the unit on the hard drive, and it will clean the hard drive with magnetic pulses. Make sure to leave it on for at least 10 minutes. This procedure will leave no trace. Use it as an emergency disk crasher in the event you need to make an immediate and permanent erasure of sensitive data. Keep the unit on standby next to the computer. If it is ever needed, turn it on and place it on top of your computer case; within seconds, the hard drives will be corrupted beyond repair. If the computer later is seized for inspection or as evidence, the hard drives will be unusable and corrupted.

An Antiseizure Device

As an additional safeguard, you can install a booby trap switch that turns the system on if the computer case is removed or tampered with without the "proper" opening method. This requires a small 12-volt dry-cell battery (with a small drain 12-volt charger tapped into the unit's power source) connected to a $39 inverter (installed inside the tower computer case). Locate a switch on the computer cover that will trip if the "proper" deactivation procedures are not followed. Use a regular on/off switch inside one of the unused floppy plates that can be accessed to turn on the deactivator (on/off switch) prior to opening. If this isn't done—and only the owner would know to do this—when the cover is removed, the unit activates (the switch is closed to inverter, and it operates as a self-contained power source); 15 seconds later, the hard drives will be trashed. Attach the AC erasure unit to the underside of the hard drives using duct tape or nylon tie straps.

This trap is difficult for the computer investigator to avoid. Unless forewarned by informants or the suspect, the technician is likely to first learn of this system when the case is removed. Quick removal of the extraneous equipment may not be possible before significant corruption has occurred.

System in Operation

If the system is in operation when the premises are entered, the investigator will need to decide how to proceed. Should it be shut it off? If so, when? Where? Power can be terminated at the wall plug or at the computer switch—many investigators recommend pulling the wall plug. This method avoids the possibility that the on/off switch had been modified to become a self-destruct device trigger. If information is being downloaded or uploaded via telephone modem line or network connection, should it be allowed to continue or should the line be cut or unplugged? Consider the implications for these and other foreseeable events that could affect the quality or quantity of evidence on the system.

External Inspection

The system to be searched should be inspected externally for evidence. For example, look around the area for notes and other documentation, which may not only be evidence but also contain decryption/encryption codes, passwords, macro commands, and the like.

Check the printers. If they contain ribbons, ensure that these are taken as evidence. With a little practice they usually can be read, at least in part. If the system is operational, photograph the screen image before unplugging the system. If the monitor is dark, check closely for burned-in images. The images just might contain clues that may assist in accessing the information sought as evidence.

Be sure to identify, tag, and document the system configuration, include photos, video recordings, and schematics for complex environments. This will assist in reassembling the system if it must be recreated in another location. It also will help explain to a judge and jury what was encountered when entering the facility to be searched and the configuration of the system.

In searching the hardware, remember that all peripherals may have memory and that memory may contain important evidence. Some items to consider are multiplexers, routers, bridges, printer servers, and repeaters. Sometimes, these are overlooked during a search, where less-experienced investigators concentrate solely on the hard drive and diskettes of a suspect's computer. Retrieving evidence from these areas will depend on the specific type of device.

Searching Access Controlled ("Secure") Systems

During a search, the investigator may be confronted with a system that is secured physically or logically. A physical access control normally will present no major problem. For example, many brand name systems come with CPU key locks. Usually, the keys will either be in the system or in the vicinity and can be used to unlock the system. As a last resort, using tools, the CPU cover can be removed and the lock disabled.

A logical access control system may pose a more challenging problem. The access control software may be a unique program, but more likely, it will be a standard software access control package. These software security programs normally require, or at least provide for, a unique user ID and password.

Today's packages vary in sophistication. Some may be circumvented easily, using a "control break" during the system boot or a "control c" or by simply booting the system using a DOS diskette in the floppy disk drive. Others may not be that easy to defeat.

Before attempting to break into a system, remember to evaluate all the risks. These risks include initiating a potential virus, software time bomb, or reformatting command to destroy the evidence by your attempted system access.

The best way to get around such controls is by having good sources (informants) who can provide the necessary user IDs and passwords. It also is possible that, during the physical search, the investigator will find the necessary information stuck inside a rolodex, desk drawer, or system reference manual.

If the system security controls cannot be circumvented and time allows, the software publisher may be able to assist if a "master key" or "administrative user" option is available. The publisher also may be able to guide you around the access controls.

Although you may not be able to trust the suspect(s), he or she can be "compelled" to relinquish that information. That's another risk that you may have to evaluate.

Compelling Suspects to Provide Access Information

The following information (from Don Ingraham, Assistant District Attorney, Alameda County, Oakland, CA) provides the supporting information that can be used to obtain a court order to compel a suspect to provide system access information (Note: There is a disagreement within the legal profession as to the legality of this approach):

- *Problem.* Can a suspect whose computer is in the possession of law enforcement to be searched, be lawfully ordered to divulge the password?
- *Caveat.* This opinion does not address the risk that a suspect might use the opportunity to command the destruction of the potential evidence, which actually occurred in the Equity Funding case.
- *Conclusion.* Yes, if the fact of his or her divulgence is immunized and not used as evidence of that person's authority and control of the computer. A password authorizes the computer to access and recover the specified files: It does not create the data but simply permits access to data already in existence. Such data was not created under compulsion but speaks for itself, just like writing exemplars, blood samples, or fingerprints.
- *Analysis.* At least three decisions of the United States Supreme Court and a recent decision of an appellate division in California suggest that such an order can be made and enforced through a court's contempt authority.

Among the decisions analyzed were *Fisher* v. *U.S.* and *U.S.* v. *Doe.* In *Fisher* v. *U.S.* (1976), 425 US 391, 48 LED2d 39—invoices and IRS summons for the suspects records, which he gave to his attorney who entrusted them to the accountant, on whom the summons was served—such disclosure did not involve Fifth Amendment self-incrimination, because the potential exists: "a party is privileged from producing evidence but not from its production"; there was no violation of the attorney/client privilege because these records could have been seized from the suspect if he still had them; and there was no violation of the Fourth Amendment because the summons was so narrowly drawn as to be limited to materials of significant relevance to the investigation.

U.S. v. *Doe* (1983), 465 US 605, 79 LED2d 552, reversed a lower court's suppression of the business records of the suspect in a government contracting fraud investigation, including the records of his bank accounts in the Grand Caymans: The records sought were created voluntarily. The U.S. Supreme Court affirmed the lower court's conclusion that the act of enabling their production would permit the inference that the suspect could be identified with them; and therefore, the suspect would be entitled to immunity as to their acquisition. In other words, his compliance with the order could not be used as proof of complicity in the crime they will be used to prove.

Footnote 13 to this opinion, 79 LED2d 561, clarifies that restriction:

by producing the documents, respondent would relieve the Government of the need for authentication . . . (which would) establish a valid claim of the privilege against self-incrimination. This is not to say that the Government was foreclosed from rebutting respondent's claim by producing evidence that possession, existence, and authentication were a "foregone conclusion." Clearly, independent proof on those critical points would have to be established by other evidence.

Systems with Passwords

If you seize a system protected by a password and do not trust the suspect or the suspect refuses to cooperate, you must attack the system just like any hacker attempting to penetrate it. There are several ways to attack the system:

- Look for passwords written down on documents on or near the computer system.
- Try words and numbers that can be related to the suspect, such as date of birth or mother's maiden name.
- Call the software publisher or vendor and request its assistance. A court order may be necessary. All publishers will deny any backdoor to their security-protected software; however, it would be a surprise if there was no backdoor.
- Use a software product that can identify the password. Many are software-dependent. One software publisher guarantees its program can penetrate Microsoft software, WordPerfect, Lotus 1-2-3, and others. The program attempts various passwords at approximately 500,000 attempts per second.
- Use a software program such as a dictionary software product to attempt a "brute force" attack, which attempts to randomly guess the password starting at A and going to Z.
- You may be able to use a keyword search based on information determined through your investigation. Note: The same approach is possible when attempting to guess the key for an encrypted file; however, the more modern encryption products usually are too sophisticated for such an approach.

SEARCHING MEDIA

The first thing to remember is that the conduct of the search may affect the admissibility of the evidence obtained. Computer evidence is ephemeral, it can be destroyed with the touch of a keyboard. It also is easy to manufacture "evidence" or taint real evidence through application of disk editing utilities that write directly to the storage media. As an example, imagine a file exists on a floppy drive that contains a copy of a relevant memo. Someone who desires to incriminate an innocent person may be able to modify the language in the memo, using a disk editor, and leave no trace of the access when the file is listed in a directory or accessed through the associated application software. To deal with the issues of reliability and completeness of the electronic evidence it is critical that the search procedures allow for results that can be replicated by anyone, even experts retained by the defense in a criminal investigation.

Investigators must realize that what is occurring with regard to computer evidence is very similar to the history surrounding use of DNA evidence in criminal trials. There was a great deal of resistance initially as to the admissibility and reliability of DNA-derived evidence. After investing heavily in the scientific tools and techniques that allowed crime labs to conduct validated testing protocols, the evidence went through a time when it was novel and defense attorney's did not know how to respond to the overwhelming scientific basis for the conclusions presented by forensic DNA examiners. This period ended with the O. J. Simpson trial in California. This trial showcased how weaknesses in handling and preservation techniques could be exploited to cast doubt on the reliability of the conclusions drawn from the evidence. Although the science of DNA evidence remains sound, the introduction of such material, by itself, no longer is any guarantee of a swift plea bargain or a jury's acceptance of the evidence.

Similarly, evidence obtained through computer media searches has enjoyed an initial period of novelty and impact. The CIA traitor Aldrich Ames may have been undone in part by the search of his personal computers at home and in his office. Some key evidence in the Starr investigation was obtained by searching personal computers and recovering files and copies of e-mail messages.

The highest profile application of these techniques to date has been in the Department of Justice antitrust proceedings against Microsoft. The effective use of "smoking gun" e-mail messages, retrieved or recovered from personal computers and application backup files, contributed substantially to the government's case against Microsoft. As powerful as these findings have been, investigators must realize that the very success they enjoy is creating increased awareness by defense attorneys of the protocols and procedures. It must be expected that defense attorneys, to serve their clients, will begin to question every aspect of the electronic evidence life cycle.

To counter potential defense objections to electronic evidence, investigators in high-technology-crime units must understand and apply rigorous procedures dealing with the search, identification, and preservation of electronic evidence. In effect, the investigator may expect to be subjected to the same sort of scrutiny that the LAPD crime lab suffered during the O. J. Simpson trial.

To avoid such problems, it is important that the evidence search process begin with the creation of a "bitstream image" of the system to be inspected using reputable and specialized backup software programs. Such images differ from conventional backups in a very fundamental way. Whereas a backup will make copies of all *files* on a media source (floppy diskette, hard drive, etc.), the bitstream process involves copying every bit and byte on a media source, whether in a file or just a few stray clusters left over from a long-deleted file.

As previously noted, most microcomputer disk operating systems (OSs) do not *physically* overwrite files "deleted" from a media storage device. Rather, the operating systems typically use a flag in the file allocation tables to tell the OS that the space currently assigned to a file no longer is reserved and may be reused to hold new data. This means that, especially for files that may contain many clusters, portions of the file may survive long after it has been "deleted." The bit stream backup then may be used to create an exact duplicate of the media source to be searched. We will call this exact duplicate of the entire media source a *forensic search image*. Saving this image to a recordable media, such as a write once read many (WORM) compact disk (CD) allows the investigator to examine the contents without making any changes to them.

Once a forensic search image has been created from the bitstream backup, it is possible to search for relevant files and materials. Even if the investigation unit has no specialized search utilities, a great deal of evidence still can be gathered by careful application of common disk editing utilities. When actually looking for evidence on a system, the first thing to do is bring up the directory structure. In searching an MS-DOS-based system, for example, look first for directories and their subdirectories.

This may help point out the right direction when looking for evidence. Slowly and methodically search each directory, subdirectory, and then individual files for evidence. Remember, some files may have "camouflaged" filenames to make them appear worthless. First look for *.doc and *.txt and other common word-processing files, as these are usually suffixes for files containing text. Files with suffixes of *.wk, *.wk1, and *.wks are examples of spreadsheet files. Be extremely careful with files ending in .com, .exe, and .bat. These usually are programs; once accessed, they will cause the computer to do something—something you may not want it to do, such as reformat the disk.

Remember, the investigator must never, ever examine the original storage media (hard, floppy, or other drives), e.g., using Windows itself. The operating system makes changes to the files, such as date of last access, that may affect the evidentiary value of the conclusions of the investigator. However, if accessing a forensic search image on a CD, it is acceptable to use Windows, the File Manager, and the Windows Explorer to examine the files through that path.

Hidden Files

If a file is locked with an invisible character,[2] it is possible to type <Alt 255> in a suspected location within the filename, such as immediately before or after the dot separating the first eight characters from the last three characters of the filename. If that fails, files can be renamed generically, using a command such as copy loa*.* loans.new. This will take all files with names beginning with loa and followed by any other characters—including invisible characters—and rename them loans. This will eliminate any hidden characters in the file names and allow normal access.

Using a disk utility program, you may be able to "see" the invisible character space. It would be represented by a blank space. Rename the file and then access it.

In DOS, even "inaccessible" files can be copied to other disks using the DOS command Copy a* *b:. This will copy all files in a given directory on disk drive a: to disk drive b:. Repeat the command for all accessible directories on the suspected computer disk. The copies will retain all the hidden characters embedded in the original file names.

Reading Graphics Files

If dealing with graphics files, graphics conversion software that can convert vector to vector, raster to raster, and vector to raster files should be part of your tool kit. Vector images usually are created by CAD or drawing, chart, or graph software applications. Raster images are made up of dots, called *pixels*, arranged in a rectangle, called a *bitmap*. Raster images normally are created by scanners or paint software. Fax formats also are rasters.

You may not be able to convert from raster to vector. Another point to remember is that you should convert metafile formats to raster because converting to a vector format may convert only a part of the original image or none at all. This is because metafiles contain both vector and raster components.

General Conduct of Searches

A general guide for conducting a system search should include the following:

1. Immediately get people away from the computers.
2. Photograph and videotape the area, screen, front and back of each system and peripherals. Remember liability issues may arise and photographs and videotape could support your procedures against such claims.
3. If you decide to unplug the system, do so at the wall (using the switch may invite an unwanted action, such as reformat the hard drive or initiate a virus).
4. If an older system, "park" the hard drive.
5. Leave a system disk in the drive and tape it to prevent booting from the hard drive.
6. Label all hardware, documentation, disks, and so forth.
7. Take all documents along with the system.
8. Look for documentation containing passwords.
9. Before removing the equipment, check for magnetic fields at doors and so on (use a compass).
11. Use surge protectors.
12. Use your own software to examine the system.
13. Create bitstream backup copies from the original storage media, to allow restoring to the exact condition.
14. Create forensic search images of seized storage media for review. Never use the evidence itself.
15. Secure the original media sources as critical evidence.
16. Review, search, and inspect the "forensic search image" system for relevant evidence.
17. Document all steps taken.
18. The defendant may help—but don't let him or her near the machine and ensure the defendant's rights aren't violated.
19. Ensure a chain of custody is maintained and completely documented for all access and use of evidentiary materials.
20. Prepare summary reports of findings that present information and support conclusions using a minimum of technical jargon. Often visual images are more effective than reams of printouts and file listings.

COLLECTING, TAGGING, AND MARKING EVIDENCE

When collecting evidence, you generally can use normal evidence collection procedures. However, it is crucial that the system be tagged in such a manner as to allow rebuilding it for such reasons as conducting subsequent system examinations and presenting the system as evidence in court.

When tagging the equipment, it is important to tag the ports and both ends of cables to facilitate putting the system back together exactly the way it was found.

TRANSPORTING EVIDENCE

When transporting evidence several factors are important to consider:

- If transporting the evidence in a radio-equipped vehicle, shut off all the equipment to prevent damaging the information on the media through radio waves.
- Be careful to keep the equipment away from moisture, high humidity, and excessive heat or cold.
- Be sure to maintain a documented chain of custody.

Figure 17–1 The general crime scene.

A HIGH-TECHNOLOGY-CRIME SCENE

Figures 17–1 through 17–4 depict a general crime scene that you may observe during an investigation. Assuming the systems were running at the time of the search, would you know what to do and in what order?

Figure 17–1 depicts what could be three stand-alone microcomputers. However, they actually are part of a local area network that includes several other systems in another room. The systems are running Microsoft Windows NT, and each system has a separate output to a telephone line. One also is used as the interface to the Internet.

Figure 17–2   Close-up of the shelf unit.

Figure 17–3 Close-up of the bottom shelf.

Figure 17–4 Portion of the desk not shown previously.

Figure 17–2 provides a different angle of some of the hardware. At first glance, the top shelf contains a laser printer and scanner. The second shelf holds the monitors and mouse interfaces. The third shelf contains the keyboards. The bottom shelf (Figure 17–3) holds the two CPUs, a hub, consolidate power controller, an "A-B" switch, a box for CDs, a pack of tools, a small fire alert device, and some books. The books may give some indication of applications on the network.

The systems look alike, however, the one on the right is the server and the one on the left is a workstation. What at first glance may be a normal setup may not be. The CD box, or the fire alert device, or any one of the devices actually may be an explosive device that could be triggered remotely.

So, the investigator must be cautious when approaching a high-technology-crime scene, just as in conducting drug searches of a "meth" manufacturing facility.

Figure 17–4 shows a notebook system that includes an external Zip drive, diskettes, CD case containing applications on CD, a wireless telephone, an indication of an internal modem attached to the telephone, and on the left side of the notebook computer, a cable connected to the hub shown in the other photographs.

Of interest to the high-technology-crime investigator, in addition to the desktop system and local area network hardware, is that the notebook computer indicates mobility, which means that it obviously is used at other locations. So much for stating the obvious. However, you must understand the need for this mobility on the part of the high-technology criminal. Is it for the convenience of working at home, at another location, on the road? Probably, and that means there may be more evidence in the suspect's car, home, or other offices. Possibly the suspect has accounts with one or more ISPs that could contain additional evidence. Having good sources and detailed information from those sources before conducting the search would greatly enhance the ability of the investigator to collect all relevant evidence during the search.

If a source is being used to gather information, be sure to show the source pictures of hardware and try to determine what is at the crime scene. If a notebook computer is there, can the source determine why a notebook computer is being used, where it is being used, or any other details about the systems, such as applications, versions, brand names, or models. The notebook pictured also has ports for video and cellular phone hookups.

NOTES

1. The information provided is not all-inclusive, as the operating systems, applications, and hardware constantly are changing. Therefore, the information presented should be used only as a guide. Specific systems require specific forensic procedures.

2. Every application has various places where it stores information. This example is just that, an example. Applications like Microsoft Explorer, Microsoft Office, Microsoft Windows, Netscape, and others provide additional places that keep a historical record of what site or documents were last accessed. For example, with Microsoft Windows, click on the Start key and then click on Documents. There you will find an audit trail of what documents were last accessed. The Recycle Bin is another great place to find a file that the miscreant thought had been erased because it was deleted from the directory.

PART IV

High-Technology-Crime Investigation

Challenges for the Twenty-First Century

OBJECTIVE

The objective of this, the last part of this book, is to look into a crystal ball and predict what working in the global information environment will be like for the twenty-first century high-technology-crime investigator. Chapter 18 deals with the future of technology and its impact on the global information environment, the future of high-technology-crime security, the criminal justice system, and the future of the high-technology-crime investigation profession.

18

The Future of High-Technology Crime and Its Impact on Working in a Global Information Environment

MICROPROCESSORS

Pundits have said and continue to say that the little, silicon chip computer soon will reach its physical limits. In this event, what will happen? What will be the replacement? These are interesting issues on which to speculate. The technology industry, in order to survive, will continue to improve but how will it do that?

We will see a new era of integration of all the current technology: intranets, cellular telephones, pagers, and private branch exchanges. Already we're seeing cellular phones and pagers being incorporated into watches. In the not too distant future, watches as we know them will not exist. They will be information devices that provide satellite-supported voice, video, and data from anywhere in the world. They will be solar powered, with the ability to store that power for extended periods of time.

Cable televisions will be sold as a completely integrated unit with built-in intranet and Internet access—actually, GII access—which includes telephones. After all, we can make telephone calls via the Internet, albeit not as clear or "user friendly" as we would like, but it is getting there.

We won't have to reprogram or make any changes to our home information and entertainment system to get the information that we want while denying that same access to our children. This future system will "scan" you and, based on specific biometrics of your physical profile and voice identification, automatically configure itself according to your previous instructions.

Miniaturization will continue, as well as mobility, flexibility, integration, lower costs, and increased communication, and information collection—all with untold possibilities.

HIGH-TECHNOLOGY CRIMES AND THE MISCREANTS THAT COMMIT THEM

High-technology crime is expected to increase in number of incidents and sophistication. High-technology criminals will use sophisticated attack programs not found on the Internet. They and others will continue to find an increasingly profitable job market. They will be the new "hired killers" of the global organized crime rings, drug cartels, terrorists, governments, and espionage agents. They will be hired to steal information and "kill" systems through denial of service or information destruction.

Some high-technology devices are being used today (see items 2, 4, and 5). It is only a matter of time before we see

1. Terrorists, using a computer, penetrate a control tower computer system and send false signals to aircraft, causing them to crash.
2. Terrorists use fraudulent credit cards to finance their operations.
3. Terrorists penetrate a financial computer system and divert millions of dollars to finance their activities.
4. Terrorists bleach U.S. $1 bills and using a color copier, reproduce them as $100 bills, and flood the market with them to try to destabilize the dollar.
5. Terrorists use cloned cellular phones and computers over the Internet to communicate using encryption to protect their transmissions.
6. Terrorists use virus and worm programs to shutdown vital government computer systems.
7. Terrorists change hospital records, causing patients to die from an overdose of medicine or the wrong medicine by changing computerized tests and analysis results.
8. Terrorists penetrate a government computer and cause it to issue checks to all its citizens, destabilizing the economy.
9. Terrorists destroy critical government computer systems that are processing tax returns.
10. Terrorists penetrate computerized train routing systems, causing passenger trains to collide.
11. Terrorists take over telecommunication links or shut them down.
12. Terrorists take over satellite links to broadcast their message over televisions and radios.

HIGH-TECHNOLOGY SECURITY

We are seeing the uses of high-technology tools to monitor prisoners and track vehicles and people. One is a camera device installed on public streets that can compare a database of the digitized faces of criminals or others and match them with people walking on the street.

Such high-technology devices will increase the debate of privacy and individual freedom. Some people will argue that, if you do nothing wrong you have no reason to fear these new security measures. The debate over the use of sophisticated high-technology devices will intensify in the future. Who will win the argument is anybody's guess. However, as before, most people are willing to give up more freedoms for more security.

INFORMATION SYSTEM SECURITY

Information systems security will continue to increase in complexity and sophistication. In the future, the gap will close between sophisticated attacks on systems, PBXs, cellular phones, and other devices and defense against them. New attacks will still hold the edge; however, the future will find quicker recoveries, countermeasures, counterattacks, and new defenses all working together to provide a "layered defense."

The information systems security profession will become one of the most important and dominant professions in the twenty-first century, gaining executive management recognition, support, and authority. This will be coupled with a more aggressive defense and high-technology-crime prevention program, which will include tracing the source of the attacks and counterattacking.

Law enforcement agencies will become serious targets of the global high-technology criminals. We will begin seeing a law enforcement investigator who is also the department's information systems security officer.

CRIMINAL JUSTICE SYSTEMS

In the future, like today, all major branches of the criminal justice systems will be trying to catch up with the global information environment. High technology will continue to be added in piecemeal fashion, but through associations and networking, criminal justice agencies will be quicker to adopt the high technology used by others. In time, this will evolve into informal and formal on-line groups within the global criminal justice systems, which will develop cooperative processes to share information about new techniques, tools, and methods to provide more effective and efficient processes.

In the future, secure local, national, and global links will be established to track criminals regardless of their location. High technology will assist in the investigation of high-technology crime, but once the criminal is apprehended, anywhere in the world, the prosecution and incarceration would be done on a global scale, using teleconferencing as the medium. Therefore, because of the global dependence on the GII and Internet, the United Nations will support global high-technology-crime international laws to allow for the investigation, apprehension, and prosecution of these offenders. All or most of the information-dependent nations will support such processes, since they are likely to be victims of these global attackers.

LACK OF TRAINING, MANAGEMENT SUPPORT, AND SOMETIMES EVEN INTEREST

In 1995, Dr. Kovacich conducted a small, fairly informal survey of his fellow High Technology Crime Investigation Association members. The purpose of the survey was to determine their preparedness, support, and capability to successfully investigate high-technology crime.

From the tabulated results, it would appear that most association members believe they lack the training, resources, and management support to adequately address high-technology-crime issues. In addition, they believe that high-technology crime is increasing, because of cheaper, more powerful, easier to use computers and more computer users. Also interesting to note, and not adequately addressed, is the potential risk to law enforcement agencies based on outside personnel or agencies being responsible for maintaining and operating their information systems.

Although limited in scope, this survey is still believed to provide a reliable baseline as to the status of high-technology crimes and their investigation as perceived by HTCIA members in law enforcement and the investigative profession and have expertise in that area.

The survey and its conclusions were made in 1995. Do you believe significant changes have taken place that would change the results of that survey? If you are an investigator in a U.S. federal government agency, especially the FBI, you may say yes. If you are at the state or local level (where there usually is less money and a lower priority for such endeavors), you probably have not noticed any meaningful changes.

High-technology-crime investigation will develop into a formally recognized, distinct profession. The profession is developing now and will follow in the footsteps of the industrial security profession with the certified protection professional (CPP) designation, the certified fraud examiner (CFE), the certified public accountant (CPA), the certified information systems auditor (CISA), and the certified information systems security professional (CISSP).

To make this a reality, a consortium must put together or a nationally recognized nonprofit association must sponsor such a certifications program. Any attempt by a profit-oriented group would be unsuccessful because its rationale for doing so would be questioned. Furthermore, it would lack law enforcement support, making it somewhat meaningless. The consortium could be made up of federal law enforcement agencies, police associations, and the High Technology Crime Investigation Association.

By whatever means, in the future, such a designation will be needed to ensure that those involved in high-technology-crime investigation have the honesty, integrity, experience, and knowledge to be considered experts in their the profession. This will be accomplished by passing a rigorous certification test and background check, after meeting a minimum criteria vis-à-vis years of related experience and formal education.

In the future, colleges and universities will begin offering more high-technology-crime investigation courses and eventually a major in that field under the criminal justice or information systems security program.

THE "MUST HAVES" OF THE HIGH-TECHNOLOGY-CRIME INVESTIGATOR

Although the profession of high-technology-crime investigator is in its infancy, it has untold potential. The challenges are many. The high-technology-crime investigator must know and understand:

- People.
- Laws.
- High-technology devices, such as computers, telecommunications.
- Investigative techniques.
- Project planning.
- Report writing.
- Evidence seizure and collection methods.
- Information systems security.
- Electronic commerce.
- Office politics.
- Every high-technology environment in which he or she will work.

A profile of a *successful* and *professional* high-technology-crime investigator is one who

- Enjoys "playing" with high-technology devices, equipment, and games.
- Enjoys working with people, especially technically oriented people.
- Enjoys the challenge of "the hunt" and chasing the high-technology miscreants.
- Takes each investigation as a personal challenge to his or her ability.
- Believes that, if the investigation does not end in the successful identification of the miscreant, the miscreant is smarter than the investigator, which is a major driving force in the investigator's relentless pursuit of the miscreant.

- Keeps current on technology and related crimes and understands the implications of new technology, the opportunity to use it as a tool for criminal deeds, and its implications in conducting an investigation.
- Keeps current on latest investigative tools, techniques, and related sources of information.
- Is an active member in high-technology-related associations and constantly networks with peers to keep abreast of current and related events.
- Enjoys constant change and gets bored if there are no changes.
- Is customer support oriented and driven to meet all expectations.
- Accepts and uses new, unique investigative methods.
- Loves working in the global information environment.
- Loves conducting high-technology-crime investigations.
- Loves life and has fun.

HOPE FOR THE FUTURE

In the hands of the juvenile delinquents and global miscreants, high-technology crime can steal from those who honestly labored for their possessions; destroy businesses; and cause major disruptions, chaos, and even death through telemedicine.

An Wang (1920–1990) said, "When we enter society at birth, we receive an inheritance from the people who lived before us. It is our responsibility to augment that inheritance for those who succeed us. I feel that all of us owe the world more than we received when we were born." A professional high-technology-crime investigator does just that.

Thus far, the miscreants are winning the high-technology war—and it is a war. It is part of the global information war taking place now and that is likely to increase in intensity in the twenty-first century. It is the new crime scene, the new battlefield.

As high-technology-crime investigators, we must hope for the best but also plan for the worst.

References and Recommended Reading

Aburdene, Patricia, and John Naisbitt. *Megatrends 2000*. New York: Avon Books, 1990.

Allen, H. E., and C. E. Simonsen. *Corrections in America: An Introduction*, 4th ed. New York: Macmillan Publishing Company, 1986.

Anonymous. *A Hacker's Guide to Protecting Your Internet Site and Network, Maximum Security*. Indianapolis: SAMS Publishing, 1997.

Association of Certified Fraud Examiners (ACFE). Computer Fraud, seminar, San Francisco, 1993.

Association of Certified Fraud Examiners (ACFE). High-Tech Fraud, seminar, San Francisco, 1995.

Banks, Michael A. *How to Protect Yourself in Cyberspace: Web Psychos, Stalkers and Pranksters*. Scottsdale, AZ: The Coriolis Group, 1997.

Bellovin, Steven M., and William R. Cheswick. *Firewalls and Internet Security*. Reading, MA: Addison-Wesley Publishing Company, 1994.

Bequai, August. *Techno-Crimes: The Computerization of Crime and Terrorism*. Lexington, MA: D. C. Heath and Co., 1987.

Bintliff, R. L. *Complete Manual of White Collar Crime Detection and Prevention*. Englewood Cliffs, NJ: Prentice-Hall, 1993.

Boni, William C., and Kovacich, Gerald L. *I-Way Robbery Crime on the Internet*. Boston: Butterworth–Heinemann, 1999.

Breton, Thierry, and Beneich Denis. *Softwar*. New York: Holt, Rinehart and Winston, 1984.

Brown S. E., F. Esbensen, and G. Geis. *Criminology Explaining Crime and Its Context*. Cincinnati: Anderson Publishing Co., 1991.

Buchsbaum, Walter H. *Personal Computers Handbook*. Taipei: Author, 1981.

Burger, Ralf. *Computer Viruses: A High-Tech Disease*, 3rd ed. Grand Rapids, MI: Abacus, 1989.

Carroll, John M. *Computer Security*. London: Butterworth Publishers, 1977.

Cheswick, William R., and Steven M. Bellovin. *Firewalls and Internet Security: Repelling the Wily Hacker*. Reading, MA: Addison-Wesley Publishing Co., 1994.

Clark, Franklin, and Ken Diliberto. *Investigating Computer Crime.* Boca Raton, FL: CRC Press, 1996.

Computer Emergency Recovery Team (CERT). Internet Security, Information Systems Security Association conference, Toronto, Canada, 1994.

Datapro Research Corporation. *Balancing the Scales: Computer Crime Legislation Update.* Delran, NJ: Author, 1986.

Deloitte, Haskins, and Sells. *Computer Viruses, Proceedings of an Invitational Symposium.* New York: Deloitte, Haskins, Sells, 1988.

DeMaio, Harry B. *Information Protection and Other Unnatural Acts: Every Manager's Guide to Keeping Vital Computer Data Safe and Sound.* New York: Amacom, 1992.

"Drugs." *Crime Science,* Arts & Entertainment Channel (September 3, 1995).

Edwards, Mark J. *Internet Security with Windows NT.* Loveland, CO: Duke Press, 1998.

Felten, Edward W., and Gary McGraw. *Java Security.* New York: John Wiley and Sons, 1997.

Fialka, John J. *War by Other Means: Economic Espionage in America.* New York: W. W. Norton and Company, 1997.

Fites, Philip, and Martin P. J. Kratz. *Information Systems Security: A Practitioner's Reference.* New York: Van Nostrand Reinhold, 1993.

FitzGerald, Jerry. *Business Data Communications.* New York: John Wiley & Sons, 1984.

Forgione, Dana. "Recovering 'Lost' Evidence from Microcomputers." *White Paper* (June–July 1998).

Futrell, M., and C. Roberson. *An Introduction to Criminal Justice Research.* Springfield, IL: Charles C Thomas, 1998.

Garfinkel, Simson, and Gene Spafford. *Practical Unix Security.* Sebastopol, CA: O'Reilly and Associates, 1991.

Gurbani, Vijay K., and Uday O. Pabrai. *Internet and TCP/IP Network Security.* New York: McGraw-Hill, 1996.

Hafner, Katie, and John Markoff. *Cyberpunk: Outlaws and Hackers on the Computer Frontier.* New York: Touchstone, 1992.

"High-tech karma." *U.S. News & World Report* (August 21, 1995), p. 45.

"Home Page Speeds Ordering." *Information Week* (August 21, 1995), p. 64.

Icove, David, Karl Seger, and William Von Storch. *Computer Crime: A Crimefighter's Handbook.* Sebastopol, CA: O'Reilly and Associates, 1995.

"Jailhouse Takes Away Prisoners' Cash: IBM Runs Disk Head Dash." *Computerworld* (August 14, 1995), p. 116.

Jones, D. A. *History of Criminology: A Philosophical Perspective.* New York: Greenwood Press, 1986.

Kabay, Michel E. *The NCSA Guide to Enterprise Security: Protecting Information Assets*. New York: McGraw-Hill, 1996.

Kenney, John P., and Harry W. More. *Principles of Investigation*, 2nd ed. St. Paul, MN: West Publishing Co., 1994.

Knightmare, The. *Secrets of a Super Hacker*. Port Townsend, WA: Loompanics Unlimited, 1994.

Kovacich, G. L. "Hackers: From Curiosity to Criminal." *The White Paper* (1994).

Kovacich, Gerald L. *The Information Systems Security Officer's Guide*. Boston: Butterworth–Heinemann, 1998.

Landreth, Bill. *The Cracker. Out of the Inner Circle: A Hacker's Guide to Computer Security*. Bellevue, WA: Microsoft Press, 1985.

"Lawyers Access Own Version of Info Superhighway." *Communications News* (July 1995), p. 40.

Leibholz, Stephen W., and Louis D. Wilson. *Users' Guide to Computer Crime: Its Commission, Detection and Prevention*. Radnor, PA: Chilton Book Company, 1974.

Levy, Steven. *Hackers: Heroes of the Computer Revolution*. New York: Anchor Press, 1984.

Li, X., and N. B. Crane. *Electronic Style: A Guide to Citing Electronic Information*. Westport, CT: Meckler Publishing, 1993.

Martin, James. *Security Accuracy and Privacy in Computer Systems*. Englewood Cliffs, NJ: Prentice-Hall, 1973.

McClain, Gary. *Twenty-First Century Dictionary of Computer Terms*. New York: Dell Publishing, 1994.

McGraw, Gary, and Edward W. Felten. *Java Security: Hostile Applets, Holes, and Antidotes. What Every Netscape and Internet Explorer User Needs to Know*. New York: John Wiley and Sons, 1997.

Melvern, Linda, Nick Anning, and David Hebditch. *Techno-Bandits* Boston: Houghton Mifflin Company, 1984.

MCI. *Invisible Criminal*. VHS videotape, 1994.

Naisbitt, John. *Megatrends*. New York: Warner Books, 1982.

Naisbitt, John. *Megatrends Asia*. New York: Simon and Schuster, 1996.

National Research Council. *Computers at Risk*. Washington, DC: National Academy Press, 1991.

Norman, Adrian R.D. *Computer Insecurity*. New York: Chapman and Hall, 1983.

Ohmae, Kenichi. *The Mind of the Strategist*. Middlesex, England: Penguin Books, 1982.

Parker, Donn B. *Crime by Computer: Startling New Kinds of Million-Dollar Fraud, Theft, Larceny, and Embezzlement*. New York: Charles Scribner's Sons, 1976.

Parker, Donn B. *Computer Security Management*. Reston, VA: Reston Publishing Company, 1981.

Pettinari, D. *Using Internet to Communicate with the Public on LE Issues.* Available from FTP: polcomp.ilj.org/pub/polcomp. File: 720.12A.txt. (July 20, 1995).

Platt, Charles. *Anarchy Online Net Crime, Net Sex.* New York: Harper Paperbacks, 1996.

Roberts, Ralph. *Computer Viruses.* Greensboro, NC: Compute! Publications, Inc., 1988.

Rose, Lance. *Netlaw: Your Rights in the Online World.* Berkeley, CA: Osborne/McGraw-Hill, 1995.

Ruthberg, Zella G., and Harold F. Tipton, eds. *Handbook of Information Security Management, 1994–95 Yearbook.* Boston: Auerbach Publications, 1994.

Schwartau, Winn. *Information Warfare: Chaos on the Electronic Superhighway.* New York: Thunder's Mouth Press, 1994.

Schwartau, Winn. *Information Warfare: Cyberterrorism: Protecting Your Personal Security in the Electronic Age,* 2d ed. New York: Thunder's Mouth Press, 1996.

Schwartau, Winn, *Time Based Security.* Seminole, FL: Interpact Press. 1998.

Schweizer, Peter. *Friendly Spies: How America's Allies Are Using Economic Espionage to Steal Our Secrets.* New York: Atlantic Monthly Press, 1993.

Shaffer, Steven L., and Alan R. Simon. *Network Security.* Cambridge, MA: AP Professional, 1994.

Spencer, Donald D. *The Illustrated Computer Dictionary.* Columbus, OH: Charles E. Merrill Publishing Company, 1980.

Stang, David J., and Sylvia Moon. *Network Security Secrets.* San Mateo, CA: IDG Books Worldwide, 1993.

Steele, Guy L., Jr, Donald R. Woods, Raphael A. Finkel, Mark R. Crispin, Richard M. Stallman, and Geoffrey S. Goodfellow. *The Hacker's Dictionary.* New York: Harper and Row, 1983.

Sterling, Bruce. *The Hacker Crackdown: Law and Disorder on the Electronic Frontier.* New York: Bantam Books, 1992.

Stoll Clifford. *The Cuckoo's Egg.* New York: Doubleday Books, 1989.

Tafoya, W. "A Delphi Forecast of the Future of Law Enforcement." Dissertation submitted to Graduate School, University of Maryland, 1986.

Tafoya, W. "Into the Future, a Look at the Twenty-First Century." *Law Enforcement Technology,* p. 16.

Toffler, Alvin. *Future Shock.* New York: Bantam Books, 1971.

Toffler, Alvin. *The Third Wave.* New York: Bantam Books, 1980.

Toffler, Alvin. *Powershift.* New York: Bantam Books, 1990.

Toffler, Alvin, and Heidi Toffler. *War and Anti-War.* Boston: Little, Brown and Company, 1993.

Toffler, Alvin, and Heidi Toffler. *Creating a New World Civilization*. Atlanta: Turner Publishing, 1994.

U.S. Department of Justice, Bureau of Justice Statistics. *Computer Crime, Electronic Fund Transfer Systems and Crime*. Washington, DC: Government Printing Office, 1982.

U.S. Department of Justice, Bureau of Justice Statistics. *Computer Crime, Electronic Fund Transfer Systems Fraud*. Washington, DC: Government Printing Office, 1986.

U.S. Department of Justice, Office of Justice Programs, Bureau of Justice Statistics. *Directory of Automated Criminal Justice Information Systems 1993*. Volume 2, *Corrections, Courts, Probation/Parole, Prosecution*. Washington, DC: Government Printing Office, 1993.

U.S. Department of Justice, Office of Justice Programs, Bureau of Justice Statistics. *Dedicated Computer Crime Units*. Washington, DC: Government Printing Office, 1989.

U.S. Department of Justice, Office of Justice Programs, Bureau of Justice Statistics. *Organizing for Computer Crime Investigation and Prosecution*. Washington, DC: Government Printing Office, 1989.

Vold, G. B., and T. J. Bernard. *Theoretical Criminology*, 3d ed. New York: Oxford University Press, 1986.

Walker, Bruce J., and Ian F. Blake. *Computer Security and Protection Structures*. Stroudsburg, PA: Dowden, Hutchinson and Ross, 1977.

Wood, Charles Cresson. *Information Security Policies Made Easy*. Sausalito, CA: Author, 1994.

Appendix

Recommended Websites for Reference

The websites listed here were on-line when we surfed the I-way. The list is not all-inconclusive but a sampling of what may be of interest to the high-technology-crime investigator.

ASSOCIATIONS

at http://www.gocsi.com (Computer Security Institute)

at http://www.acfe.org (Association of Certified Fraud Examiners)

at http://www.asis.com (American Society for Industrial Security)

at http://www.icsa.com (International Computer Security Association)

at http://www.intlissa.org (International Information Systems Security Association)

HACKERS SITES

at http://www.2600.com

at http://www.unitedcouncil.org

at http://www.phrack.com

at http://www.underground.org

at http://Lopht.com

INFORMATION SYSTEMS SECURITY

at http://www.infosecuritymag.com

at http://www.securitymanagement.com

at http://www.issa.org

at http://www.icsa.com

at http://www.ics2.org

at http://www.securityinfo.com

at http://www.crypto.com

at http://www.cs.purdue.edu/coast/coast.html

at http://www.telstra.com.au/info/security.html

at http://www.nsi.org/compsec.html

at http://www.iss.net/vd/library.html

at http://www.ntbugtraq.com

at http://www.tno.nl/instit/fel/intern/wkinsec.html

at http://www.cs.purdur.edu/coast/hotlist

at http://java.sun.com/security

at http://spam.abuse.net

at http://cs-www.ncsl.nist.gov

at http://www.ncsa.com

at http://www.rootshell.com

at http://www.microsoft.com/ie/security

at http://www.netscape.com/assist/security

AUDITING

at http://www.isaca.org

at http://www.iia.org

GOVERNMENT

at http://www.piperinfo.com/~piper/state/states.html

at http://www.ustreas.gov

at http://www.usdoj.gov

at http://www.fbi.gov

at http://www.ifs.univie.ac.at.~uncjin/uncjin.html

LAW ENFORCEMENT

at http://www.ncjrs.org

at http://www.nlectc.org

at http://police.sas.ab.ca

at http://wings.buffalo.edu/student-life/public-safety/other

at http://innotts.co/~mick2mc/ukpolice.html

at http://www.lookup.com/Homepages/91900/home.html

LAW

at http://www.law.indiana.edu/law/lawindex.html

at http://www.internetlawyer.com

at http://law.house.gov

at http://www.americandream.com

at http://www.ilpf.org

at http://www.discovery.org/iltfrls.html

TERRORISM

at http://interlog.com/~vabiro

at http://www.site.gmu/~cdibona

at http://www.tezcat.com/~top/terrorist

at http://www.terrorism.com

at http://www.xensei.com/users/humcom/police.htm

CERTS

at http://www.auscert.org.au

at http://www.cert.org

at http://ciac.llnl.gov

at http://www.assist.mil

at http://fedcirc.llnl.gov

at http://www.first.org

at http://www.cert.dfn.de/eng/dfncert

at http://www.naisirc.nasa.gov/nasa/index.html

at http://www.cert.dfn.de/eng/csir/europe/certs.html

FRAUD

For general information regarding on-line fraud scams, contact http://www.
ftc.gov/bcp/scams01.htm. Other groups that can help follow.

American Compliance Institute at http://www.compliance.com

Coalition Against Insurance Fraud at
http://www.insurancefraud.org

Computer and Network Security at
http://www.netsurf.com/nsf/v01/01nsf.01.01.html

The Federal Web Locator at http://www.law.vill.edu/Fed-
Agency/fedwebloc.html

GPO access databases at http://www.acess.gpo.gov/
su-docs/aces/aaces002.html

Ignet at http://www.ignet.gov/ignet

Online Fraud Information Center at http://www.fraud.org

U.S. Department of Justice at http://www.usdoj.gov or
http://www.ncjrs.org

National Health Care Anti-Fraud Association at
http://www.nhca.org

Internet Wiretap at http://www.wiretap.spies.com

Statistics News Information Prevention at http://www.newc.com/
crimeprevention/white/whitecollarcrime.html

Fraud Information Center at http://www.echotech.com/fmenu.htm

Internet Anti-Scam at http://www.nerdworld.com/nw1319.html

AUSTRALIAN CRIMINAL JUSTICE AND
CRIMINOLOGY MAILING LIST

The Australian Criminal Justice and Criminology Mailing List (CrimNet)
provides a forum in which criminal justice professionals, practitioners,
academics, and students discuss issues and exchange information on conferences, new publications, and significant new developments.

To subscribe, send the message "subscribe crimnet" to majordomo@
law.usyd.edu.au.

CIVIL JUSTICE

Civil Justice (CIVIL-JUSTICE) provides information on legislation, studies,
policy papers, and campaigns aimed at restricting victims' rights and
weakening liability laws. To subscribe, send the message "subscribe civil-
justice firstname lastname" to listproc@essential.org.

CRIMINAL JUSTICE DISCUSSION LIST

The Criminal Justice Discussion List (CJUST-L) is a forum for the free and open discussion of criminal justice issues and problems, theoretical or real. To subscribe, send the message "subscribe cjust-l firstname lastname" to listserv@cunyvm.cuny.edu.

FUTURE LAW DISCUSSION

To subscribe to the Future Law Discussion (FUTUREL), send the message "subscribe futurel firstname lastname" to listserv@vm.temple.edu. If there are problems, e-mail Richard Klein at rklein@vm.temple.edu.

JOURNAL OF CRIMINAL JUSTICE AND POPULAR CULTURE

The *Journal of Criminal Justice and Popular Culture* (CJMOVIES) publishes reviews of all types of popular culture artifacts and original essays pertaining to the intersection of popular culture and criminal justice. To subscribe, send the message "subscribe cjmovies firstname lastname" to listserv@albany.edu.

JUSTICE INFORMATION DISTRIBUTION LIST

The Justice Information Distribution List (JUSTINFO) provides criminal justice professionals accurate, current, and useful information on criminal-justice-related issues through a biweekly newsletter sponsored by the National Criminal Justice Reference Service (NCJRS). To subscribe, send the message "subscribe justinfo firstname lastname" to listproc@ncjrs.aspensys.com.

MODEL UNITED NATIONS BULLETIN

To subscribe to the *Model United Nations Bulletin* (MODELUN), send the message "subscribe modelun firstname lastname" to listserv@indycms.iupui.edu.

WEEKLY UNITED NATIONS NEWS

To subscribe to the *Weekly United Nations News* (UN-NEWS), send the message "subscribe un-news firstname lastname" to listserv@unmvma. unm.edu.

OTHER SOURCES OF INFORMATION

Canadian Training Institute at http://www.cantraining.org/

Charles University Faculty of Law, Prague, Czech Republic, at http://whois.cuni.cz/cgibin/who.iso-8859-1?db=uk&lan=english&ask=7.4

Crime Mapping Research Center at http://www.nlectc.org/cmrc/

Federal Bureau of Investigation at http://www.fbi.gov

Home Office Research and Statistics Directorate at http://www.open.gov.uk/home_off/rsd/rsdhome.htm

Inter-Law's 'Lectric Law Library at http://www.lectlaw.com/

International Centre for Criminal Law Reform and Criminal Justice Policy, University of British Columbia, at http://www.law.ubc.ca/centres/icclr/index.html

National Archive of Criminal Justice Data (NACJD) at http://www.icpsr.umich.edu/NACJD/home.html

National Center for State Courts at http://www.ncsc.dni.us

National Conference of State Legislatures (NCSL) at http://www.ncsl.org

Scandinavian Research Council for Criminology, University of Iceland, at http://rvik.ismennt.is/~tho/NSfK.html

Swedish National Police College Library at http://www.police.se/gemensam/phs/bibl_e.htm

United Nations Centre for International Crime Prevention (UNCICP), Vienna, Austria, at http://www.ifs.univie.ac.at/~uncjin/uncjin.html

United Nations Online Justice Information System (UNOJUST) at http://www.ncjrs.org/unojust

University of Illinois at Chicago, Office of International Criminal Justice at http://www.acsp.uic.edu

University of South Florida, Department of Criminology at http://www.cas.usf.edu/criminology/index.html

VERA Institute of Justice at http://broadway.vera.org

World Criminal Justice Library Network at
http://newark.rutgers.edu/~wcjlen/WCJLEN!.html

FedWorld Information Network at http://www.fedworld.gov

Intelligence community at http://www.odci.gov/ic

Library of Congress at http://www.loc.gov

National Archive of Criminal Justice Data at
http://www.icpsr.umich.edu/NACJD/home.html

National Criminal Justice Association at http://www.sso.org/ncja/

National Law Enforcement and Corrections Technology Center
(NLECTC) at http://www.nlectc.org

Congressional information at
http://www.access.gpo.gov/congress/index.html

U.S. House of Representatives at http://www.house.gov/

U.S. Senate at http://gopher.senate.gov

STATE AND LOCAL CRIMINAL JUSTICE RESOURCES

The C-SPAN Networks at http://www.c-span.org

CopNet at http://police.sas.ab.ca/

Crime-Free America at http://announce.com/cfa/cfa.htm

Justice Center, University of Alaska, Anchorage, at
http://www.uaa.alaska.edu/just/

National Center for State Courts at http://www.ncsc.dni.us

National Criminal Justice Association at http://www.sso.org/ncja/

Rand Corporation at http://www.rand.org/areas/CRIM.Toc.html

SEARCH, the National Consortium for Justice Information and Statistics, at http://www.search.org

State and Local Government on the Net at
http://www.piperinfo.com/state/states.html

Airborne Law Enforcement Association at http://www.alea.org/

Bureau of Alcohol, Tobacco and Firearms at
http://www.atf.treas.gov/

Center for Sex Offender Management at
http://www.csg.org/appa/csom.html

Community Policing Consortium at http://www.
communitypolicing.org

Department of the Solicitor General of Canada at
http://www.sgc.gc.ca/

Federal Bureau of Investigation's ten most wanted fugitives at
http://www.fbi.gov/mostwant/tenlist.htm

Federal Bureau of Investigation's fugitive publicity at
http://www.fbi.gov/fugitive/fpphome.htm

Federal Law Enforcement Training Center at
http://www.ustreas.gov/fletc/

Financial Crimes Enforcement Network at
http://www.ustreas.gov/fincen/

Florida Department of Law Enforcement at
http://www.fdle.state.fl.us/

International Association of Chiefs of Police at
http://www.theiacp.org

International Association of Law Enforcement Planners at
http://www.www.dps.state.ak.us/ialep

Law enforcement agencies on the Web, list maintained by Cecil
Greek, Florida State University associate professor of criminology,
at http://www.fsu.edu/~crimdo/cj.html

National Law Enforcement and Corrections Technology Center at
http://www.nlectc.org

National Sheriffs' Association at http://www.sheriffs.org

Niagara Regional Police (Canada) at http://www.niagara.
com/~nrpsweb

Office of International Affairs fugitive home page at
http://www.usdoj.gov/criminal/oiafug/fugitives.htm

Partners *Off* Duty at http://www.murlin.com/~webfx/
PartnersOffDuty/

Police Executive Research Forum at http://www.PoliceForum.org/

The Police Officer's Internet Directory at http://www.officer.com/

Law enforcement agency listings, including a link to every law enforcement agency in the world that has a home page (agencies are
listed geographically), at http://www.officer.com/agencies.htm

U.S. Customs Service at http://www.customs.ustreas.gov/

U.S. Immigration and Naturalization Service at
http://www.ins.usdoj.gov/

U.S. Marshals Service at http://www.usdoj.gov/marshals/

U.S. Postal Inspection Service wanted posters at
http://www.usps.gov/websites/depart/inspect/wantmenu.htm

The World's Most Wanted fugitives and unsolved crimes at
http://www.mostwanted.org

Zeno's forensic page at http://users.bart.nl/~geradts/forensic.html

COPFLEET-L

COPFLEET-L was established to facilitate discussion among police de-
patements about the purchase, care, and maintenance of police vehicles
and equiptment. To subscribe, send the message "Subscribe COPFLEET-L
your name" to LISTSERV@american.edu. To send a message to subscribers, e-mail COPFLEET-L@american.edu.

LEGUN-INSTRUCTORS

The purpose of "legun-instructors" is to provide an open forum for law enforcement firearms instructors. It is designed specifically for law enforcement firearms instructors. Due to the sensitive nature of the information
on this list, approval is required prior to joining the mailing list. To subscribe to legun-instructors, contact Greg Block at greg@firearmstraining.
com.

POLICE DISCUSSION LIST

The Police Discussion List (police-l) is restricted to sworn law enforcement officers. To subscribe, send the message "subscribe police-l your
name" to listserv@cunyvm.cuny.edu.

PUBLIC SAFETY COMMUNICATIONS LIST

The Public Safety Communications List was initiated for the exchange
of nonconfidential information about police, fire, and EMS telecommunications. To send a message to subscribers, e-mail them at dispatch@
tcomeng.com. To subscribe, send the message "subscribe dispatch your
name" to majordomo@tcomeng.com.

Index